9/18/87

To George:

Here's hoping the
Richie + Brad make the
Red Sox, not the [illegible]

Best wishes,

Dan Shaughnessy

D0501875

3-31-22
GIVEN TO JIM WESTLAKE
BY JOE McNAMARA (John's NEPHEW)
© LIMELIGHT

SEE PAGES 1, 12, 121, 143

John MANAGED '85-'86-'87 PART OF 88-?
BOSTON
S HAUGHNESSY BAD MOUTHED
JOHNNY All THE TIME DURING
HIS STAY IN BOSTON

ONE STRIKE AWAY

ONE STRIKE AWAY

The Story of the 1986 Red Sox

Dan Shaughnessy

A Peter Weed Book
BEAUFORT BOOKS PUBLISHERS
New York

*To my father, William J. Shaughnessy, who
loved words and introduced his sons to Fenway Park*

Copyright © 1987 by Dan Shaughnessy

All rights reserved. No part of this publication may be reproduced or trans-
mitted in any form or by any means, electronic or mechanical, including
photocopy, recording, or any information storage and retrieval system now
known or to be invented, without permission in writing from the publisher,
except by a reviewer who wishes to quote brief passages in connection with
a review written for inclusion in a magazine, newspaper, or broadcast.

Library of Congress Cataloging-in-Publication Data

Shaughnessy, Dan.
  One strike away.

  "A Peter Weed book."
  1. Boston Red Sox (Baseball team)—History.
I. Title.
GV875.B62S53 1987   796.357′64′0974461   87–1139
ISBN 0–8253–0426–1

Published in the United States by Beaufort Books Publishers, New York.

Designed by Irving Perkins Associates

Printed in the U.S.A. / First Edition

10 9 8 7 6 5 4 3 2 1

ACKNOWLEDGMENTS

T HANKS to fellow Grotonian Peter Gammons who helped me break into the business, and to Bill Tanton of the *Baltimore Evening Sun* who gave me my first full-time job. Thanks to best friends, Kevin Dupont and Lesley Visser, who made life easier and more fun during the hungry years. Thanks to Ken Nigro, who showed me how a beat should be covered, and to Peter Pascarelli, Peter May, and Steve Fainaru, three people who made it a pleasure to travel with a pro sports team. Thanks to those at *The Boston Globe* for their help: the late Jerry Nason offered encouragement to a Holy Cross sophomore; former sports editor Dave Smith made room for a lot of BNBL stories; and the late Ray Fitzgerald set an example for every young sports writer. *Globe* colleagues Bob Ryan, Leigh Montville, Mike Madden, Will McDonough, John Powers, Jack Craig, Ian Thomsen,

Jackie MacMullan, Neil Singelais, Bob Duffy, Don Skwar, Bill Griffith, and Larry Whiteside have been of considerable assistance over the years, and sports editor Vince Doria has given me a chance to cover Boston's best beats. Thanks to the others at the *Globe* who helped me tell the story of the 1986 Red Sox, particularly systems editor Charlie Liftman and fellow reporters Dave O'Hara, Joe Giuliotti, and Chaz Scoggins. Also thanks to Ed Kleven, Clark Booth, and Sox historian George Sullivan.

I was twenty-three years old when I first went on the road with the Baltimore Orioles in 1977 and learned a great deal from all members of that exemplary organization. The Red Sox front office was very helpful during my first year on the Boston baseball circuit and I owe special thanks to traveling secretary Jack Rogers and Dick Bresciani, Josh Spofford, and Jim Samia of the PR staff.

Thanks to my mother, Eileen Shaughnessy, who reads every word in Groton, and to all the Shaughnessys and Wits in New Hampshire, Colorado, Arizona, Michigan, Ohio, Georgia, and on Cape Cod.

And to Marilou, my proofreader, inspiration and lifelong companion, special thanks for helping Sarah and Kate's dad write his first book.

Dan Shaughnessy
December 1986
Newton, Massachusetts

CONTENTS

1

ONE STRIKE AWAY

SATURDAY night, October 25, was yielding to Sunday morning when Dave Henderson swung his bat. The muscular outfielder clocked Rick Aguilera's 0–1 fastball and drove it over Shea Stadium's left field fence where it smacked off a sign that read, "Newsday, it's a hit!" The home run gave the Red Sox a 4–3 lead in the tenth inning of the sixth game of the 1986 World Series in which Boston was ahead three games to two. Shea's digital clock flashed midnight when Henderson reached the visitor's dugout, and before the half inning was over, the Sox added another run on a Wade Boggs double and a Marty Barrett single. It was finally going to happen. After sixty-eight years the Olde Towne Team was about to win another World Series.

The industrial meadow surrounding Shea Stadium was dark and quiet when the Mets came to the plate in

1

the bottom of the tenth. A few fans trudged toward the parking lot to beat the traffic as countless New Yorkers watching on television simply turned back their clocks one hour and went to bed.

Red Sox fans, meanwhile, inched closer to their sets. At last it was going to happen. In Stoughton, Massachusetts, Tom Mulvoy cradled his week-old son in front of the TV screen and thought about someday telling his boy that together they watched the Red Sox win the 1986 World Series. Recent generations of Boston fathers and sons had not been so lucky. In a plush high-rise apartment in the heart of downtown Boston, Bob Rodophele, a loyal season-ticket holder, cohosted a championship party. A bottle of Korbel Extra Dry (vintage 1978 not permitted for obvious reasons) was on ice but wouldn't be opened until the Red Sox popped their own champagne. Rodophele wore his Sox hat and kept score on a huge multi-colored scorecard. On the island of Nantucket, Steve Sheppard and Karin Ganga-Sheppard looked at each other as their friends focused on the television. Steve and Karin had been married at St. Mary's Church on April 19, 1986, and concluded their wedding vows with, "Till death do us part—or until the Red Sox win the World Series." With a 5–3 lead and two outs and none on in the tenth, Sheppard still wasn't worried about his marriage. "I couldn't let myself think it," he said. "I never felt secure." Back on the mainland fans were more optimistic. Car horns honked on the Massachusetts Turnpike from Stockbridge to Boston and the same sounds broke the midnight air on the Daniel Webster Highway in Nashua, New Hampshire, and on Boston Post Road from Bridgeport to New Haven. It was finally going to happen and people not usually caught up in baseball games were braced to celebrate with the rest of the region.

As the magic moment approached, crusty skeptics—and there are plenty who follow the fortunes of this team—began to wonder, "What is it going to feel like?" No one under the age of seventy-five could actually remember. Now, with victory at hand, some fans permitted themselves to speculate on the possibility of a winter without regret, a winter without hot stoves roasting slumping superstars and managerial blunders. What would it feel like to close the curtain on a Sox season and not say, "Wait till next year"? Would the emotions of victory match the anticipation of repeated near misses?

Since 1918 Red Sox fans had been deprived of the pleasure of a National Championship. So much so that the prefix long-suffering had been permanently attached to the Fenway faithful sometime in the middle of the twentieth century.

In January 1901 the Boston Americans, aka Pilgrims, were charter members of the upstart American League. The Pilgrims bought Cy Young from St. Louis for $3,500, and Young won thirty-three games at the age of thirty-four. Two years later Boston beat Pittsburgh five games to three in the first modern World Series. Over sixteen thousand attended Game One in Boston and Cy Young had to help out at the ticket booth. (Imagine Jim Rice behind a ticket window asking, "How about a pair under the roof down the third base line in section twenty-seven?")

In 1907 the Pilgrims became the Red Sox. Boston won five of the first fifteen World Series, including the 1918 fall classic when a fourth-year left-hander named Babe Ruth extended his consecutive Series shutout string to 29.2 innings before allowing a run against the Chicago Cubs. The Sox won that World Series, 4–2. Fifteen months later, on January 3, 1920, owner Harry Frazee sold Ruth to the New York Yankees for $125,000. Frazee insisted that the Ruth deal was the only way he could retain the Red Sox, but then a year later he made $2 million financing a stage production of "No, No, Nanette."

Those who believe that the Red Sox will never win again usually mark this as the turning point. Since the sale of the Babe, Sox fans have supported bad teams, mediocre teams, and talented teams that somehow have failed to fulfill their potential. Since the sale of Ruth, New York has won twenty-nine championships; Boston, zero. The 1946 Red Sox were loaded with sluggers and able pitchers, but lost the seventh game of the World Series, 4–3. St. Louis scored the winning run when Enos Slaughter scrambled from first base on a hit to left-center by Harry Walker. The popular theory is that the Sox lost the Series because shortstop Johnny Pesky hesitated with a relay throw from the outfield while Slaughter didn't. But Sox slugger Ted Williams compiled no extra base hits with only one RBI in the Series, and was outhit by a talkative rookie, Cardinal catcher Joe Garigiola. Two years later another powerhouse Boston team finished in a first-place tie with the Cleveland Indians. A one-game playoff was held at Fenway Park. When Sox manager Joe McCarthy opted to start journeyman Denny Galehouse, the Tribe routed Galehouse en route to an 8–3 victory.

In 1949 the Red Sox finished the season in New York needing only one win in two games to clinch the American League flag. The Sox blew a 4–0 lead in the first game and lost 5–4 on Johnny Lindell's eighth-inning homer. New York won the finale by a 5–3 count. The 1967 Red Sox overcame 100 to 1 odds to win the American League pennant and took heavily favored St. Louis to the seventh game of the series in Fenway Park—but again the Sox were losers. Manager Dick Williams started Cy Young winner Jim Lonborg on two days' rest in Game Seven and Bob Gibson beat Lonborg and the Red Sox, 7–2. In 1972 Boston led the Tigers by half a game and needed to take two of three in Detroit in the final series of the season. The Sox lost the first game 3–1 as Luis Aparicio fell down rounding third base on a Carl Yastrzemski shot to center. And the next day they were eliminated.

In 1974 the Red Sox led the American League East by seven games on August 23 and led third-place Baltimore by eight games on August 29, but finally finished third themselves, seven games behind the Orioles. The Sox won the first game of the 1975 World Series and led, 3–0, in Game Seven before Bill Lee threw an ill-timed blooper pitch to Tony Perez. Cincinnati's proud first baseman deposited Lee's insult somewhere near the Citgo sign that rests atop Kenmore Square. In the ninth inning when Sox manager Darrell Johnson summoned rookie Jim Burton to stall the Red Machine, Burton gave up a two-out, two-on bloop single to Joe Morgan, and the Reds were 4–3 winners. The 1978 Sox season remains one by which all future folds will be measured. The mighty Red Sox led the Yankees by a whopping fourteen games on July 19 and eventually fell three and a half games behind New York before tying for the lead on the final day of the regular season. Yet another one-game playoff was hosted at Fenway and the Sox were 5–4 losers as Bucky Dent plopped a three-run homer into the left field screen off Mike Torrez. It was left to Carl Yastrzemski to make the final out against Rich Gossage. Starting in 1972, the Red Sox were in first place after the All Star break seven times in fourteen seasons, yet managed only one division flag over this span. Sox fans adopted "Won't Get Fooled Again" as their official song.

This was the legacy the 1986 Red Sox lugged into the bottom half of the tenth inning at Shea Stadium on the morning of October 26, 1986. Boston's precious 5–3 lead was entrusted to a twenty-four-year-old Texan with 94.2 innings of big league experience—Calvin Schiraldi— whose first name hinted that historical forces might be at work once again. No one is quite sure when the link was first observed between the sixteenth-century beliefs of theologian John Calvin and the fortunes of the Boston ballclub, but the two seem in perfect harmony. Calvin taught that some are chosen to be among the elect and some are not. Could it be that the Red Sox are victims of predestination or fate? Scholar A. Bartlett Giamatti, lifelong Sox fan, president of the National League and former head of Yale, observed, "There's an almost Calvinistic sense of guilt at success, that we must re-enact the Garden of Eden again and again. There's a sense that things will turn out poorly no matter how hard we work. Somehow the Sox fulfill the notion that we live in a fallen world. It's as though we assume they're here to provide us with more pain."

Calvinist clouds of self-doubt aside, it was the Mets' turn to bat and Mr. Schiraldi was set to slam the door. Wally Backman went out on a fly to left and Keith Hernandez lined to center. Two outs. No one on base. A 5–3 lead. Cake. Hernandez, the Met backbone, went into the clubhouse and later admitted that at that point he'd planned to "go out and get drunk and stay up all night." Aguilera was on the bench and said, "My heart was breaking." Hands in pockets, Met manager Davey Johnson sat down and smacked his head against the back of the dugout wall.

Across the field the Red Sox were standing on the top step of their dugout, waiting for the final out. Oil Can Boyd was slamdancing with anyone in his vicinity and Roger Clemens said, "I was sure we had it won." Mets assistant equipment manager John Rufino had already loaded twenty cases of Great Western champagne and had it carted over to the Red Sox clubhouse. Foil was peeled from the tops of the bottles. Bruce Hurst had won the MVP vote by a 4–1 count, and the championship trophy was making a rare appearance in the Red Sox locker room. An NBC crew was set up in the clubhouse and cellophane had been hung on the players' lockers to protect clothes from champagne spray. Commissioner Peter Ueberroth would present the trophy to Red Sox president Jean Yawkey and chief operating officer Haywood Sullivan and then read a congratulatory telegram from President Reagan. Hurst would get the MVP and it seemed probable that a statue of Henderson would soon stand next to Sam Adams at the front of Faneuil Hall in downtown Boston.

There was one happy pocket of fans in the Shea Stadium stands where Red Sox wives rose and cheered as Gary Carter came to bat. Yet one Boston wife remained seated. Most of the young women who marry ballplayers are high school sweethearts from southern California, Texas, Florida, and other sunny places that produce major league ballplayers. Sherry Gedman, like her husband Rich Gedman, the stoic Red Sox catcher, grew up forty miles from Boston. Unlike the other wives, Sherry did not marry into the Sox family—she was born into it and she knew that it was too early to celebrate.

As Carter came to the plate, Met scoreboard operator Mike Ryan pushed the wrong button and "Congratulations Boston Red Sox" flashed prematurely on the electronic message board. Ryan, a native of Pittsfield,

Massachusetts, was red-faced and at least one person was prompted to recall the *Chicago Herald Tribune*'s "Dewey Defeats Truman" headline in 1948. Meanwhile the revered baseball broadcaster Vin Scully was telling America that Marty Barrett had been named Player of the Game.

Carter singled to left on a 2–1 pitch. Pinch hitter Kevin Mitchell was next and he stroked an 0–1 pitch to center for another single. Sox pitching coach Bill Fischer visited Schiraldi at the mound, after which Schiraldi quickly got two strikes on Met third baseman Ray Knight. *One strike away.*

Knight singled to center, scoring Carter, moving Mitchell to third. "I did what I wanted to, but he hit it over the second baseman's head," Schiraldi said later.

Sox manager John McNamara summoned Bob Stanley, the human dartboard ornament of Fenway Park. Stanley was one of the most likeable and approachable personalities on the ballclub, but his hefty contract, hefty midsection, and chronic ineffectiveness turned Sox fans on him by 1985. Seven months earlier, after getting roughed up in the Sox home opener, Stanley said, "All I know is this. When I stand out there and save the final game of the season and we win the pennant and I'm waving in the air, I'll be waving to my wife and family. The rest of 'em can go to hell." The insertion of Stanley at this crucial juncture almost certainly was greeted with both anger and anguish back in Boston.

A week earlier, on the eve of Game One of the World Series, Stanley said, "I always play like it's the World Series when I'm hitting fly balls to my son Kyle. He's five years old. I'll say, 'Okay, seventh game of the World Series. Two outs in the ninth. Here's a pop up.' If he catches the ball, we win the World Series. If he drops it, it's a foul ball and we win the World Series on the next one."

Mookie Wilson, the fleet, switch-hitting Met outfielder, was the only batter Stanley faced. Stanley worked the count to 2–2. *One strike away.* Just like playing in the back yard with five-year-old Kyle.

Wilson fouled off a curveball. *One strike away.*

Wilson fouled off another curveball. Stanley lacked an out pitch and Wilson was able to spoil the Steamer's strikes. For the fourth and final time, a Sox hurler delivered a pitch with the championship *one strike away.*

This time the ball sailed in toward the batter. Wilson jackknifed away from the pitch and a weary Gedman lunged to his right. The ball grazed Gedman's glove and bounced to the backstop. Wild pitch. Mitchell danced across the plate and it was 5–5. Knight took second and the NBC crew set a record for moving equipment out of a locker room.

In Roslindale, Massachusetts, thirty-five-year-old Ed Duggan got up from his chair and walked out of his house, leaving his mother and brother to see the finish on television. A Sox fan his entire life, Duggan knew what was coming. He walked alone down dark Sycamore Street toward Cummins Highway, toward Roslindale Square, toward another date with disappointment.

Stanley said it was the first time his fastball had ever broken in toward a left-handed batter (some of the Mets thought it was a spitter). "Usually my ball goes backward toward a left-handed hitter," said the Charlie Brown reliever. "This one went the other way. I've never seen one of my pitches do that and, hey, I didn't try to throw it like that. It just happened. That's the story of my life, isn't it? I had the chance to be the hero; instead I'm the goat."

Stanley's official pitching line for Game Six: 0 innings

pitched, 0 hits, 0 runs, 0 walks, 0 strikeouts, 1 wild pitch. He threw only one wild pitch during the 1986 regular season. The pitch to Wilson should have been ruled a passed ball. Gedman got his glove on the fastball and admitted, "Any time the ball hits my glove, I feel it should be a passed ball."

After the wild pitch Stanley threw three more pitches to Wilson. Wilson hit two more fouls, then dribbled a slow grounder just inside the first base line. Boston's weary war horse Bill Buckner was playing behind the bag and failed to charge the ball. The ball bounced twice then bounced a third time and stayed down, skipping under Buckner's glove, between his legs, and into history. When Knight scored from second with ease, the Red Sox had provided a capsule summary of their last sixty-eight years in the span of one half inning.

In Stoughton, Massachusetts, Tom Mulvoy, holding his week-old son, snapped off the TV. "Welcome to the club," he said to tiny Stephen Mulvoy. On the twenty-ninth floor of the plush apartment building in the heart of downtown Boston, Bob Rodophele slumped into a sofa, clutching the still unopened bottle of Korbel Extra Dry. On Nantucket Island Steve Sheppard said, "Knowing in my heart of hearts they couldn't do it, I could bet my marriage on it. We were willing to sacrifice our marriage for the good of the team. But even that didn't work. They get you every time. They always find a way to blow it." In Roslindale, Ed Duggan was still walking alone toward the city square when the sounds of defeat broke the quiet autumn night. He knew what had happened. "People were pouring out of houses and bars and slamming car doors," he remembered. "I could tell they were agitated. The cars started coming down the street and there was rubber screeching all over the place. I knew the Red Sox had lost."

Buckner won the goat horns. In Boston they were ready to lynch McNamara and Stanley in addition to the hobbling first baseman, but across the land Buckner was the fall guy. He earned a spot in World Series lore— alongside Fred Bonehead Merkle and Mickey Owen of dropped-third-strike fame. "I did concentrate on that ball," Buckner said. "I saw it well. It bounced and bounced and then it didn't bounce, it just skipped. I can't remember the last time I missed a ball like that, but I'll remember that one." The veteran first baseman won't have to remember: He'll be reminded of the little league grounder for the rest of his life.

In the weeks and months after the Series, Buckner was the butt of cocktail party jokes across the land. A New York broadcaster announced that the Mets' victory parade finished with the team bus going through Buckner's legs. In Wellesley, a man wearing a baseball Halloween costume tied a ball to a string and let it dangle around his ankles, like a monkey's tail. When guests asked who he was, the man would bend over, extend his empty mitt, look back at the ball between his legs and announce, "I'm Bill Buckner." At the end of the year, Joe Namath, on national television, selected Buckner's error as the most memorable sports moment of 1986.

Buckner's gaffe certainly wasn't the reason the Sox lost and Wilson thought he might have beaten it out, even if Buckner had fielded the ball cleanly (Stanley insisted that he had Wilson beaten). Buckner's greatest sin was not knocking it down. If Buckner bobbled the ball or failed to throw to first in time to get Wilson, the Sox would have been in a bind, but the only way Knight could score was if the ball went right through Buckner's legs. Which it did.

A single question remained, one that will haunt

McNamara forever. What was Buckner doing in the game? Dave Stapleton had been Boston's late-game defensive first baseman in all seven post-season victories. Why wasn't Stapleton inserted to pinch run for the hobbling Buckner when Buckner was hit by a pitch in the top of the tenth?

"Normally with Buckner we pinch run for him," McNamara said after the game. "We didn't have to tonight and he has very good hands."

Managers McNamara and Davey Johnson made dozens of controversial moves in Game Six. McNamara was roasted for lifting Clemens after seven innings, though it was claimed he had a blister on the middle finger of his right hand. After throwing 135 pitches, Clemens was pulled even though he'd retired five straight batters. Clemens would never second-guess his own manager, but later admitted, "I could have kept on throwing a few more fast balls. If he wants me to go out for another inning or two, I don't care if it's my worst day. I'll get people out." Mike Greenwell pinch hit for the man with the 24–4 record and struck out on a pitch in the dirt. McNamara said Greenwell was a good low-ball hitter. The Boston manager was also critiqued for letting the left-handed Buckner hit with the bases loaded against lefty Jesse Orosco with two out in the eighth. Buckner was batting .148 (4–27), had stranded twenty-four of twenty-five baserunners at that juncture, and McNamara had Don Baylor's thirty-one-homer, right-handed bat on the bench. Buckner lined to center, ending an inning for the fourteenth time in six games. The selection of Stanley as the man to replace Schiraldi was also second-guessed. When the questions began coming the next day, McNamara spread his arms in a Christ-like pose and said, "This is an outstanding second-guess situation.

You got me. But I don't second guess myself at all about anything that happened in that game."

Johnson took heat for the following moves: 1. Pinch-hitting Danny Heep for shortstop Rafael Santana in the fifth inning. Heep hit into a doubleplay and sub-shortstop Kevin Elster made a ninth-inning error. 2. Not double-switching when Jesse Orosco replaced Roger McDowell in the eighth. This forced Johnson to lift Orosco for a pinch hitter in the bottom of the inning. 3. Not having Howard Johnson bunt after he had failed on one attempt with runners on first and second and no outs in the ninth. 4. Pinch-hitting Lee Mazzilli for Orosco in the eighth, creating a situation that forced powerful Darryl Strawberry to take a seat on the bench as new pitcher Aguilera filled the number five spot in the batting order. This turn of events prompted Strawberry to pout like a baby during the Mets' shining moment, even though Strawberry had stranded all fourteen runners he'd seen in the first six games. 5. Letting Carter swing at a 3–0 Schiraldi pitch with two on and one out in the eighth (Carter hit a sacrifice fly). 6. Pitching to white-hot Barrett with Boggs on second and two out in the tenth.

Each of the above can be justified and Johnson was not nasty when asked to explain his strategy. "I leave the second-guessing to the sportswriters and to the fans," said the Met manager. When all else fails a manager can always look a questioner in the eye and say, "I can see that you know nothing about baseball." This tactic is employed more often than people realize and usually indicates the questioner is zeroing in on the unthinkable: an admission of error by a major league manager. McNamara's refusal to acknowledge that some of his moves were worth challenging was both maddening and foolish. If baseball decisions were obvious and universally accepted, there would be no need for managers, and the game would be a lot less fun.

Even a casual fan could see that McNamara goofed by leaving Buckner in for the tenth. Bone spurs, strained Achilles' tendons, a chronic ankle injury, and residue from nine cortisone shots had made Buckner a defensive liability. He was utterly immobile. Logic failed when McNamara tried to explain his non-move. Buckner could have been pinch hit for in the eighth (something the Sox didn't do all year), pinch run for in the tenth, or simply replaced for defensive purposes before the bottom of the tenth. McNamara did nothing, which is contrary to how he managed in every other post-season game in which Boston led. Game One of the World Series is the best example. With the Sox leading 1–0, Buckner made an out to end the top of the eighth. Stapleton came in to play the final inning and a half and made a key play on a Knight bunt attempt in the bottom of the ninth. Two days prior to Game Six, McNamara had taken Buckner out with the Sox leading in the eighth. Perhaps the manager wanted Buckner to share in the field celebration. Nothing else makes sense.

It's ironic that Sox fans would be upset because Dave Stapleton *wasn't* playing. Stapleton batted only thirty-nine times in 1986, hitting .128. It marked the sixth consecutive season in which his batting average declined. According to the official player ranking system of the Elias Sports Bureau, Stapleton was dead last among 692 major leaguers in 1986. He placed nineteenth in each of five statistical categories for AL first basemen, and ranked 109 among the 109 players grouped in the first base/outfield/DH category. The Red Sox dumped Stapleton one week after the Series ended.

The Red Sox need a copious crypt to stash the skeletons that haunt the franchise and Buckner, McNamara, Stanley, and Schiraldi were gaining first-ballot admission into the Red Sox Hall of Shame. Outside the Mets locker room Boston television journalist Clark Booth found former Sox pitcher Mike Torrez, who served up the infamous three-run homer to Yankee shortstop Bucky Dent in Boston's 1978, 5–4, playoff defeat. "I'm off the hook. I'm off the hook," Torrez was claiming and as the camera rolled, he added, "You know, it's unfortunate but it seems like Boston always runs into things like this."

The rest of the midnight confessions were predictably sad.

Stanley, who with Jim Rice and Dwight Evans was a survivor of the 1978 race, echoed Torrez. "I guess 1978 was a rotten feeling, but this is the bottom." The next day, Stanley got a telegram from a nun in Marblehead that read: "Get in there and kick some ass. God be with you."

Down the hall in an interview room McNamara snapped when asked about the history of the Red Sox in seventh games. "I don't know nothin' about history and I don't want to hear anything about choking or any of that crap."

"We had the game won," admitted Houdini Henderson. "I'm beginning to think somebody up there is writing a script to make it interesting. We have to put this game behind us. I know I can."

Getting through the night proved to be a difficult task for the Sox and their fans. On Sunday when a reporter started to ask McNamara what he felt when he first woke up, the Sox manager interjected saying, "I never got to sleep."

Saturday night marked the end of daylight savings time and Sox legions were saddled with an extra hour of morning mourning. Eddie Andelman, Boston's rowdy, rotund king of sports talk shows, set up a studio in the lobby of the New York Hilton and commiserated with angry and sad Sox fans until 4 A.M.

"I got up and I barked at the dog," remembered John Iannacci of Lunenberg, Massachusetts. Richard Beaser, a senior staff physician at Boston's Joslin Diabetes Center, noticed a lot of high blood sugar counts. "Patients were not taking care of themselves up to standards," Dr. Beaser remarked. "I noticed a deterioration of people's attention to their diet. People were ignoring their health because they were caught up in the World Series."

Those new to the Boston area finally understood why fans and writers had been so skeptical all summer. Meanwhile the telephone company was busy connecting New Englanders who'd migrated to other states and found themselves wanting to call hom for comfort. Longtime Red Sox chronicler Peter Gammons was reminded of a New Haven bar owner who said after the '78 playoff: "They killed our fathers and now the sons of bitches are coming to get us."

This classic game featured five errors, poor baserunning, sloppy throws, and managerial paralysis. The Red Sox left fourteen men on base and according to *New York Post* guest columnist George Steinbrenner, "Stranded more men than Zsa Zsa Gabor." In the first three innings Boston had eight hits and ten baserunners, but scored only twice. In the first inning Rice failed to score from first base on a two-out, 371-foot double off the outfield fence by Evans. Six innings later Rice was gunned down at the plate while trying to score from

second on a single to left by Gedman. The game took
four hours and two minutes and ended at 12:39 A.M. on
Sunday, October 26 (bumping *Saturday Night Live* off
the air for the only time in the program's eleven-year
history).

Sox fans will always remember where they were at
that moment. Red Sox folds are like assassinations,
blackouts, and blizzards. The community is galvanized
by the event, somehow endures the crisis, and later
everybody remembers exactly what they were doing
when it all happened. No less than thirteen pitches
could have produced the final out and brought the
championship to Boston, but each time the Mets stayed
alive.

There was, of course, another game to be played. The
Red Sox and Mets were rained out on Sunday, October
26, and finished the 1986 World Series Monday night
in Shea Stadium. Thousands of angry Bostonians promised they would not watch, yet Game Seven drew a 58.9
local rating, meaning of Boston sets actually turned on,
80 percent were tuned in to the ballgame. This was the
highest single program response in the history of Boston
television—a rating that television critics believe will
never be matched.

The Red Sox took a 3–0 lead in Game Seven and
seemed in command with Met menace Bruce Hurst on
the mound. But not a single Boston fan took any comfort
from this. And, true to form, the Red Sox gave up eight
runs in the final three innings and lost the game, 8–5.
It marked the fourth time in four tries since 1918 that
the Red Sox had lost a seventh World Series game. But
everyone in New England knew that the series was lost
two days earlier. "We let it get away Saturday night,"
admitted McNamara. "Saturday night's ballgame was

the thing that was tough." The heroic Hurst added, "We had the chances to put the Mets away and we didn't. We won together; we'll lose together." Sad Stanley told a television audience, "I'm sorry and as bad as you people feel, I feel much worse, believe me."

Columnist Michael Madden, father of two heartbroken, teen-age daughters, wrote: "I had told them about boys, taking candy from strangers, accepting rides in black Trans-Ams, and never to trust anybody named Rambo, but I never told them about the Red Sox. Now they will have a lifetime like mine and yours. When they were three, I should have trained—no demanded and commanded—them to like the Yankees. I would never have let a friend or a boy do this to them: but I allowed the Red Sox."

Boston psychologist Tom Cottle had to deal with a more serious problem. Hosting a call-in radio show on WHDH, Dr. Cottle took a call from a woman who sounded inebriated and suicidal. "She had a history of mental problems," he said. "The Sox had kept her aloft and what had happened in the last forty-eight hours was enough to make her want to kill herself." Dr. Cottle calmed the woman, then talked to her off the air, and arranged for treatment. "I encountered several people like that," he said later. "People were physically, mentally, totally disrupted for a few days. They were grieving as if a grandparent had died."

A week after the World Series ended, motorists on Highway I-8 in Mission Valley, California, saw a message on the First United Methodist Church billboard: "Should the Red Sox Give Up?" This was a tease for a Sunday sermon delivered by Reverend Mark Trotter. According to the Reverend Trotter, "It had to do with hope and not giving up and the quality of a Christian life." The Reverend said he saw the Sox loss portrayed as a Greek tragedy. "I wanted to contrast that attitude with what I perceive is a Biblical attitude that our fate is not determined. There's always a possibility for winning the World Series—even for the Red Sox."

At the same time the nationally syndicated cartoon strip "Tank McNamara" ran a series in which a futuristic schoolteacher explained the derivation of the word *Boston*, which had become synonymous with failure. The usage was, I Bostoned that exam. "Once there was a large and prosperous city called Boston," the teacher said. "What was the fate of this fabled lost city? Why did all of its half-million residents move away within a two-week period in the late twentieth century? There was no volcanic activity in the area. Many anthropologists now believe it was shame."

Back in the real world the *Globe* was flooded with angry letters after a page one Game Seven account ran under a sub-headline "And Boston is Mudville Once Again." Many readers missed the reference to Ernest Lawrence Thayer's poem, "Casey at the Bat," which ends with the line, "But there is no joy in Mudville: Mighty Casey has struck out." Some readers thought the paper was trashing the city.

Thayer grew up in Worcester, Massachusetts, the hometown of Rich Gedman, and attended Harvard. When he wrote "Casey" in 1888, he certainly had Boston in mind. Boston even appears in *The Best Loved Poems of the American People*, selected by Hazel Felleman and published in 1936 by Doubleday & Co. (who owned the 1986 Mets). Thayer's poem opens, "It looked extremely rocky for the Boston nine that day;" and ends "But there is no joy in Boston: Mighty Casey has struck out."

It remains unclear when Boston was changed to Mudville, but obviously Ernest Lawrence Thayer was either a prophet or a time-traveler.

The Red Sox were the story of the 1986 World Series. Met fans will glow when recalling the miracle comeback of Game Six, but baseball bards will mark this as the Series the Red Sox *lost* before crediting the Mets with the victory. In New York the story was the Mets championship. Everywhere else in Baseball America, the story was the Red Sox loss.

For seven months they had turned back every challenge and spit in the face of historians and critics who predicted a collapse. They asked only that they be judged by their deeds and maintained that they were not accountable for the sins of their predecessors. But the weight of the Red Sox uniform proved too great and before it was over, they'd composed their own sad song. Future Red Sox players will be asked about the mistakes of Messrs. McNamara, Stanley, and Buckner, and may plead their innocence. But the legend will live—until the Sox win the World Series.

Eighty-three championships have been played and eighty-three winners have been crowned. The 1986 Red Sox are the only team in Series history to come within one strike of winning—then lose.

But the Red Sox also came within one strike of losing—then won. On Sunday, October 12, Boston trailed the California Angels, 5–2 in the ninth inning of the fifth and what appeared to be the final game of the American League season. The Angels had a 3–1 lead in games and were making preparations for their first trip to the World Series. Former Angel MVP Don Baylor spiked a two-strike, two-run homer off Mike Witt, then Angel manager Gene Mauch pulled Witt and called on

Gary Lucas to pitch to Gedman. Gedman pointed to center field and asked that a banner be removed. The banner read "Another Boston Choke." Lucas threw one pitch and it hit Gedman. Mauch summoned Donnie Moore to pitch to Henderson.

Henderson had batted .196 with one homer in limited play for the Red Sox since being acquired from Seattle in August. He was batting against Moore because regular center fielder Tony Armas had twisted an ankle early in the game. Henderson got off to a bad start, tipping a Bobby Grich drive over the center field fence for a two-run homer. In the eighth he struck out against Witt. Dave Henderson was a guess hitter who seemed to be guessing wrong as he looked especially bad fouling off two Moore fastballs after the count went to 2–2.

The 1986 Red Sox then earned a spot in New England sports history as Henderson leaned over the plate, swung his Wonderboy club, and made solid contact with Moore's forkball—driving it far over the left field fence.

Henderson's home run put a special glow on the Red Sox season. There would be no disgrace after Boston fought off elimination with the most dramatic comeback in their history. Boston baseball fans forgave past heartbreaks and fell in love again.

The 1986 Red Sox accomplished many things. They had the MVP, the Cy Young Award winner, the American League batting champ, and the AL Manager of the Year. They finished first after almost everyone picked them to finish fifth in their division. They beat the Angels in a thrilling seven-game playoff series and came within a strike of winning the World Series. They also rekindled New England's passion for baseball. The region, bound by baseball boredom in the early eighties, had turned to the wonderful Larry Bird and the perennial champion Celtics. The Patriots made a stunning charge to the Super Bowl, and Marvelous Marvin Hagler of Brockton was a world champ. But then along came the 1986 Red Sox to touch off baseball fever, a feeling that had been absent for years. People *cared* again.

2

SPRING TRAINING AND THE
ARRIVAL OF DON BAYLOR

SOME of them checked into the Winter Haven Holiday Inn. Newcomer Sammy Stewart opted for an apartment near several nice fishing holes, while tryout hopeful Joe Sambito commuted from his home in St. Petersburg. Jim Rice settled into his Winter Haven house and drove his classic Chevys to work every day.

Boston didn't give the Red Sox much thought when the local nine started spring training on the weekend of February 23, 1986. The bats, balls, and gloves went south early but the hearts and hopes stayed behind in the frozen north. There was still a lot of talk about the Patriots' Super Bowl loss, and the Celtics had just returned from a grueling sixteen-day west coast tour. The Red Sox made some news during the winter, but most of it was negative. The team, a perfectly boring 81-81 in 1985, had finished an aggregate 56½ games out of first place in the three previous seasons. Before Christmas '85 Boston fired black minor league instructor Tommy Harper, which resulted in Harper filing a race discrimination suit against the ballclub. Harper claimed he was canned because he spoke out against the team's policy of allowing the Winter Haven Elks Club to leave complimentary passes for white members of the Red Sox organization. The ballclub retorted that Harper's contract was not renewed because of his poor performance, and stated, "The Boston Red Sox have never had any official or unofficial relationship with the Elks Club of Winter Haven. The Red Sox Baseball Club has not and will not take any action against any employee to discourage an employee's opposition to racisim in any form."

A trio of trades also spiced the off season. On November 13, 1985, the Sox acquired pitchers Calvin Schiraldi and Wes Gardner plus outfielders LaSchelle Tarver and John Christensen from the Mets in exchange for pitchers Bobby Ojeda, Tommy McCarthy, Chris Bayer, and John Mitchell. Boston General Manager Lou Gorman, director of baseball operations for the Mets from 1980–84, had good reports on the four new Sox. No one would have predicted that Schiraldi and Ojeda would become pivotal figures in the 1986 World Series. At the annual baseball meetings Gorman unloaded relief pitcher Mark Clear in exchange for Milwaukee Brewer utility infielder Ed Romero, a move interpreted as addition-by-subtraction by Boston fans. Sox coach Rene Lachemann managered Romero at Milwaukee and thought he would be a valuable backup infielder. A week after the Romero deal Gorman swapped erratic shortstop Jackie Gutierrez for Oriole pitcher Sammy Stewart. It was the first Boston-Baltimore trade since

June 1960 when the Orioles sent Willie Tasby to Boston for Gene Stephens. Gorman, who also had worked in the Baltimore organization, was friendly with Oriole GM Hank Peters and knew the Orioles were looking to deal Stewart, who was going into the final year of his contract. As Boston was convinced that Glenn Hoffman could handle the everyday duties at short, the inconsistent Gutierrez became expendable.

The deal the Red Sox *didn't* make proved more controversial than any they did. The Red Sox turned down the St. Louis Cardinals' offer of pitchers Joaquin Andujar, Kurt Kepshire, Jeff Lahti, and Rick Horton for Bruce Hurst. Andujar had won twenty in 1984 and again in '85 and the St. Louis quartet had compiled an aggregate record of 39–25 in 1985. The twenty-seven-year-old Hurst, meanwhile, was saddled with a lifetime mark of 42–46. Sox fans suggested drug tests for management when word leaked that this offer was rejected and Hurst admitted, "If the Red Sox had a chance to get four pitchers like that, including Joaquin Andujar, and I've been hovering around .500, it probably doesn't make sense."

Cold cash was another hot topic during the off season. Three Sox players went to salary arbitration. Marty Barrett asked for $435,000 instead of the club's figure of $325,000. Barrett won. Rich Gedman asked for $1 million instead of the club's $650,000. The Red Sox won. The Sox also won the tiebreaker—a celebrated dollar war with batting champion Wade Boggs, who asked for $1.85 million and was awarded the club's $1.35 million. Boggs was extremely bitter at the Sox arbitration tactics and came to spring training with a sourball pinched between his cheek and gum. "When you get two-hundred-forty hits and hit .368 and people say you don't contribute, you've got to have some doubts about whatever you do," said the defending American League batting champ. Boggs was royally roasted by fans who have a hard time relating to a man who's upset because he's only making $1.35 million a year to play baseball. One radio station jabbed Boggs by taking up a collection to keep Wade happy. Boggs's bloody arbitration war ended February 23, the day most of the pitchers and catchers arrived in camp.

Winter Haven, Florida, is located near the middle of the Citrus State. Visitors from the north fly into Orlando International Airport, drive an hour past Disney World, Circus World, and several other palaces of awakening desires, before reaching the land of lakes. There are no beaches in Winter Haven, in fact the city seems to be further from salt water than any other town in the state. The Sox play at Chain O' Lakes Park, right next to the Citrus Dome—a huge building with an orange roof cut like a an orange peel. Every spring the locals invite the players to a beer and barbecue feast—men only—where hundreds of grown men stand in long lines hoping a Bob Stanley will spill sauce on them. Something like the Cannes Film Festival, only more glamorous.

Olympic swimming medalist Rowdy Gaines is from Winter Haven and the city brags about him at every border. Nothing moves fast. There is time to sit and watch the ospreys build nests in the right field light towers. The traffic is slow, people talk slow—even the fast food is slow. The folks with the money are on the coast. Winter Haven is a town of trailer parks, hamburger joints, jacked-up jeeps, and rednecks. Bingo is big; houses are small; the midnight sky is pitch black, and the Elks Club is all white.

A pizza and pipes emporium is a local attraction. One

can hold the anchovies while listening to a huge organ probably last used for the filming of Vincent Price's *The Abominable Dr. Phibes.*

Dining in a Winter Haven coffee shop, a reporter asks the waitress where she's from. "LA," she replies. Stunned to find a young woman from Los Angeles working in Winter Haven, he strikes up a conversation only to find that in Winter Haven, *LA* means Lake Alfred.

Despite what Delta and Eastern Airlines would like you to believe, central Florida weather isn't perfect in late February. The brochure featuring an endless line of palm trees, toasting bodies, and pina coladas can blow from one's hand when an occasional bone-chilling breeze sweeps across the land of lakes. Sometimes it even rains. But it's always warmer than February-in-Worcester, and the Red Sox have been happy with their Winter Haven home for over twenty years. The days start early. Minor leaguers work out at the lower diamond and often get special batting instruction from Carl Yastrzemski or Ted Williams. The major leaguers dress in the clubhouse down the right field line at Chain O' Lakes Park, and indefatigable hitting coach Walter Hriniak is usually working with one of the veterans in the batting cage adjacent to the right field bullpen. The first few days are painless and short—lots of stretching, throwing, hitting, and fundamentals. Pitchers practice covering first base and work on pickoff plays, outfielders rehearse the proper cutoff throws, and reporters discuss possible trades and try to figure out this year's roster.

Spring training is a casual time for every ballclub. Fans enjoy a unique closeness during the month of March. The stands are filled with the very old and the very young. There is no public drunkenness or yahoos who chant "Yankees suck" between pitches. There's nothing trendy or ugly about spring training baseball crowds. Old men come out to sit in the sunshine, reminisce, and watch young men play baseball.

Fans are able to put up in the same hotel where many of the players stay and, with the players removed from the pressures of the regular season, may even establish normal, neighborly relationships with their heroes. It's more meaningful than a smudged autograph on a cocktail napkin, signed by a young star who won't make eye contact. Vacationing Bostonians who share a motel ice machine with the likes of Dave Stapleton will probably be more forgiving when they watch him strike out in August.

Dinner conversation is an integral part of spring training—not the banter that goes on during a meal, but the restaurant reviews that dominate conversations the next morning. Everybody asks everybody else where they ate the night before. Considerable time is spent discussing veal scallopini and rack of lamb. There isn't much nightlife in Winter Haven. The pool-side lingerie show at the Holiday Inn was a big attraction every Tuesday in March 1986. Three watering holes, all in a row, attracted the fast and slow crowds during spring training evenings. Christy's Restaurant lounge served as the scene of many late-night baseball discussions (Tony Armas learned he wasn't going to be traded there). And Christy's is only a short stumble from the Holiday Inn bar, Paddy O'Shea's, which caters to Irish Bostonians and a core of regulars. Flanking the Holiday Inn on the other side is the Howard Johnson's motel, which features a lounge called Rumors. Here even though Wade Boggs and Tim Lollar are honored with nameplates on barstools, Sox officials placed Rumors off limits for minor league players.

The 1986 Red Sox staggered through spring training. They lost their exhibition opener to Detroit 3–0 with LaSchelle Tarver hitting into a triple play. There weren't many jobs up for grabs, a situation which fans found surprising after Boston's 81–81 finish in 1985. Veteran pitcher Bruce Kison retired at the start of camp due to an injured right shoulder while second baseman Jerry Remy found he couldn't do much on a left knee ravaged by seven operations. The Sox lost thirteen of their first nineteen exhibition games and surrendered the coveted Polk County trophy, held by the winner of the Boston/Detroit–Winter Haven/Lakeland series. As the team approached the final week of the grapefruit season, there was absolutely no evidence to suggest a good year. The Red Sox lacked speed, the defense was mediocre, and veteran outfielders Tony Armas and Jim Rice looked sluggish after inactive winters due to injuries. Rice was coming back from surgery on his left knee and Armas was recovering from a torn left calf muscle. For the first time in his life, the Sox center fielder hadn't played much winter ball and he looked rusty and broken down when he got to Florida. Including right-fielder Dwight Evans, the Sox had an outfield that would be an aggregate one hundred years old on July 2, 1986.

GM Gorman walked around camp defending the Ojeda trade and the Hurst non-trade, but it didn't look like the Sox got much from the Mets. Schiraldi was a Florida bust: he compiled a 14.50 ERA in five appearances, developed a sore arm, and was shipped out. Gorman admitted, "He hasn't pitched well. He hasn't earned a spot based on what he's done. If he has to go down and pitch his way back, that's what he'll have to do." Gardner looked as if he might make the team, but it was clear that outfielders Tarver and Christensen needed considerable seasoning. The Stewart-Gutierrez deal was jeopardized when the Orioles, dissatisfied with Gutierrez's psychological condition, appealed to American League President Bobby Brown to rescind the deal. Dr. Brown ruled that the trade would stand, but Sox fans were beginning to have doubts about Stewart. The Gomer Pyle sound-alike was awful in his early outings, but simply shrugged and said, "Spring training don't mean dawg."

Of more concern was Clemens, who was knocked around Florida ballparks in his first five spring outings. Six months after shoulder surgery he was reluctant to throw his A-1 fastball. In his first five spring starts he gave up twenty-nine hits, 9 walks, and nineteen runs in nineteen innings while striking out only 8. The spring progressed, but Clemens didn't and the young righty became reluctant to talk. "I got no comment about the way I pitched," he snapped after getting hammered by the White Sox in Sarasota.

Later in the season Clemens talked about his injury and his spring ordeal: "When we had the operation, Dr. Andrews was in there and he said, 'Your rotator cuff is very, very strong. There's no problem with that, no problem with your arm; there's just one little thing'— about the size of my small fingernail—'a piece of cartilage that flared up.' There's no knowing why it flared up, but it did and when I threw and my rotator cuff rotated, it rubbed and it rubbed and it rubbed and that's what wore me down. They went in there and took that little baby out. When I first started playing catch, about two weeks, three weeks after the surgery, I could tell there was nothing there. I could get right back on top of the ball and there was no little jolt in the back of my shoulder. I had to take it at my own pace. The first couple games I got knocked around a little—basehit, basehit, basehit. And that's frustrating. I wanted to go ahead and cut loose, but I just had to stay within myself. I worked real hard on my breaking stuff and I shut all the reporters out because I got tired of answering the questions, because if everybody keeps saying, 'How are you feeling? How are you feeling?' or 'Are you hurting? Are you hurting?' or 'Are you tired? Are you tired?' you'll start believing it yourself. You got to shut out all the negative things. That's the only way you can do it. You're always going to have negative things or criticisms and you got to be able to accept that, but at certain points to try and make progress, you've got to shut those things out and go on. And that's what I did it for. I figured I'd answer all the questions when it got done and I knew I was there. There weren't too many points where I was scared. But I was worried and I was very puzzled."

In the midst of Clemens's spring struggle pitching coach Bill Fischer told the young righty to stop throwing so many breaking balls. When Clemens was told that his spring fastball had been clocked at 93 miles per hour, he gained new confidence and aired it out in his final spring start against the Tigers. On the last day of spring training Clemens pitched seven innings and allowed only three hits and a run while walking one and striking out nine. He was overpowering and afterward said, "I'm satisfied with where I am right now."

Clemens was not the only Red Sox pitcher to make headlines in Florida. Dennis "Oil Can" Boyd set the stage for a kaleidoscopic season by reporting to camp weighing only 133 pounds. When Boyd's routine medical tests revealed a liver malfunction, the brass called a press conference and announced that Boyd would undergo tests at the University of Massachusetts Medical Center in Worcester, Massachusetts. It would be the first of many vague press releases concerning Oil Can in 1986. While the team announced that Boyd would check into the Massachusetts Hospital and would be unavailable for comment, the Can had other ideas. Following the advice of his agent, Dennis Coleman, the confused Boyd remained in his Winter Haven home overnight and talked with confused reporters.

"Yes, I've lost some weight," he said. "But I'm still at one thirty-eight, which if anybody would have bothered to check it out, was the weight I pitched at while I was in college. It's no big deal. I'll report to the doctor when I get there and hopefully I'll be right back."

Sox owner Haywood Sullivan was steaming the next day when Boyd's whereabouts were still uncertain, but the Can finally checked into the UMass Medical Center and the Sox immediately shifted into the loose-lips-sink-ships mode. "I am instructed not to say anything on Oil Can," McNamara said. Meanwhile speculation ran rampant and Boyd was rumored to have everything from a drug problem to the bubonic plague. A week later moments after Gorman announced "nothing is wrong with Oil Can. . . . He doesn't have any kind of hepatitus," team physician Dr. Arthur Pappas announced that Boyd had contracted a noncontagious form of hepatitus—the result of a virus that caused him to tire quickly, diminished his appetite, and produced a weight loss. Boyd was back in Winter Haven March 13 and so was his agent, Coleman. Sox pitchers Bob Stanley and Al Nipper were angry with Coleman after he mentioned their names in a television interview. Coleman charged that a double standard existed: Boyd's illness started rumors of drug abuse while Stanley and Nipper had not faced such speculation when they were injured the year before. Stanley confronted Boyd's agent at the Holiday

Inn, and there was considerable tension in the clubhouse when the Can returned.

Good Friday brought a special gift to the Boston Red Sox just when it was needed most. The New York Mets were in Winter Haven. After near misses in 1984 and '85, the Mets were touted as a team ready to take its place at the top of baseball. They were a consensus pick to finish first in the National League East and it didn't take a lot of imagination to picture Davey Johnson managing in the 1986 World Series.

Met Mozart Dwight Gooden pitched against the Sox on March 28 and surrendered a home run and a single to Boston designated hitter Mike Easler. But Easler's name was being tossed about the pressbox long before he solved Dr. K. In Friday's editions of *The New York Daily News* reporter Bill Madden floated a rumor that the Red Sox and Yankees were contemplating a deal that would send Easler to New York for Yankee designated hitter Don Baylor. Gorman would not comment on the rumor before the exhibition game, but the trade seemed plausible. The Sox had held an organization meeting Thursday night and it was known that McNamara thought highly of Baylor. McNamara was a coach with the Angels when Baylor enjoyed his salad days in California. It was also known that Easler had told management he wouldn't mind a change of scenery if the Sox were planning on sitting him down against lefties. Gorman and Haywood Sullivan were spotted talking on cordless telephones during the Sox-Mets contest, and after Boston's 10-inning, 6–5 victory over the Mets (ironically, the same score that the Sox would lose to the Mets by in another ten-inning game in October), Gorman, Sullivan, and McNamara met at first base. "We may have an announcement soon," admitted Gorman as he left the field.

The deal was done. It marked the first time Boston and New York had consummated a trade since the Sox acquired Danny Cater in exchange for future Cy Young winner Sparky Lyle on March 22, 1972. "I think a lot of Don Baylor," said a surprised Bill Buckner. "But Mike Easler was swinging the bat real well, and he's going to have a good year. I was surprised we traded him to a team we're trying to beat. I thought that was a no-no."

In Fort Lauderdale Yankee MVP Don Mattingly had some prophetic fears about shipping Baylor to the enemy. "I'm afraid to look at his numbers at the end of the year after he plays in Fenway Park. I wish him well, but I hope he doesn't hurt us."

The popular Reverend Mike Easler (imagine trading an ordained minister on Good Friday) left these words with his former teammates: "I feel they have the talent, but it's important to put it in their minds. There's got to be more belief—more of each individual's commitment to winning. They have such quality athletes. I can't pinpoint it. It's funny. I just can't understand what's wrong. Even the pitching staff, they say, is questionable. I don't think it is."

Thirty-six-year-old Don Baylor wanted out of New York because the Yanks planned to use him as a designated hitter only against left-handed pitching. He also wanted to get away from their blustering owner George Steinbrenner. Baylor had turned down a trade to the White Sox, but was happy to come to Boston where he owned a .350 batting average with 17 homers and 65 RBI in 82 career Fenway games. The Red Sox knew they were getting a right-handed power hitter who could take advantage of Fenway's left field wall. They also knew they were getting a leader.

Baylor arrived on Monday, March 31. Roger Clemens said, "As soon as he walked into this clubhouse, there wasn't any doubt who the leader was."

Minutes after buttoning his Red Sox jersey (number 25, which Ed Romero happily yielded), Baylor said, "You have to be on the field and play every day and play hard. I don't go around soliciting leadership. I play the way I play. I've learned from some guys I played with—like Frank Robinson."

Frank Robinson had a great influence on the young Don Baylor. They played together only briefly in 1971, but Baylor came up through the Orioles' system and had long looks at Robinson in spring trainings before he was promoted to the big club in '71. Robinson was one of the most feared players of his time. He played hard all the time and the opposing team was the enemy. He came up in the National League when pitchers named Don Drysdale and Bob Gibson would snarl at hitters, then knock them on their behinds. There wasn't a lot of fraternization in those days. Gibson and Robinson didn't even like talking to teammates at All Star games.

"They're the enemy," Robinson said while visiting Boston as a coach with the Orioles in the summer of '86. "They're the bad guys. There's no way you can concentrate on doing everything you can to beat them if you're talking about going out to dinner later. I'm not talking about intentionally trying to hurt somebody. You stop short of that. But there's going to come a time when you've got to knock somebody on his rear end or pitch somebody inside. I'm not saying you don't speak to the other team, but just say hello, and that's it."

Robinson on leadership: "Number one, the people have to respect you. That's the most important thing.

Most of the time, you have to lead by example. If you're doing it, you don't have to say as much. You have to be playing every day and producing. If you get to a point where you're not doing it on the field anymore, you become more of a cheerleader."

Robinson saw the impact Baylor had on the 1986 Red Sox and noted, "I don't think it can be emphasized enough. I don't know if the Red Sox are going to win this thing or not, but he can make the difference between your being a so-so club and an outstanding one."

Baylor made a difference. He led with his bat and he led with his presence. He brought dignity and professionalism to the clubhouse. He made no demands for togetherness and harmony, but his subtle means of sculpting the team had a tremendous impact. The Sox had a long history of clubhouse cliques and pettiness. The old joke about the team was that they went to dinner in twenty-five separate cabs. Some team. Pitchers looked at their inflated earned run averages and blamed the defense. Hitters blamed the pitchers for Boston's abject mediocrity. When Baylor walked into the clubhouse, he found twenty-three men anxious to change their image. As always the Red Sox had the talent, but they needed a leader. Rice wore the captain's hat, but it never quite fit. Rice played hurt and never made excuses, but he did not lead.

Baylor led. He got to the park early, left late, and worked hard. He never forced himself on his teammates, but his dignity and dedication, coupled with a winning record, gave him the credentials to lead. "I think whatever influence I do have is because of my professionalism," Baylor said.

There is a common misconception about leaders of sports teams. Fans hear that a player is supposed to be a clubhouse leader and they assume that means he is always giving "Win one for the Gipper" speeches, high-fiving teammates, and cheering from the sidelines. While cheerleaders are useful, they are not necessarily the leaders. Pittsburgh's Willie Stargell led without saying much of anything. Fans would watch the Pirates and listen to Stargell's post-game descriptions and be none the wiser. But Stargell was the man/child who insisted that his teammates never get down, and he'd lead them in a conga-line around the post-game buffet table after a win *or* a loss. Stargell would insist that the radio still play after a tough defeat. When the Pirates fell behind the Orioles, three games to one in the 1979 World Series, Stargell turned the music up. Then he hit a two-run homer to put the Pirates ahead for good in Game Seven in Baltimore.

Baylor was born in Austin, Texas, on June 28, 1949, the first of three children of Lillian and George Baylor. George Baylor was a baggage clerk for the Missouri Pacific Railroad and had to be away from home a good deal. Lillian Baylor was a cashier at the local high school and spent much of her spare time in activities with the Sweet Home Missionary Baptist Church. Don Baylor was bigger than most kids his age and he wasn't afraid to be one of the first three black students to enter O. Henry Junior High School in Austin. At Stephen F. Austin High School, where he became a three-sport star, he dislocated his right shoulder twice in one football game, and his throwing arm has never been the same.

Lou Gorman was director of minor league clubs when the Baltimore Orioles drafted Baylor in 1967. Don Baylor, who had football, baseball, and basketball scholarship offers from Stanford, Texas, and other major colleges, asked for a tuition clause; the Orioles agreed and George Baylor signed for his seventeen-year-old son. Four years later, while he was still in the minor leagues, Don Baylor married Jo Cash, a University of Texas student. Don Baylor, Jr., was born in 1972 and toured the American League with his father in the summer of '86. When Don and Jo Baylor were divorced in 1981, father and son grew closer than ever. Don Jr. was born with amblyopia (lazy eye) but received the finest medical care and had no trouble fielding fungoes with the Red Sox all summer.

Prior to coming to the Sox, Baylor played for four division champions and thirteen winning teams in sixteen seasons. He got a valuable head start in the Baltimore organization, a system that flooded baseball with players and managers in the sixties and seventies. The Orioles developed a strict stylebook and throughout their system players were taught the same way. It's easy for a young player to get confused when he's taught to do something one way at the A level, then taught another way at AA. The Orioles were consistent in their teaching and won consistently—but there was a drawback. Baltimore was loaded with quality outfielders, which made it difficult for a young star to reach the majors. Baylor was Minor League Player of the Year in 1970 when he hit .327 with 22 homers and 107 RBIs. He led the International League in four offensive categories and felt optimistic heading to Miami for spring training with the Orioles. But the Orioles were the defending World Champs, had won two straight American League pennants, and didn't need a talented rookie rusting on the bench behind Robinson and Blair. "It was one of the hardest decisions I ever made," Weaver said years later.

"I mean, how do you tell a kid like that to go back to the minors for another year?"

Baltimore won the American League flag again in '71, but lost a seven-game World Series to the Pirates. Down on the farm Baylor was still the best thing to hit Rochester since Kodachrome. Confident that Baylor was ready to step in, the club traded two-time MVP Frank Robinson to Los Angeles. Baylor was Baltimore's left fielder in 1972 and Weaver went to work getting the powerful youngster to pull the ball. "I knew he had thirty homers in that bat, but he wasn't pulling the ball the way he could," said the diminutive skipper.

One of Baylor's first trips to Boston provided Weaver and Co. with a few laughs. The visitor's dugout at Fenway Park is on the third base side and the cozy contours of the ballpark make it impossible for anyone in there to see what's happening in the deepest corner of left field. The Sox had a couple of runners on board when someone dropped a hit down the third base line toward the left field corner. "We all saw Donnie go into that corner," said Weaver. "But it seemed like he never came out. Apparently the ball was rattling around one of them doors down there, but all we saw was the Red Sox running around the bases. We were leaning out of the dugout trying to see what was happening down there when the ball finally came out."

The left side of the Orioles' infield, shortstop Mark Belanger and third baseman Brooks Robinson, introduced Baylor to the Major League Players Association with which both were involved. In 1986 Baylor served as league rep and seemed to be on the telephone any time he wasn't working on his hitting with Walter Hriniak.

A working knowledge of baseball's Basic Agreement

came in handy when Baylor went into the final year of his contract with the Orioles and was traded to Oakland along with Mike Torrez and Paul Mitchell in exchange for Reggie Jackson, Ken Holtzman, and Bill Van Bromel. A's owner Charlie Finley was in the process of strip-mining his ballclub and immediately cut Baylor's salary twenty percent to $36,000. Baylor got it back after the '76 season when he signed a six-year $1.6 million pact with the California Angels.

In California Baylor developed into the kind of power hitter Weaver predicted. He hit 95 homers and knocked in 323 runs in his first three years with the Angels, including '79, his MVP year, when he hit .296 with 36 homers and 139 RBI. However, life in Anaheim was not always heavenly. He was denied opportunities to go to the World Series when the Angels lost playoffs to the Orioles (1979) and Brewers (1982). The loss in Milwaukee was particularly tough because the Angels led the best-of-five series 2–0 before dropping three straight in Brewtown. During the sixteen-year history of five-game playoff series (the playoffs were upgraded to seven-game sets in 1985), this marked the only time that a team failed to win after taking the first two games.

There was one other regrettable incident while Baylor was in California. Due to a fractured left wrist, he struggled through the 1980 season—on the disabled list for over six weeks and only five homers in ninety games. In 1981 he staggered out of the blocks, getting but two hits in his first twenty-seven at bats. Then he picked up the *Anaheim Register* and read something that shocked him. California GM Buzzie Bavasi had critiqued the new Angel scorebook that featured Baylor, Rod Carew, and Fred Lynn on the cover. "What's Baylor doing in that picture with two hitters?" columnist John

Hall reported Bavasi as saying. Baylor erupted. He stormed into Bavasi's office threatening to quit.

But Baylor didn't quit. He played three more seasons for the Angels before taking the free agent route a second time. He signed with the New York Yankees and had his only .300 season (.303) there in 1983. Then three years with Yankee owner George Steinbrenner was all Baylor could take. He had a no-trade clause in his contract but agreed to leave New York for Boston. It was an easy decision. Fenway Park is a yard tailored to suit a right-handed pull-hitter, the Sox planned to DH him in every game, and Baylor had a pleasant relationship with McNamara (who coached him in California) and Gorman (who drafted him for Baltimore).

Boston knew what they were getting—a classy veteran power hitter who would also lead. Baylor looked extremely fit when he arrived in Winter Haven. He was two hundred pounds of solid muscle and his shoulders tapered to his waist as if he had a yield sign inside his jersey. His stomach protruded slightly, but there was no fat on Don Baylor. He always seemed to be sweating. He had small ears, chocolate-brown eyes, a mustache, and a smile with a fashionable Lauren Hutton gap between his front teeth. He bought a lot of his clothes in Europe and dressed better than most of his younger, more casual teammates. His voice was gentle with a slight rasp, but his words always commanded attention. Baylor had played everywhere, with everyone, and seen everything a major leaguer could see—except his name in a World Series box score.

He instituted the Kangaroo Court, which had been successful under judge Frank Robinson in Baltimore. Sox players would be fined small amounts for minor offenses. Baylor was judge and Rice collector—a very effective tandem. Baylor kept track of player offenses in a blue spiral notebook (a designated hitter has plenty of time for such details) and announced the offenses before every Sunday home game. Eating close to game time brought a $5 fine. There were similar penalties for pitchers who gave up hits on 0–2 pitches, hitters who failed to advance baserunners, fielders who overthrew cutoffs, and other such offenses. "We've had it on other clubs I've been on," said baseball's Judge Wapner. "It makes you concentrate. From now on when guys don't take the extra base or when you don't advance the runner that's a fine."

McNamara was delighted to see Baylor set up the court. "I know how he is and how he can affect a ballclub in more ways than one."

Yelling at opposing pitchers was a Baylor specialty. "Designated hitting can be a very boring job," he admitted. "Yelling keeps me in the game. I know they can hear me. That's why I've been hit forty-five times in the last two seasons. But that's all right. They know I'm waitin' for one of their second basemen or shortstops to be around the bag."

Baylor's kamikaze baserunning earned respect around the league, but his ability to be hit by a pitch made him a legend. When he came to Boston he already held the American League record for most times hit by a pitch in a career (192). His body seemed to be made for the terrible task. A muscular six one, 210 pounds, Baylor would lean over the plate and hold his ground. He rarely attempted to get out of the way of a pitch and showed pain after getting hit only once—when Nolan Ryan froze his left wrist in 1973. "I stand on the plate," he said when he joined the Red Sox. "I feel like the inside of the plate is mine and I'll stand there until I can't take it anymore."

In his first year with the Sox Baylor would set an American League record for getting hit by pitches. He was plunked thirty-five times and, in many cases, the pitcher would be the offended party, sometimes charging the plate. It was an interesting reversal of the relatively new practice of batters charging the mound. In the late seventies and early eighties, baseball witnessed a rush of these. Old-timers claimed it was a result of the American League's designated hitter rule. Knowing they themselves wouldn't have to listen to any chin music, pitchers were more comfortable making hitters dance. Charging the mound became the hitters' only response. Baylor somehow managed to turn the beat around. Baylor's failure to duck, coupled with his apparent painlessness, infuriated several pitchers who hit him. But to no avail. Drivers who crash into parked cars can't quibble because the car didn't get out of the way. "I don't like to show anything," Baylor said.

He had it down to a science. When he'd see the pitch coming, Baylor would turn and expose his back to the ball. "I don't feel anything back there," he says. "It's when the pitches get down by your hands that you are worried. I don't want anyone putting the ball on my hands. That's where I'm doing my work."

If the umpire doesn't believe he was hit, Baylor shows them a white mark on the spot where he was hit. White men turn red, then black and blue, but a black man gets a white spot on his flesh when he's struck by a fast travelling baseball.

Baylor's arrival in Winter Haven was the first indication that things might turn around for the 1986 Red Sox. Lou Gorman and Chicago White Sox GM Ken Harrelson were working on another trade the day Baylor came into camp. The White Sox were dealing Tom Seaver—a man with baggage tags marked Cooperstown—and McNamara made it clear to Gorman that he wanted Seaver. Tom Terrific pitched for McNamara in Cincinnati and the two had always enjoyed a good working relationship. Boston was willing to part with Tony Armas but wanted a prospect to go along with Seaver. Gorman asked for pitcher Bruce (son of Chuck) Tanner or outfielder Ken Williams. Harrelson did not want to part with a prospect and was aware that there were growing doubts about Armas's bat speed and his ability to patrol large center field acreage. "He's got a broken-down body," observed Kansas City General Manager John Scheurholz. When the Red Sox–White Sox proposal got hot, Chicago's veteran scout Ellis Clary was dispatched to Winter Haven and watched Boston four straight days. The deal collapsed when Harrelson refused to toss in an enricher.

Steve Lyons was the man most disappointed when these talks vaporized. The twenty-five-year-old Lyons had spent most of spring training in McNamara's doghouse and repeatedly asked reporters, "Where am I going?" He'd hit .264 in his rookie season (1985) and shown flashes of brilliance afield. Lyons had speed and versatility, and could force the action, qualities which Boston lacked. He felt he was ready to play every day and he didn't mind saying so. McNamara thought Lyons came into camp too heavy and too cocky for a kid with only 133 big league games on his resume. There was some grumbling when Lyons tried to duck a six-hour bus trip to Miami the day after he'd gotten a cortisone shot in his sore arm. Back in Boston there was considerable fan pressure to play Lyons regularly, but the manager and certain veterans scoffed at the thought.

They saw Lyons as a rowdy teenager. They disapproved of his style and manner. Baseball encourages conformity. Managers want ballplayers who keep quiet, spit tobacco, and grumble "let's get these guys" between innings. The tradition-steeped Red Sox believe in conformity more than most organizations. Free spirits and deep thinkers are chased. In Boston, where you played the party line or you didn't play at all, Lyons stood out like a punk rocker at George Will's breakfast club.

Lyons was always polite, always preening, and his teammates cringed when they heard him say, "To be honest to myself, I don't feel like you lose anything when I'm in the lineup." He had the curly hair, pearly teeth, and blue eyes of a television anchorman, but he also had terrible baseball instincts, which is why he never cracked the lineup. He made enough mistakes in the field and on the basepaths to earn the nickname Psycho. Ironically three months after the spring deal collapsed the Sox would acquire Tom Seaver in exchange for Steve Lyons.

The final days of spring training are the most fun for fans who love to scour the waiver wire, but it's a tough time for young men wondering about their careers. Sox utilityman Dave Stapleton was one of these.

Cheryl and Dave Stapleton had their second son on February 1, 1986, and four weeks later the family of four moved into Winter Haven's comfortable Holiday Inn. Twenty-month-old Shaun Stapleton was already walking better than Bill Buckner and was a fixture in the motel courtyard. "It gets tough with the two babies sometimes," the struggling thirty-two-year-old said, "but my wife is great. She takes care of things and makes sure I get my sleep."

Stapleton needed his sleep. His six-year big league career had been on the decline and had to have a good spring to stay up. After playing in 301 games in the 1982 and '83 seasons (hitting .264 and .247 respectively) Stapleton lost his first base job when the Sox traded for Buckner in 1984. The one-time starter from Fairhope, Alabama, played in only forty-three games in '84 and '85 and was now fighting for his professional life.

April 2 was Good News Day for the Stapleton family. The popular freckled infielder made the cut and would travel north with the team once again. Standing around the Lakeland batting cage at Joker Marchant Stadium before yet another meaningless game with the Tigers, Stapleton said, "It's a weight off the old shoulders. I definitely had some jitters. My stomach was really moving around when I saw all the veterans going. I hope I can do something to show that their decision is justified."

While Stapleton shook hands around the cage, Joe Sambito sat in the visitor's dugout and did a radio interview with Sox broadcaster Joe Castiglione. Sambito was another grateful survivor of the cut and he had a story to tell. One of the best relief pitchers in baseball in the late seventies and early eighties, Sambito ruptured the medial collateral ligament in his left elbow while pitching against St. Louis in April 1982. He had some pain but stayed in the game and picked up his fourth save of the young season, the seventy-second of his career. A month later he had elbow surgery. A tendon was taken from his right leg to reconstruct the ligament, but the operation left him with almost no feeling in his left hand—not a good situation for a man who makes his living throwing left-handed fastballs. He had two more operations a year later and worked hard on hand exercises. Sambito didn't pitch again in 1982 or 1983 but kept at his hand exercises and in '84 came back to pitch in thirty-two games for the Astros. Houston trailed in twenty-nine of those thirty-two games. Sambito did not register a single save, and a year later was released at the end of spring training. He signed with the Mets, but didn't pitch well in Flushing Meadow (12.66 ERA) and was shipped to Tidewater (AAA) in June. The Mets released him in August. He felt like throwing in the towel but gave it one more shot. On January 31, 1986, the veteran lefty signed a Red Sox contract that would earn him $275,000 if he made the team. Sambito came to spring training intent on proving that he could still get hitters out. He was never overpowering but did what Frank Tanana did after arm problems: made the conversion from power to finesse. McNamara was impressed and Sambito made the team on April 2.

Sambito and Stapleton smiled, but Mike Stenhouse and Mike Brown did not. Stenhouse, a journeyman player with a Harvard degree, hit .333 in Florida but lost in the numbers game. He was asked to report to Pawtucket and said he'd think about it. Brown compiled an ERA of 0.75 in the Grapefruit League before he was axed. He requested a trade and fired this salvo in an effort to expedite his departure: "For fifty years pitchers have stunk here and for fifty years they've been changing them. Whatever they're doing is not working. They act like they've got five guys who won twenty games on this staff." Stenhouse and Brown both reported to Pawtucket but would be back to make significant contributions before season's end.

Boston's twenty-four-man roster didn't impress the experts. The Sox had finished fifth in 1985 in the American League East. And in a poll of 210 members of the Baseball Writers Association of America, a whopping 120 scribes picked the Sox to do so again. *Sports Illustrated* listed Boston sixteenth in a rating of the twenty-six major league teams and quoted an anonymous Sox player as saying, "I read all winter where we were going to make amends for last year's disappointment. Then the games start and baserunners are being picked off, cutoff men are being overthrown, we're grounding into doubleplays, and balls are falling in. Nothing's changed." *Inside Sports* picked them fifth and predicted a 79–83 finish. *Sport Magazine* followed suit and wrote, "The Red Sox are the most boring team in baseball. . . . This collection of slow and aging vets has lost together for too long." *The Sporting News*, baseball's bible, also picked them fifth and stated, "Realistically, the Red Sox are encouraging false hope." Closer to home, there was a discernible lack of blind provincialism. The Red Sox pre-season analysis in *The Boston Globe* by this writer was superimposed on a giant number five—large enough for George Scott's uniform jersey—and led with this grand slam: "Fifth place is their middle name. Dull. Sluggish. Passive. Unimaginative. All of the above have been used to describe the 1986 Red Sox edition that schlepped through spring training in central Florida. Even the boldest prognosticator can't fathom the thought of this club finishing higher than fourth in the American League East." After Baylor was acquired, the same smug scribe wrote, "At least it's an attempt to breathe some life into a brain-dead team."

Sox players were understandably insulted. "Everybody's so negative," said Wade Boggs. "What do you think people thought of the Tigers before they won in eighty-four? If we stay healthy and play up to our ability, I think we can win."

Boggs's statement was unusually strong because there weren't many players talking pennant when the team prepared to leave Florida. The most optimistic Boston vet of them all—Mike Easler—had been shipped to New York and most of the regulars were predicting improvement without any grand promises.

"I'll tell you one thing," said Dwight Evans, the senior continuous service Sox player, "there's a new feeling here. I don't know if that means we're going to be a better ballclub or not, but I think we can; and in all the years I've been here, I can't remember having a feeling like this. This team might surprise a lot of people."

There was one fearless prediction. The 1986 New Year's day strip of "Pogo" featured a mouse telling two sleeping companions, "Wake up, wake up. It's a brand new year. This is the year the Red Sox win the pennant." Leave it to Boston to have their only published first-place prediction appear on the funny pages.

The Sox carried an 11–16 record into their final spring game, a high noon matinee against the Tigers on Saturday, April 5. Detroit manager Sparky Anderson didn't bring his best unit to Winter Haven, but it probably wouldn't have mattered. After being knocked around for a month, Roger Clemens threw caution aside and fired silver bullets. He abandoned his curveball and blinded the Tigers with white heat—just like in the young days. Clemens was waiting for an opportunity to air out his arm and chose the final exhibition game. He pitched seven innings, allowed three hits and no runs, and struck out nine while walking one. "I'm very satisfied with where I am right now," he said.

Clemens's performance in the final pre-season game was lost in Sunday's news because loose cannon Dennis Boyd rolled off the deck again. An hour before Clemens took the mound, McNamara marched into the press room (where writers eat hamburgers and which is known as Locke-Ober South) to announce, "Mr. Boyd was late again today and has been fined a day's pay. There's not going to be one set of rules for twenty-three and another set for Oil Can. Clemens had a little problem today, but he called in. I don't think it takes talent to be on time." Gedman, Buckner, Rice, and Baylor were in McNamara's office with Boyd when the fine of approximately $2,150 was levied. "They just wanted everybody to know what was going on," said Rice.

As the Red Sox charter flight from Orlando to Detroit lifted off the ground later that day, newcomer Sammy Stewart announced, "American League, here we come." Boyd joined Baylor during the flight and the troubled hurler got some counseling. "We had a talk in private, but I wasn't going to force myself on him," said Baylor. "We talked about basic things—what it takes to play in the big leagues. You can have all the talent in the world, but if you get bothered by personal problems, you're not gonna be around. I remember Mike Norris when he came up with Oakland in seventy-six. He was a young kid like Can, and he missed buses and planes. Eventually it catches up with you. Mike Norris probably will never pitch in the big leagues again, and that shouldn't happen to a young guy with talent like that."

Clemens's performance and Baylor's presence gave the Red Sox two powerful, new weapons when they touched down at the Detroit Airport on the night of April 5, 1986.

3

K DAYS WITH ROGER ONE

Home plate was crooked at Tiger Stadium. Bob Stanley, Bill Buckner, and Marty Barrett, the three wise men, were the first to notice that it was a little too far back and tilted slightly in the direction of right field. Wade Boggs, the man with the vision to hit .368, got down on his hands and knees like a golfer sizing up a putt and said, "It's off. They're cheatin' already." Groundskeeper Frankie Fenech was summoned and Boggs drew a line for the Detroit field marshall. "If it were moved up to here it would be straight."

Fenech was hot and snapped, "Now let me tell you something, pal. The plate is lined up with the pitching rubber and second base. I don't know what everybody's worried about."

The plate was never moved.

There was another mild Motown controversy. The

Cincinnati Reds traditionally start play before any other team in baseball, but Boston and Detroit were getting a twenty-eight minute jump on the 2:05 scheduled start at Riverfront. J. Kenneth Blackwell, vice mayor of Cincinnati, accused Sparky Anderson of underhand tactics and McNamara's name was also dropped. The good people of Cincinnati apparently thought that Anderson and McNamara, two men who'd managed and been fired by the Reds, had conspired to deny the city its annual first-ball boast. McNamara chuckled when he heard the charge.

John Francis McNamara had one of the best reputations in baseball. He'd been in the game thirty-five years and cultivated lifelong friends at every stop on the way to Boston. The son of a railroad man who immigrated from Ireland and landed in Boston just after the turn of the century, McNamara was born June 4, 1932, in Sacramento, California. His father, a worker with the Union Pacific Railroad, died when John was twelve and his mother was left to raise her six children alone. The kids went to school and church without fail, and young John, an altar boy, was introduced to baseball by uncles who lived across the street. He signed with the St. Louis Cardinals after he graduated from high school in 1951, but he was a small catcher who couldn't hit. He spent the 1953 and '54 seasons in the Army and worked toward an accounting degree at Sacramento State College. When he returned to pro ball he struggled to hit .200 and the Cardinals released him in 1955. McNamara wanted to stay in baseball and played for Sacramento and Lewiston, Idaho, before getting his big break in 1959. Lewiston manager Hollis Lane retired and twenty-six-year-old John McNamara was offered the job. Two years later Kansas City A's farm director Hank Peters made Lewiston the A's full-time farm club, and McNamara began his association with one of the most innovative and productive organizations in baseball. In the A's camp he came under the tutelage of legendary pitching coach "Sailor" Bill Posedel.

In 1963 McNamara was the A's Double-A manager at Birmingham. The Triple-A manager was Haywood Sullivan. When the A's moved to Oakland in '68, Peters made McNamara a big league coach and by '70 McNamara was a thirty-seven-year-old big league manager. Charlie Finley fired him and replaced him with Dick Williams after one full season, and McNamara coached with the Giants before taking over the woeful Padres in 1974. Fired early in the 1977 season, he went to California to coach under Jim Fregosi for a year. When the Reds were looking for a man to replace Sparky Anderson in 1979, McNamara got the call. He won his first division title in '79, but was fired again in the middle of the 1982 season. Peters was General Manager of the Orioles in '82 and wanted McNamara to replace Earl Weaver, but McNamara didn't want to follow another legend. Seeking to move near his children on the west coast, he took the Angels' job and managed California for two years until he resigned to rejoin Sullivan in Boston.

A small man with silver hair, a prominent nose, and year-round sunburn, McNamara is not an imposing figure but he projects presence. He has the soft voice of a librarian, but his steely blue eyes penetrate cement walls and don't miss a thing. McNamara keeps a mental file on everyone and everything around him. He knows who is feuding with whom, whose father is sick, who is having domestic problems, and who is goofing off in the outfield during batting practice. He projects eternal calm and everlasting control.

McNamara has carried his mother's values into middle age and never misses Sunday mass. He loves talking about his children; and he positively glows when his son Mike, now a Marine lieutenant, comes to visit. McNamara has often said that his ballplayers helped him relate to his children when they were young. "I was around young players all the time and I knew the lingo and sometimes it surprised my kids."

Most of his former players love him. McNamara is a father figure to Reggie Jackson. When the slugger was a minor league prospect in 1967 McNamara managed him and at a Birmingham restaurant that wouldn't serve Jackson because he was black, McNamara pulled the team out of the eatery. "That's what John McNamara is about," Jackson wrote in his 1984 biography. "He was and still is like blood to me."

McNamara has no tolerance for foolishness and, like all managers, hates it when reporters refer to him as "coach." A major league manager would rather be addressed as hairball than coach. The Sox manager can be particularly rough on out-of-town writers. He isn't much of a self-promoter and, unlike Earl Weaver and Tom Lasorda, is not comfortable schmoozing in the dugout. "He treats out of town reporters like they just used his toothbrush," noted one rebuffed scribe.

He trusts his coaches and leaves them alone. In 1986 Joe Morgan was in charge of the bullpen, Walter Hriniak was in charge of the hitters, Bill Fischer was in charge of the pitchers, and Rene Lachemann was the scout and overseer of the camp. McNamara worked closest with Fischer because he believes pitching is the most important aspect of the game.

He isn't particularly interested in bunting or trick plays, but seethes when fundamentals are botched. He is not a tinkerer. And in 1986 the Sox lineup would not change much from day to day, as seven players accumulated more than 520 official at bats.

Though universally respected as a solid baseball man and a stabilizing force, John McNamara had been fired three times and owned a lifetime major league winning percentage of but .483 (751–805) when he was hired by Boston. His Angels were 81–81 in 1984 and the Red Sox went 81–81 in McNamara's first year in Boston. His record was at best mediocre and he needed a pennant-winning year to prove he was more than one of baseball's good-old-boys who circulated from city to city without controversy or celebration.

The 1986 Red Sox season started dramatically enough when leadoff batter Dwight Evans hit Jack Morris's first pitch over the left field fence, marking the only time in baseball history that anyone has homered on the first pitch of the first big league game. The Sox hit three more homers off Morris and Evans's blast might have been perceived as a happy harbinger—if not for the manner in which they gave the game away. Boston hit four home runs and overcame a 4–2 deficit with three runs in the top of the seventh, then lost it when reliever Sammy Stewart yielded a two-run homer to Kirk Gibson on an 0–2 pitch. A lifelong product of the Baltimore system where George Bamberger and Earl Weaver said a pitcher should never waste a pitch, Stewart violated one of his new manager's cardinal rules. Meanwhile Boggs went 0–5, struck out three times, and still claimed the plate was crooked.

Boston's second game was worse. Oil Can Boyd

handed a 4–2 lead to the bullpen in the eighth, which failed again. Joe Sambito and Bob Stanley coughed up a couple of runs, and when the Sox went ahead in the tenth, Stanley and Steve Crawford surrendered the game in the bottom of the inning. It looked like the 1986 season would be Raging Bullpen Redux. In '85 Boston lost 31 games after the sixth inning and compiled only 29 saves, second-fewest in the American League. The brass and the bullpen gang had promised more relief in 1986, but the first two games had fans back home rolling their eyes and saying, "Same old Sox."

"We'll be better," promised Stanley. "We'll be all right. We'd better be or we'll all be shipped to Russia or someplace."

The Sox did not leave Detroit empty handed. It snowed during batting practice on April 10 and frosty Al Nipper threw 149 pitches en route to a 4–2 victory. The save went to Joe Sambito, his first in almost four years.

The next night in Chicago pitching coach Bill Fischer was walking Clemens out to the bullpen where Roger would warm up for his first start when he was called over to the stands. There Fischer was given a small rock by a wild-eyed old man who said, "Hold on to this and you'll win the pennant." Fischer stuffed the stone into his warmup jacket, where it would stay all season. Clemens beat the White Sox that night, throwing 129 pitches in 8.2 innings of a 7–2 victory. It was his first win since August 3, 1985, and evened the Red Sox at 2–2. Twenty-four hours later Tom Seaver beat Boston and fielded questions about his trade possibilities. "If that happens, it happens. It's not something I think about when I go to work."

The Sox were delayed getting out of Chicago and

spent considerable time hanging out at O'Hare International Airport before the trip to their Fenway homecoming. Tony Armas, who failed to knock in a run in Boston's six-game season-starting trip, bought beers for everyone in sight to toast the birth of his fifth child, Antonio. The Armas home in Newton, Massachusetts, was the House of Antonio. The center fielder, a Newton resident, was named Antonio Rafael Armas and his wife's maiden name was Antonio. Their five children were Griselda, Maria Luisa, Antonio, Antoinette, and baby Antonio. "It's not unusual where I come from," said the native Venezuelan.

Nearby Bob Stanley prepared for a homecoming roasting from the Fenway critics. Stanley walked around the terminal shaking hands with teammates and saying, "Hi, I'm Lou Stanley. You might think you hear some booing when they introduce me at the ballpark tomorrow, but they're really just saying 'Lou.' They introduce us in numerical order and I told Bruce Hurst, number forty-seven, not to worry. He'll hear the boos, but they'll be leftovers from me, number forty-six. It will be brutal."

The commercial flight was late and uneventful. As the plane's cabin lights came on approaching Boston's Logan Airport well after midnight, Sammy Stewart bellowed, "Wake up, John McNamara, it's time to go to sleep." The comment got a big laugh, but McNamara mumbled, "That Stewart is a real wise-ass." One week earlier a Boston television station had videotaped McNamara apparently snoozing on the Sox bench during an exhibition game. Making full use of modern editing techniques and sound effects, the station aired a segment that McNamara considered humiliating and unfair. "I'm not very pleased," the manager said after he learned of the spoof. "They spliced it together, and it was a time when we were reviewing some things. I didn't like that very much."

The city of Boston observed its annual religious and civic holiday on Monday, April 14—the Red Sox home opener at Fenway Park against the World Champion Kansas City Royals. Fenway is the only spot in New England where the fusion of church and state goes unchallenged; people go there to worship and nobody complains about public prayer because everyone in New England is praying for the Sox to win a championship.

Opening Day '86 marked the seventy-fifth anniversary of the changeless green theater with the asymmetrical field lines and the reach-out-and-touch sight lines. Built in 1912 in the center of Boston's "Emerald Necklace," Fenway Park was squeezed into a geometric gem with the Boston and Albany Railroad tracks on one side and Boston's cowpath streets on the other. It is cozy.

Thirty-three-year-old Sambito, a Brooklyn native and a veteran of nine big league seasons, had never been in the ballpark. "I've got a lot of relatives here and when I was a kid we came to Boston for a lot of visits, but I never went to a game. I had seen Fenway, but only once. When I was a teenager, I was in that observatory at the top of the Prudential Tower. Somebody pointed out the ballpark to me. It looked like a little green dot. I'm really impressed now that I see it. I expected the left field wall to be twenty feet behind the shortstop. The toughest thing about the park is getting here. I was driving around for forty minutes. I could see the stadium, I just couldn't reach it."

A beautiful April afternoon turned ugly when the Sox bullpen checked in. Ed Romero's error turned a 2–2 tie into a 4–2 deficit and Stanley relieved Boyd in the eighth, surrendering a pair of run-scoring singles as 34,764 hooted. "It's what the people wanted to see, I guess," the lumpish pitcher said with a shrug. "I was prepared for it, but it doesn't give you too much confidence." Then Stanley uttered those words that sounded hollow and foolish at the time, but proved semi-prophetic: "When I'm standing out there and save the final game of the season and we win the pennant and I'm waving in the air, I'll be waving to my wife and family. The rest of 'em can go to hell."

Boston's home opener was a public relations disaster. Having your million-dollar-per-year relief pitcher tell the flock to "go to hell" after blowing up in a six-run inning is *not* the way to start a season.

A couple of injuries slowed things in the first month. Starting shortstop Glenn Hoffman was shelved with a wide range of problems. On Easter Sunday Hoffman turned his right ankle running out a grounder against the Blue Jays in Winter Haven. He started the first two games of the season and made a damaging error in the second one in Detroit. As Ed Romero started the next fifteen games in Hoffman's place, McNamara seemed to have a different reason for resting Hoffman each day. Ankle problems, dizzy spells, blurred vision, and nervousness about his wife who was overdue with their first child were all cited. Romero was a capable fill-in but proved to be the very definition of a utility player: leave him in long enough and he'll start to hurt the cause. The Sox, worrying whether Hoffman would ever be ready, began searching for a shortstop. They were not content to continue the season with Ed Romero at short every day.

Reliever Wes Gardner had a more specific problem.

On the opening day roster Gardner represented Boston's only return in the controversial Ojeda trade. Messrs. Schiraldi, Tarver, and Christensen were all in Pawtucket while Ojeda was throwing zeros as the Mets steamrolled through the National League. Gardner pitched one inning of relief in a 12–2 blowout victory at Chicago, then a muscle tear in his shoulder put him on the shelf and he was disabled April 14 with surgery to follow.

The Sox wallowed in the familiar waters of mediocrity through April, but there were flashes of better things to come. On a Thursday afternoon against the Royals, Clemens ran his record to 2–0 on the strength of a tie-breaking two-out grand slam by Baylor. Clemens said, "If we keep pitching this well and we keep the team in the game, the guys are gonna be popping the balls in the seats and we're gonna come out on top."

Boston vaulted over the haunting .500 barrier for the final time April 26 when Nipper beat the Royals in Kansas City. The next day's game was rained out and was followed by a day off, which meant Clemens was working with six days' rest when he took the Fenway mound to face the Seattle Mariners on April 29.

The Patriots and Celtics were the major sports stories in Boston on that soon-to-be-famous Tuesday. In Foxborough the Pats had selected SMU running back Reggie Dupard in the first round of the NFL draft that morning. Over on Causeway Street the Celtics were primed for an Eastern Conference semi-final playoff showdown against Dominique Wilkins and the Atlanta Hawks. While tickets for the Celtics were impossible to get, only 13,414 filed into Fenway to see the Sox and the lowly Mariners game, which was not aired on AM radio in Boston because of the Celtic game.

Before things began, Bill Buckner told Nipper that Clemens would strike out eighteen Mariners. "The way he's been throwing and the way they've been striking out, eighteen seemed like the number," Buckner said later. "It's pretty tough to predict twenty."

The 1986 Mariners were sultans of swish. When they ran into the Clemens express, they were en route to shattering an American League record with 1,148 strikeouts, only fifty-five short of the major league mark held by the 1968 New York Mets. Seattle's K-Nine fanned 166 times in their first nineteen games in '86. They were scarcely prepared for Clemens who was 3–0, had punched out ten Tigers in 6.2 innings his previous start, and was working with six days' rest.

Spike Owen, Clemens's once and future teammate, led off for Seattle and struck out swinging on a 3–2 fastball. Phil Bradley and Ken Phelps went down in identical fashion in the 1-2-3 first. Clemens had six strikeouts in the first three innings. Leading off the fourth, Owen sliced an 0–2 curveball to right for a single. Making one of his rare starts at first base, Judge Baylor took a mental note to fine Clemens $5 for surrendering a hit on an 0–2 pitch.

It was then the game took on a new tone. Clemens struck out eight straight batters after Owen's hit and Baseball America stood at attention. Associated Press and UPI flashed the news throughout the land. Boston right-hander Roger Clemens had twelve strikeouts after five innings and fourteen after six, including eight straight. The eight straight tied an American League record, and Clemens will always have Texas soul brother Don Baylor to thank for his two records. With Owen on first and two out in the fourth, Baylor backpedaled on a foul pop by veteran Gorman Thomas.

The ball clanged off Baylor's rusty glove and Clemens had a second chance to whiff the ancient Mariner. Thomas was caught looking at a 3–2 fastball to end the fourth.

Halfway across the country Clemens's mother, Bess Wright, and two of her daughters, Janet and Bonnie, were watching the game on television—thanks to the satellite dish at the West Houston Bowl lanes. Unfortunately, others wanted to switch to the NBA Rockets playoff games and the Clemens clan was outvoted. Janet wanted to scratch a few eyes out when Roger's image was switched off to make room for twin towers Ralph Sampson and Akeem Olajuwon.

While Clemens's mother and sisters tried to find another satellite dish, the Mariners were swinging and missing at a record clip. After fanning Thomas, Clemens punched out five consecutive Seattle hitters, giving him the eight straight. Nolan Ryan (Angels '72 and '73) and Ron Davis (Twins '81) were the only other American Leaguers who had struck out eight straight batters. Owen, Clemens's sure-handed shortstop at the University of Texas, broke the strikeout string with a fly to center.

In the middle of his streak the K kids appeared in the right field bleachers. This peaceful gang from Newton decorated Fenway by plastering a giant red *K* placard on the green wall behind the last row of bleachers in right after every Clemens strikeout. The K kids hadn't planned on attending the weeknight April contest but heard Clemens ringing up the strikeouts (on FM radio) and rushed to the park with enough placards to paper the place.

Clemens struck out Bradley to start the seventh, then walked toward the Sox dugout. McNamara clutched his heart and said, "Roger, what's wrong?"

"I've got to clean my spikes," said the Rocket Man.

Ken Phelps whiffed for a third straight time, but then Thomas crushed a 1–2 fastball and drove it into the center-field bleachers to give Seattle a 1–0 lead. After the top of the seventh, homeplate umpire Vic Voltaggio, a ten-year veteran of big league ball, shook his head and told the batboy that this was the best pitching performance he'd ever seen.

In the bottom of the seventh Dwight Evans got the run back with interest, smashing a Mike Moore pitch to center for a three-run homer. Meanwhile, Clemens told McNamara that his legs were tired and starting to cramp, but his arm felt fine. After ringing up two more strikeouts in the eighth, he retreated to a chair in front of his locker while the Sox hit. Nipper informed the twenty-three-year-old Texan that he was within one strikeout of tying a major league record. Owen led off the ninth and whiffed on a 1–2 fastball. Phil Bradley was next and ran the count to 2–0 while looking past Clemens at the Fenway messageboard that read: "Roger Clemens has tied the major league strikeout record for strikeouts in a nine-inning game with nineteen." Clemens was tied with Steve Carlton, Nolan Ryan, and Tom Seaver. He threw three more fastballs, all strikes, and Bradley took the last one as homeplate umpire Voltaggio signalled Clemens into the record books. Third baseman Wade Boggs jogged over to shake Clemens's hand. In 111 years, covering almost 150,000 games, no big league pitcher had ever fanned twenty batters in a nine-inning game.

Players in the Sox dugout worried about the precious baseball. Clemens still had the 20-K ball and was getting ready to pitch to Ken Phelps. What if Phelps homered or just hit a foul into the seats? That ball could be lost forever or scooped up by some disco king walking to a nightclub outside Fenway. Not to worry. Phelps grounded to short for the final out, and the ball was safe.

There weren't many sportswriters or photographers to record the magic moment. Most of the locals were either scrutinizing the NFL draft or watching the Celtics dissect the Atlanta Hawks. Dancing Dave O'Hara, the veteran Boston baseball scribe for the Associated Press, found himself grumbling high above courtside at the crusty Garden while Clemens made history at Fenway. *Globe* Sox regular Larry Whiteside did the same. The popular Sides, who had the night off, stopped at Fenway, watched two innings, then drove over to Causeway Street where Larry Bird and Co. were set to burn Atlanta. When the Garden scoreboard flashed, "Roger Clemens has twelve strikeouts after five innings," Vince Doria, the *Globe* sports editor who was also watching the Celts, asked Whiteside for the Fenway press box number. "Gee, he only had five when I left," Whiteside said, indicating that six strikeouts in two innings were needed to hold his attention. While the Celtics raced toward a 119–108 victory, several photographers and local camera crews retreated from the Garden and bolted to catch the last inning at Fenway.

Yet it was a camera-toting fan—the ubiquitous Joe Hickey, known for his photos of the Red Sox and their families taken on team cruises and during spring training—who snapped the best shot of the final strikeout. The picture appeared in *Sports Illustrated* and became the official photograph of Clemens's record-setting performance. Roger obtained dozens of matted copies and presented each of his teammates with autographed souvenirs.

When Ken Phelps grounded to short for the final out, Stormin' Gormin resisted the temptation to applaud from the on deck circle. "I wanted to tip my hat," said Thomas, who fanned only once. "He was that good."

"I saw Catfish Hunter pitch a perfect game and I saw Mike Witt pitch a perfect game and Tom Seaver pitch some great games—but that was the most awesome display of pitching I've ever seen," McNamara said.

Debbie Clemens rushed down to the rail in front of the box seats to hug her husband as the small crowd stood and applauded. There wasn't much sleep at the Clemens's apartment in Malden that night. Clemens was up calling his mother, brothers, and sisters.

In Houston Janet picked up the phone and heard, "Sis, I'm in the Hall of Fame."

Roger Clemens lay awake for several hours, then drifted into a strange dream in which he was arrested after delivering a head-slap to a fan who charged the mound in the middle of a game. "That's when I woke up," he remembered. "The police were taking me away for hitting the dude in the head."

Wednesday, April 30, was a wild day in the Sox public relations department. The Hall of Fame placed one of the first calls and requested Clemens's ball, cap, glove, and spikes, plus the official score sheet. *Newsweek, Sports Illustrated, People, The New York Times, The Washington Post, USA Today*, and the *CBS Morning News* were among those requesting interviews.

Clemens threw 138 pitches at the Mariners, 97 strikes. He struck out the side three times and was clocked at 97 miles per hour (95 MPH consistently) on a gun used by a Toronto Blue Jays scout. He had two strikes on five of the ten batters who did not strike out. The Mariners put only ten balls in play, and but two were pulled. Clemens did not have a three-ball count after the fourth inning. He struck out more batters in one evening than former teammate Mike Trujillo fanned during the entire 1985 season (nineteen in eighty-four innings). Some skeptics believe that Seattle's penchant for punch-outs tainted the record (Boston pitchers struck out sixteen Mariners the next night). It should also be noted that Clemens did not have the advantage of pitching to pitchers—a soft spot Seaver and Carlton exploited in their nineteen-strikeout performances.

Two historical footnotes should be remembered: 1. Clemens came perilously close to losing the game. He trailed 1–0 after six and a half innings and would have lost it except for Evans's timely blast; 2. Fanning twenty without sacrificing any control was the most impressive aspect of the feat. If there is any justice, the game will be remembered as Clemens's 20-strikeout/zero-walk performance. The Rocket Man himself admitted, "If the record's ever broken, I don't think anybody will walk in a game like that."

William Roger Clemens was born August 4, 1962, in Dayton, Ohio. His natural father, Bill Clemens, was a truck driver for a chemical plant. Bill Clemens was on the road frequently and did not encourage his older sons, Richard and Randy, to play sports. Richard, Randy, Brenda, and Janet were born before Roger, and the future pitcher was still an infant when Bill and Bess Clemens separated. Roger never met his real father and that was the way Bess Clemens wanted it. She married again, and a tool and die man named Woody Booher became Roger's stepfather. Woody and Bess then had Bonnie.

Bess Lee was born in Tennessee and moved to Ohio when she was a junior in high school. She was pretty, vivacious, and popular. She married young and started a family immediately. Raising her children properly became her goal in life. She didn't like the way things went with Bill Clemens, and it especially bothered her when he discouraged oldest son Richard from playing sports. Bess made sure that didn't happen with Randy and saved enough Top Value Stamps to get him his first baseball glove. Ten years older than Roger, Randy was a good athlete. He played basketball and baseball all the time. He never grew to be six four and 215 pounds, but he was good enough to play both sports at Mississippi College.

Woody Booher was a giving, loving father. He never left the house without a kid or two; and he'd let little Roger ride on the back of his motorcycle. When Booher suffered a second heart attack and died in 1970, Roger was only eight and just starting his baseball career.

Most exceptional athletes are driven by a role model, usually a father or older brother. Randy Clemens was there for Roger. Randy was the star athlete in the family and Roger spent his early years going to Randy's games, serving as batboy, and playing catch with the older kids whenever possible. Randy looked out for his kid brother. He had a summer job maintaining the baseball fields and drove the tractor that dragged the infield. And as he knew all the little league coaches, he got them to bend the rules to let Roger get a head start.

Roger began school a year early. He was big for his age and Randy made sure that he was always matched against older kids. It wasn't until after his stepfather died that Roger started to excel. Randy remembers his brother striking out nineteen batters and hitting a pair of homers in a little league game. In one inning he threw only nine pitches. When he wasn't pitching, he played first base, shortstop, or left field. Sometimes he even caught. When he got older and played doubleheaders, he'd pitch the first game and catch the second. He was big and threw hard.

"I just had a tremendous amount of fun playing

sports," Clemens recalls. "My mother made sure I had all the right equipment and plenty of it. I mean I played sports. People would be having a little softball game in their yards a few streets down and next thing you know me and my friends, we'd be in the game."

When he wasn't playing, he talked sports. "He talked about them constantly," remembers his mother. "He was then like he is now. He was never showy, he didn't brag. But I think he knew."

Richard moved to Houston in 1971. Like his step-father Woody, he knew the tool and die industry and there weren't any jobs for Vietnam Vets like himself in Dayton, Ohio, in 1971. But there were jobs in Houston.

Richard's move to Houston proved significant to Roger's development as one by one the Clemenses followed Richard to Texas. Roger was a high school freshman when he went out to Houston to live with his brother Randy and his wife, Kathy. She was an elementary school teacher and saw to it that young Roger kept his grades up. Meanwhile Bess Wright, who'd taken the name of her third husband (a marriage that quickly ended in divorce), stayed in Ohio with daughters Janet and Bonnie.

It was a bold step for a fourteen-year-old, even though Roger's mother had told him that she would be following soon. The Clemenses wanted to leave the climate and the memories of Dayton behind. Houston had the heat, the jobs, and baseball.

Randy directed Roger's high school career, leaving nothing to chance. There would be no more twenty-game seasons with five rainouts and five snow-outs in America's Rust Belt. Roger would play big-time high school baseball. He would have the finest facilities and meet top-level competition.

Roger attended Dulles High School, the biggest

school in Texas. "It was just humongous," he recalls. "As a freshman and sophomore, I had like a 12–1 record. I was dazzling and all that stuff. I thought I was Lord K again, or whatever they say. And Randy said that when Mom moved down there, the decision where we were gonna live would be based on where I could get the best competition."

In Roger's sophomore year at Dulles, he and Randy attended a Texas 5-A playoff game between Spring Woods and Bellaire. It was big-time high school baseball and Roger's eyes were the size of catcher's mitts. "He saw the competition and the uniforms and it excited him," remembers Randy.

Randy Clemens talked to coach Charlie Maiorana, a dedicated baseball man who played by the rules and won consistently. The baseball program at Spring Woods was Maiorana's baby. There were radar guns, pitching machines, and a field that was better than most diamonds in the minor leagues. Ironically, the left field line at Spring Woods measured 315 feet, which is the same length marked at the bottom of the foul stripe on Fenway's left field wall. Maiorana manicured his ballpark religiously and secured the premises with a chain link fence. There was no electronic force field only because Maiorana couldn't afford one.

The decision was made. Bess Wright would leave Dayton and move to a townhouse apartment off Gessner Road in Houston—just a short toss from Andy Granatelli's Tune-up Shop, Baskin-Robbins, Jack-in-the-Box, Kentucky Fried Chicken, U-Haul, Porky's Pub, gas stations, and used car lots. But Gessner Road was also located in the heart of the Spring Woods school district, where Bess took a job as a bookkeeper for a national rug chain.

Clemens played football, basketball, and baseball at

Spring Woods. He weighed 220 pounds during the fall and labored on the defensive line trying to stop running backs like Stratford's Craig James. During the winter, he ran the basketball court from end to end and his weight dropped closer to 200. Maiorana thought he was still a little heavy when he came out for baseball. "He was a big, oversized kid," the coach recalls. "You could tell he hadn't developed. He was very kiddish looking."

Clemens was the third starter on the 1979 Spring Woods Tigers. Right-hander Rick Leuchen and lefty Raynor Noble held down the top spots in the rotation and both became number one draft picks. The Tigers went 31–4 and Clemens was 6–0. There were never fewer than five scouts at a game and when Spring Woods played Stratford, Maiorana counted thirty in the stands. The coach had his players warm up in center field to keep them away from the scouts. Roger fanned eighteen in one outing. And when Noble and Leuchen were drafted, his mind fastened on the pros.

Roger was a driven young man, always thinking about baseball, always running. Maiorana wasn't sure how good he would be. The kid threw over eighty miles per hour and had a pear-shaped body, but there was no question about his willingness to pay the price. "If I'd been at Westchester and had David Clyde in high school, I'd have known he was a major leaguer," Maiorana says. "But maybe his development in high school is why he's working in a lumberyard now. Maybe things happened too quick. I'm not here to make major leaguers. Roger had ability. He had the one thing you've got to have: mental toughness. And he wanted the ball against the best teams. I can't think of anything he had trouble with in high school except English themes. Roger didn't have a car in high school. He would run all the way up here. Sometimes he'd get a ride after practice, but others he'd just sling his duffel bag over his shoulder and take off. I tell that to our kids now who drive cars that I can't afford. Roger didn't have a daddy giving him money."

"I didn't have the father image that maybe was my brother's," admits Clemens. "But I was brought up right by my grandmother and my mother and I knew that I was going to have to work to get myself off the ground. If I didn't work for it, there was no way I was going to get it. When I got to high school there with my mom, the giving sort of stopped. She wanted me to know that I was going to have to get out there and work and do it on my own."

He always had a fan club. His mother, brothers, and sisters attended most of his games and they were never shy. Janet wouldn't hesitate to holler at coach Maiorana if she didn't like the way he was handling Roger. Maiorana's courageous wife, one of the longest-living victims of cystic fibrosis in history, attended every game and the Spring Woods tradition called for players to pay respects to Mrs. Maiorana immediately after the games. Though Clemens always paid his respects, it was sometimes hard getting him away from the clutches of his mother and sisters.

After graduating from Spring Woods, Roger accepted a scholarship at San Jacinto Junior College, where his coach was Wayne Graham, who had played twenty games with the Mets and had worked part-time as a batting practice pitcher for the Astros. Clemens started throwing ninety miles per hour at San Jacinto, and, at the end of that season, he had to choose between a scholarship to the University of Texas or $20,000 from New York's National League franchise.

Dwight Gooden and Roger Clemens were the ebony and ivory Cy Young bookends of major league baseball in 1985 and '86, and the Mets could only wonder what it would have been like to have had both stoppers on the same staff. New York had the chance. Gooden was still in high school when Met scout Jim Terrell scouted Clemens four times at San Jacinto and was impressed by the eighteen-year-older's velocity and control. Terrell had just joined the Met organization after two decades in the Baltimore system and on his recommendation the Mets drafted Clemens in the twelfth round in 1981. Graham was pitching batting practice for the Astros the night the Mets invited Clemens to the Astrodome to throw in the bullpen. Clemens donned a Met uniform and started throwing. At one point he stepped off the mound and asked the catcher to make him sound better as there wasn't quite enough pop in the mitt. Then he saw Met pitching coach Bob Gibson and manager Joe Torre and he began sweating. Gibson wasn't particularly impressed with him.

The Mets were willing to offer $20,000, but Clemens wanted $25,000. He said he needed the extra money because his mother's social security checks ($450 per month) would last only as long as he was in school. Terrell went back to Houston, watched Clemens throw again, then accompanied the eighteen-year-old to his home. Terrell made his offer and Clemens explained his price. Terrell excused himself, went into Bess Wright's kitchen, and called New York. He spoke to Lou Gorman, the Mets vice president for baseball operations. Terrell explained to Gorman that Clemens would settle for $12,500 on the spot and $12,500 a year later but wouldn't take $20,000. Gorman, whose fiscal responsibility with the Mets would carry him to a pennant and make him runner-up Executive of the Year five summers later in Boston, said it was too high.

Clemens loved his experience at the University of Texas. He considered himself a Texan, and all young Texans want to play in Austin, surrounded by athletes of comparable ability. He had two requests of coach Cliff Gustafson: he wanted the ball in the big games and he especially wanted to pitch against Texas A & M in his sophomore season. Gustafson, who had coached an NCAA championship team at Texas in 1975, knew Clemens would bring him another title. Spike Owen was Clemens's first Longhorn shortstop and Calvin Schiraldi was on the staff with him when Texas won the NCAA title in 1983. Roger was 25–7 with 241 strikeouts in 275 innings in two years at Texas. He was Boston's first pick in the 1983 draft, nineteenth overall.

His right arm and shoulder worked overtime in 1983. The pressure to win the College World Series in Omaha made him throw harder than ever. The Sox shipped him directly to A-ball. After three starts at Winter Haven, Boston farm director Ed Kenney went to Lakeland to see Clemens. There the young righty threw ninety-six miles per hour and fanned fifteen. Shipped to double-A the next day, he finished the season in New Britain, where he helped the team win the Eastern League playoffs and struck out ten en route to a three-hit shutout in the championship game. Counting college and pro ball, Clemens pitched 245 innings and won two championships in 1983, though he may have damaged his perfect right arm in the process.

Boston has a history of rushing talented young pitchers to the majors, and they were intent on not making this mistake with Clemens. Accordingly the prodigy started the 1984 season in Pawtucket (triple-A), where he compiled a 1.93 ERA with 50 strikeouts in 46.2 innings before he was called up in May. Roger was a quick study. He won his second big league start and was American League Pitcher of the Month in August when he went 4–0 with a 2.89 ERA and fifty-two strikeouts in 43.2 innings, including a fifteen-strikeout no-walk masterpiece against the Royals. He never pitched in September. A mysterious injury to his right forearm kept him sidelined.

The 1985 season was a frustrating one. Clemens went 7–5 with a 3.29 ERA in fifteen starts before pain in his right shoulder put him back on the shelf. He was puzzled: each time out he'd be strong for six innings, then fade. On August 30, 1985, accompanied by his mother, Randy, and Debbie, Clemens went to Georgia, where Dr. James Andrews removed a dime-size piece of cartilage from his right shoulder.

Roger began playing catch three weeks after the operation and felt fine. He was ready for Winter Haven, ready for the season every young pitcher fantasizes about.

Things were never the same for Clemens after the twenty-strikeout game. He was hounded by fans and the media, and it became increasingly difficult for him to get his routine work done. The Sox public relations department arranged press conferences when the team went back on the road. Clemens enjoyed the attention, but he didn't want it to interfere with his rigid routines. He wanted to pitch the big games, but he didn't want a camera crew trailing him around all the time.

"I want to make the most of it now," he admitted. "I've seen what happens with the older players when they come back for those old-timers' games. They miss it, and I know I'll be like that. I'll miss it, too, so I'm trying to enjoy it now. . . . There've been a lot of things happening in my life and it's caused me maybe to get away from what I should be thinking. I've tried not to let that happen. I've been trying to keep everything in perspective and keep the outside things off my mind when I'm pitching. I think I'm doing a pretty good job of it. My friends and family all said I would change after I made it to the major leagues. But I'm still just Roger. I don't consider myself great yet."

Celtic Larry Bird, no stranger to fame and greatness, made this observation when he picked up his third consecutive Most Valuable Player trophy: "I see the guy who's going to take the spotlight away from me. His name is Roger Clemens. He'll become big, and then I'll be able to go out in public again."

Clemens's upper body is a good deal more muscular than most pitchers and his neck might be sprouting from a pair of shoulder pads. He has the complexion of a Campbell's Tomato Soup baby, but lets some stubble show through on days he pitches. His eyes are small, green, and quick as he scans a room without moving his head.

When last we spoke, he owned a black GMC truck with Texas plates that read: "Sox 21" and Debbie was expecting their first child. More miscellany from that time: his favorite recording artist was Stevie Nicks; he often wore a "United States of Texas" T-shirt under his uniform; he claimed never to read the newspaper; dressed casually and conservatively, and usually had his straight brown hair cut by his sister Janet, a cosmetologist.

Roger starts many of his answers with, "Like I said . . ." and is polite in group interview sessions, but he will flatten a reporter who tries to talk to him as he prepares to begin his running routine. Early arrivals at Fenway expect to see Clemens running alone, counterclockwise around the warning track. He also likes to run the streets of Boston with his sidekick Al Nipper.

Sensitive to controversy and criticism, Clemens hates being asked about his injuries and will steer the conversation back to the team—a trait that partially explains why Clemens, like Bird, is popular in the clubhouse. "If you know me as a person, you know I'm the type of person, if everybody else is happy, I'm happy. I like to see people smiling."

Clemens's 20-strikeout performance made people notice the Red Sox again, and it was also part of a four-game winning streak. After a 6–2 home stand the Sox flew to Seattle with a 15–10 record, one and a half games out of first place. They returned from the west coast in sole possession of first place and were never headed thereafter.

Boston swept series in Seattle and Oakland. The two-game set in Seattle was highlighted by Al Nipper's one-punch knockdown of Seattle outfielder Phil Bradley, who charged the mound after being hit. The combative Nipper, a right-handed pitcher, had the presence of mind to drop his fielding mitt and smack Bradley with a left jab. Catcher Rich Gedman was ejected during the mini-brawl, and one inning later Bill Buckner got the heave for protesting a called third strike. The Bradley bout was Nipper's first of the year, but he'd had a near miss in Fenway when Detroit's Dave Collins said some things after being plunked. Nipper's post-game remark after the Collins incident was, "Tell him to put a dress on," and two nights later a dress with blue trim was found hanging in Collins's locker with a mash note from Nipper. Collins fired back saying, "Tell him I don't date ballplayers," and Nipper, the only Red Sox bachelor, said he knew nothing about the dress.

Pitching against the team he would join in three months, Mike Brown struck out eight Mariners, who then fired manager Chuck Cottier and hired Dick Williams. The Sox flew to Oakland for the weekend, and Boston swept again. In the first game against the A's, Clemens struck out eleven in 8.1 innings and left with a 5–2 one out and two on lead in the bottom of the ninth. Stanley relieved Clemens and immediately surrendered a game-tying three-run homer to former teammate Carney Lansford. The Sox scored four in the tenth and Vulture Stanley got the win. Bruce Hurst and Oil Can Boyd won the next two in Oakland and the first place Red Sox flew to California with a five-game winning streak and a 20–10 record. They had won eight of nine and twelve of fourteen.

Though Boston dropped the first two games in California, Clemens salvaged a win on Wednesday, which became the pattern throughout the season. The Sox would never lose more than four straight games and they would be swept on the road only once. Clemens was the reason. Before the season was over he would win fourteen times after a Boston defeat.

Tiger manager Sparky Anderson spotted the change: "When Clemens struck out twenty, it lifted the Red Sox and put them in that frame of mind that enabled them to keep winning."

Boston was tied for first place when they flew home from California, and there was hope for a short summer when people would once again take radios wrapped in baggies to the beach to listen to announcers Ken Coleman and Joe Castiglione. In prior years Boston's summer solstice had been a time to hold a parade for the Celtics and start counting Wade Boggs hits.

"I was spoiled my first ten years," admitted Dwight Evans, who arrived in Boston during the final stages of the 1972 pennant race against the Tigers and Orioles. "We were always in it. The last three or four years have been tough. It seems like the season is too long and everything gets to you. Everything is magnified. The last few years were hard for me because I hadn't known anything else. I don't think I could have been like [Chicago Cub] Billy Williams and played all those years without winning or even contending. I think we have a team that can compete. It's gonna be fun. It's gonna be exciting for everybody. There's so much talent here and we haven't even begun to hit yet."

"It's fun," confirmed captain Jim Rice. "When it's not fun, you stop going to the park early. You wait and take the bus."

Of course the Sox had played only 20 percent of their schedule and twenty-six of their thirty-three games had been played against the lowly American League West, but it also appeared the there was no dominant team in the overrated East. The defending champion Blue Jays were in shambles and Detroit and Baltimore hadn't started fast. The Yankees led in early May, but their pitching looked vulnerable. As Stanley noted, "I think we have an edge on the Yankees. We're tired of losing and being damned on. Our attitude is better now and we've got a better team. All those years we relied on hitting, but now our pitching is carrying us."

Wade Boggs dared to go for the gusto. "It's not fun going home in October and watching the other people in the playoffs. The World Series is what it's all about and that's what we're striving for."

Fenway Park was dark when the '86 Red Sox took over the American League East for good. Boston did not play on Thursday, May 15, and that evening Chicago beat the Yankees 8–1. Boston would now hold sole possession of first place for the remainder of the 1986 season. There would be plenty of threats, charges from below, and doomsday predictions, but there would be no surrender. This was a jocular and more relaxed team. These were the changing Sox.

4

WOUNDED WINGS,
THE CHICKEN MAN,
AND A GIFT FROM THE HAWK

O N *Sunday, Bloody Sunday,* May 18, while thousands of Boston University seniors donned grad-
uation gowns less then a mile away, the Red Sox and
the Texas Rangers tore into each other in a way that
made it clear this was not going to be an ordinary Boston
baseball season.

The Sox and Rangers split the first two games of
the series with the lowlight coming on Saturday afternoon when Oil Can Boyd accidentally shattered Don
Slaught's cheekbone and nose with a high-riding fastball.

Sunday's bizarre contest featured four home-plate
collisions, the first of which was particularly costly to
Boston. Trailing 3–1 in the top of the sixth, Al Nipper
threw a pitch that skipped past Rich Gedman and
bounded off the backstop. Ranger designated hitter

Larry Parrish broke from third as Nipper flashed toward the plate to take Gedman's throw. Parrish, Nipper, and the ball arrived together and the Texas chainsaw tore into the flesh above Nipper's right knee as he tagged Parrish out.

It was an ugly wound. Sox physician Arthur Pappas rushed to the pitcher's side, saw blood, and cut Nipper's pants open. The doctor was able to put four full fingers into the jagged cut. It severed 85 percent of Nipper's vastus medialis (one of the three major muscles in the knee), but did not tear any ligaments. The pitcher was taken to the UMass Medical Center in Worcester, where Dr. Pappas stitched the muscle back together and predicted that Nipper would be out six to eight weeks.

"Most pitchers just try to olé the tag," Nipper said later. "But I was intent on keeping him from scoring and I paid the price. If it would save a game, I'd probably do the same thing."

Home plate was a hard-hat zone for the rest of the game. Wade Boggs and Bill Buckner crashed into Texas catcher Darrell Porter in the bottom of the tenth after Pete O'Brien had scored the tie-breaker when he jarred the ball loose from Gedman in the top of the inning. Gedman was willing to wear the goat horns, but his gaffe was erased by the follies to follow.

Boston trailed 4–3 when Ed Romero led the bottom of the tenth with a harmless fly to left. Steve "Psycho" Lyons was next and he'd already committed an error, overthrown a cutoff, botched a bunt attempt, and been picked off after stroking a one-out single to center against reliever Greg Harris. Lyons reached first and took second on a wide pickoff attempt by Harris. Marty Barrett was next and he lofted a lazy fly to shallow right near the foul line. George Wright, Texas's capable right-fielder, raced toward the stripe, dove, and momentarily gloved the flare, but the ball popped loose when Wright's glove hit the ground.

Meanwhile, back in the infield, Lyons looked like a small child trying to decide whether to go for the candy counter or the ice-cream stand. "When you make as many mistakes as I made, you don't want to make another," Lyons said afterward. "I thought he caught the ball, so I decided to get my butt back to second. I knew I'd never see the field again if I got doubled off."

As Lyons slid back into second, he was greeted by his mirror image—Barrett was also sliding into second, from the other side of the bag.

Like everyone else in the park, Wright was confused. He'd corralled the baseball and was running toward the infield when he saw two Red Sox runners at second. As Lyons broke for third, Wright threw on the run, but his hurried throw skipped to the left of Steve Buechele and went past the third baseman. Normally the pitcher would be backing up a throw from right, but this was not a normal play. Harris had been backing up homeplate and rushed to back up third just in time to have the ball skip on through his legs and into the dugout. Both Sox runners were awarded homeplate and Boston was a 5–4 winner.

Two-time Orioles manager Earl Weaver says, "You're never as good as you look when you win or as bad as you look when you lose." The May 18 Red Sox victory was the first indication that this might be a year when more than a few things would go Boston's way. Some people call it dumb luck, others insist that you make your own luck (McNamara bristled every time it was suggested that his team was "lucky"), but a pinch of good fortune is always an ingredient in championship cake.

The good karma factor came into play one night later when Boston trailed Minnesota 7–6 with two out and no one on base in the bottom of the ninth. Minnesota reliever Ron Davis appeared to be cruising until Barrett walked and took third on a double by Boggs. Buckner was intentionally passed to load the bases. Jim Rice fouled off four 1–2 pitches before drawing a walk that tied the game. Marc Sullivan, "the owner's kid," was the batter. He'd come into the game after McNamara put in a pinch runner for Gedman in the eighth. Dave Sax, Boston's only other catcher, had been optioned to Pawtucket three days earlier, so Sullivan (a .210 lifetime hitter with 5 big league RBI) had to bat. Sullivan took a strike down the middle of the plate, then took a slider in the fanny, which brought Boggs home with the winning run. So it would be that Sullivan's first game-winning RBI in two varsity seasons he would knock in with his ass.

The wave was in motion. The Sox were on a roll. Boston batters put the Minneapolis area code on the left field scoreboard (6-1-2) in the first three innings the next night and Clemens ran his record to 7–0 with a 17–7 victory. They completed the sweep with a comeback 3–2 win in a game that featured two lengthy rain delays and ended just before curfew as Twins manager Ray Miller smoldered and cursed the patient umpires. This would not be the last time that natural forces helped the Red Sox in 1986.

Six days after the rain game, the Sox found themselves playing in fog on the shores of Lake Erie. Boston scored twice in the first and carried a 2–0 lead into the bottom of the sixth. Meanwhile a rare mix of temperature, humidity, and atmospheric pressure produced a ground cover reminiscent of the final scene in *Casablanca*. Sox starter Mike Brown, beginning to wilt in the fog, gave up a leadoff walk and an infield hit. Steve Crawford came on in relief and struck out Joe Carter. Mel Hall was next and he drove a fly ball into the pea soup. When Tony Armas appeared behind second holding the baseball, one could only assume that he had made the catch. The umpires, perhaps not certain, summoned Cleveland coach Bobby Bonds to hit a few test fungoes. Evans caught Bonds's first drive, a low liner, but the second one was a high fly and few people saw it go over the right field fence. After a short delay the game, one of only six shutouts the Sox would record all season, was called. The only other recorded fog-out was at Ebbets Field in Brooklyn on June 7, 1957. Oil Can Boyd blamed Cleveland's civic leaders for poor planning, saying, "That's what you get when you build a ballpark by the ocean, man."

Brown was only one pitcher who started the season in Pawtucket before joining the Sox. New Hampshire native Rob Woodward had been called up to replace Nipper when Bruce Hurst suffered a groin pull and collapsed on the Minneapolis Metrodome mound May 31. California Cooler Jeff Sellers was next to get the call. Hurst injured his left groin in the fifth inning against the Twins and had to be carried from the field. Hurst's Utah pal Danny Ainge of the Celtics advised him that he'd better be out at least a month after being carried off. Hurst would miss seven weeks.

Sammy Stewart was the next pitcher placed on the shelf; he injured his right forearm four innings after Hurst went down. Stewart had been overpowering since his opening day misfortune, pitching more than twenty consecutive scoreless innings. He was 2–0 with a 0.56 ERA in May, and the Sox would miss his long relief help in the ensuing months. Stewart had been healthy

throughout his Baltimore career, but the Orioles unloaded the big right-hander because he was in the final
year of his contract. They thought he was out of shape,
and they were tired of dealing with his tardiness and
personal problems. Both of Sammy Stewart's children
suffered from cystic fibrosis. "I'm the last one in the
clubhouse and the first one to leave 'cause my time with
my family is very important. I have two sick children
and if I pick up my little boy from school and only got
forty-five minutes with him, I'm not gonna be comin'
in here at three o'clock. That's not Sammy Stewart. My
boy has to have therapy every day. We have to beat on
his little lungs to loosen the mucus. . . . It gets tough.
I'm so happy when he's doing good, 'cause I've seen
him where he's pulling his hair out 'cause he can't get
air. Those are the things that stick in your mind when
you're on the road."

Pitching to Dave Winfield before a hostile Yankee
Stadium crowd must seem easy compared with a parent's sleepless night when a child can't breathe.

With Stewart, Hurst, and Nipper on the disabled list,
the Sox rotation was Clemens and Boyd and Fill the
Void. Incredibly Boston was able to stay in first place
while using three starters who opened the season in
Pawtucket. John McNamara, always a pitching-oriented
manager, earned his salary (and Manager of the Year
Award) during this stretch of the season. Tossing sand-
bags into an onrushing tide, he was able to hold off the
wave. The loss of Hurst was particularly rough because
Boston didn't have another left-handed starter and he
had been leading the league in strikeouts at the time
he went down.

The Pawtucket pitchers filled in admirably, and the
Rhode Island Club supplied some additional help as

well. When Glenn Hoffman was placed on the disabled list in mid-May due to a mild heart malfunction, twenty-two-year-old Rey Quinones came up and took over as everyday shortstop for three months. Quinones had been Quinonez with a Z for three seasons before telling anyone his last name ended in *s*. Quinones was flashy in the field and had a big swing, denting the left field wall in his second big league at bat.

Mike Stenhouse, also called up from the farm, spent a lot of time reading books and taking pitches. Stenhouse was a lifetime .195 hitter with the Expos and Twins, but he'd hit .333 in Florida and McNamara decided he needed another left-handed pinch hitter more than a third catcher (Dave Sax). Mike's father, Dave, was a former major league pitcher who started the 1962 All Star game for the American League when he was a member of the Washington Senators, while Mike's brother, Dave, Jr., played at Holy Cross and was a catcher in the Toronto Blue Jays system. Mike had an economics degree from Harvard, where he led the NCAA in hitting in 1979. Ivy Leaguers are resourceful. Stuck in the hotel elevator after a late Saturday night Bob Stanley loss in Texas, Stenhouse called for help and then called room service to deliver a pizza. After the rescue Stenhouse convinced the hotel to offer free drinks and brunch to the trapped guests, while Stanley hoped that a certain Boston writer, also trapped, would be unable to file his story in time.

Stenhouse was witty, articulate, and well-read. He knew that Lake Erie was not an ocean, and his favorite newspaper was not *USA Today*.

With three pitchers on the disabled list and a host of minor leaguers helping out, it was only Clemens's early season dominance that kept the Sox ahead of the pack in the competitive AL East. The Rocket Man ran his

record to 8–0 with a near no-hitter in Texas on May 25.
Oddibe McDowell broke up his bid with a clean single
to center with two out in the eighth. Darrell Porter
homered with two out in the ninth, but Clemens was a
7–1 winner in front of his family and friends (for whom
he'd left forty tickets). "I'm the guy that used to change
his diapers," said older brother Richard. "And I can tell
you we're all very proud." Clemens beat the Twins 6–3
to improve his record to 9–0. As the season stretched
into June, Boston owned the league's lowest ERA, led
in strikeouts, and had issued the fewest walks. Boston
hadn't led the American League in ERA since the Sox
had a rookie lefty named Babe Ruth in 1914. When
twenty-three-year-old Rob Woodward beat forty-seven-
year-old Phil Niekro on June 4, the Sox had a five-game
winning streak, stood 21 games over .500, and led the
second-place Yanks by an even five games.

One night later in Milwaukee, with the Sox trailing
7–5 in the ninth, Steve Lyons stood on second base with
Marty Barrett at first. Wade Boggs was at the plate.
Boggs was hitting an even .400 and had three hits in
the game. Meatball artist Mark Clear was struggling on
the mound against his former teammates. He'd given
up two home runs in the inning, but had only one out
to go. Incredibly, as Clear delivered a pitch to Boggs,
Lyons broke for third base. Stunned catcher Rick
Cerone threw Lyons out easily and the game was over.

"He made a fool of himself," said a livid John
McNamara.

"It was a stupid play and it will never happen again,"
said Lyons between bites on a Milkbone dog biscuit.
"It's the worst thing I've ever had to put behind me.
The rest of the year I'm going to be the guy that tried
to steal third base in Milwaukee."

Lyons would be off to Comiskey Park before the end

of the month, but his walk on the wild side triggered a slump that saw Boston lose four of five. Predictably the sole victory came from Clemens, who shut the Brewers out on four hits at County Stadium. The mini-slump ended when the good karma theory was invoked again at Exhibition Stadium in Toronto. There, in the top of the tenth inning of a 3–3 game against the defending champion Blue Jays, Stenhouse pinch hit for Barrett and drew a bases-loaded walk from snowflake artist Mark Eichhorn. This would be Stenhouse's lone RBI of a season in which he'd go 2–21 with 12 walks and earn the nickname Sony, as in Walkman.

Boston was beginning to catch the attention of others in the American League. "They've won about five games in a row that they wouldn't win in a normal year," said Tiger manager Sparky Anderson. "They've shown me the same things Baltimore did in '83 and that we did in '84 and that Toronto did in '85."

Milwaukee Brewer GM Harry Dalton agreed: "They've had guys get hit by pitches with the bases loaded to win games and they had that funny play against Texas and even the fog in Cleveland helped them. Those are the kinds of things that happen when you win a pennant. They've also had great pitching and you know they're going to hit, but sometimes it takes the extra things to give you that special year."

In mid-June the Red Sox finally faced the alleged iron of the AL East and captured the undivided attention of Boston fandom. The Celtics had stomped the Houston Rockets for championship number sixteen and when the NBA playoff hangover wore off, eyes cracked open to find the local nine atop the American League East. Monday, June 16, was like a second Opening Day. Only better. The sons of John McNamara were in Yankee

Stadium with Roger Clemens (11–0) ready to face Ron
Guidry. Boston led New York by three and a half and
Baltimore by four and a half games prior to the two-
week test.

Mike Easler, the man the Sox sent to New York in
exchange for Baylor, had this to say about his former
teammates: "I knew they would be good. They always
had the potential for a great pitching staff, and those
guys all matured this year. The talent was always there.
But they had that attitude like the fans have—'When's
it gonna end? When are we gonna fall out of the trees?'
The chemistry wasn't right and, evidently, the chemistry
is right now."

Face to face with their first big game of the season,
Boston shredded the opposition, scoring three times in
the first and knocking Guidry out in the third, while
staking Clemens to a seven-run lead en route to a 16-
hit, 10–1 blowout victory. As Clemens became the tenth
pitcher in history to win his first twelve decisions, a
New York tabloid bannered "HUMILIATION" across
its back page.

Wade Boggs did not play in the first game against New
York because he was still bothered by a sore rib, bruised
when he fell on a hotel room couch in Toronto while
trying to remove his cowboy boots. Boggs took a cortisone shot in his right side and it wasn't learned until
later that he had cracked a rib. He was expecting to miss
another five games when he got to Yankee Stadium early
in the afternoon on Tuesday, June 17.

Boggs took some early batting practice in the empty
park, then went back inside to ice his sore rib. In the
clubhouse trainer Charlie Moss answered the telephone
and heard an operator say that there was a call for Wade
Boggs from Tampa General Hospital. Moss passed the

phone to Boggs and a doctor informed him that his mother had been killed in an accident involving two motor vehicles, and that his grandmother also suffered multiple injuries in the crash. Boggs went into a rage and trashed the trainer's room. Months later he still did not remember the first two and a half hours after he learned of his mother's death. The Sox closed the clubhouse and grieved as a family while John McNamara took over getting Boggs to Florida and finding his father, Winn, who had flown up for the series and was staying in a New Jersey motel. The Yankees supplied a car and batting coach Walter Hriniak with pitcher Mike Brown, who had lost a parent the year before, accompanied Boggs to the airport. There Wade met his father, and the husband and son flew home together.

Winn Boggs married Sue Nell two weeks after they met in 1945. He was a career military man who had served in the Marines during World War II and flew for the Air Force in Korea before retiring in 1967. He played fast-pitch softball for twenty-five years and went into the construction business after he left the military. Wade Boggs was born in Omaha, Nebraska, on June 15, 1958. He was Winn and Sue's third child, twelve years younger than his brother Wayne and nine years behind his sister Ann. Wade loved the routine and the discipline of military life. He woke up at the same hour every day for eighteen years, left for school at the same time, and sat down for dinner at 5:30, no exceptions. He was fussy about his bats, even as a little leaguer. When all of his teammates switched to aluminum in high school, Wade Boggs stuck with wood because that's what the professionals used.

When Boggs finally made it to the major leagues, Ted Williams was shown a snapshot of an eighteen-month-old Wade Boggs holding a baseball bat. "That kid's got a helluva stance. Everything's perfect. He ought to become a great hitter," he said.

Boggs got his start hitting a taped cork with a broomstick, then graduated to sandlot games while his family lived in Brunswick, Georgia. Winn coached his son whenever he could, but he was gone much of the time, commuting from a base in Savannah, Georgia, and Sue was the one who drove young Wade to most of his little league games. But Winn's imprint was branded on his son like a Hillerich & Bradsby bat label. The family moved to Tampa in 1969 and when Wade started his senior year of high school hitting .111 (4–36), Winn Boggs went to the Tampa Public Library and checked out Ted Williams's *The Science of Hitting*. He told his son to study the book over the weekend and Wade obeyed, going 26–32 in his last 11 games to finish the season at .485. He'd hit .522 in his junior season at H. B. Plant High and won All American honors as a high school shortstop. Yet as pro bird dogs had concerns about his speed, the Major League Scouting Bureau labeled him a nonprospect. At the urging of scout George Digby, the Red Sox drafted Boggs in the seventh round in 1976. The University of South Carolina offered him a baseball/football scholarship (he was a quarterback and all-state punter in high school), but Boggs signed with Boston for $7,500. He left home two days later and hit .263 in 57 games for Elmira of the New York–Penn league—the only sub .300 season of his life.

Wade married his high school sweetheart, Deborah Bertuccelli, after his first pro season and together they may have kept Frank Perdue in business. Boggs's stomach requires mild foods and he was already eating chicken three or four times a week when he played at Winston-Salem in 1977. It was then Boggs noticed that he always hit better after eating chicken. Debbie Boggs started fixing chicken every day and developed a two-week, thirteen-recipe rotation that eventually led to a cookbook of chicken recipes titled *Foul Tips* that the Boggses coauthored in 1984.

Starting with his .332 season at Winston-Salem in 1977, Boggs hit .306 or higher in five consecutive minor league seasons, including 1981 when he led the International League with a .335 average. But it was a slow ride to the top because he was a singles hitter who couldn't run. After hitting .306 in triple-A in 1980, the Sox left him unprotected and twenty-five major league teams passed on a chance to claim him for $25,000. When he asked his minor league manager what he'd have to do to make it to the majors, Joe Morgan told him to concentrate on his fielding and his power. He started working an extra twenty minutes a day in the field, a labor he never abandoned. He couldn't make himself any faster, but he could learn to field better and hit with more power. He went from .306 with one homer and 45 RBI in 1980 to .335, five homers, and 60 RBI in 1981. The Sox brought him north in 1982 and he took over at third base when Carney Lansford was injured June 25 and hit .361 the rest of the way. He finished the season with a .349 average, a record for American League rookies playing at least one hundred games.

Boggs brought the cocoon with him. Discipline ruled his days just as it did when he grew up in a military household. Each movement was determined by the clock. It helped him concentrate. When the Sox were at home, Boggs would leave his apartment at 3:00 P.M.,

arrive at Fenway at 3:15, and get dressed. He'd stick
some tobacco in his mouth, check his bats, and be in
the dugout by 4 P.M. He'd start playing catch at 4:10,
then take grounders for twenty minutes. After a drink
of water, and a trip to center field to meditate, he was
available for interviews. This was the pre-practice ritual.
He took regular batting and infield with his teammates,
but would always leave five minutes to sit in the dugout
runway and bounce a baseball off the wall—like a bored
teenager on the back porch annoying his parents with
a repetitive, thump . . . thump . . . thump. Wind sprints
at 7:17 completed the pre-game ritual. Once the game
started, Boggs would draw the Hebrew word *Chai* in
the dirt with his bat on each trip to the plate and take
the same route on and off the field every inning. Late
in the season four footprints from the baseline to the
dugout were clearly imbedded in the Fenway sod.
Hardball anthropologists would have no trouble locating
Boggs's home park in the 1980s.

His mother's death cracked his shell. "I had gone out
of the cocoon and didn't know where I was," he later
admitted. "I had no concentration, no inner feeling. I
had to get back into the cocoon."

It was a shattering reality. Sixty-two-year-old Sue Nell
Boggs was in the family Blazer with Boggs's grandmother, Hattie Graham, when a cement truck exited the
interstate, ran a red light, and crashed into the side of
the Blazer. A work-release inmate, the driver told police
his brakes locked. He said the Blazer did not heed the
warning when he hit his horn. Sue Boggs was pro-
nounced dead on arrival at Tampa General Hospital
while Hattie Graham suffered multiple injuries. Sue
Boggs was caring for her daughter Ann at the time, who
had been told she had multiple sclerosis in the summer

of 1985. Ann Boggs's vocal chords were ravaged by MS and she was unable to pronounce words. Miraculously, she spoke clearly for fifteen minutes at her mother's funeral service. "Everyone couldn't believe it," Boggs later told Steve Fainaru of the *Hartford Courant*. "She got up and spoke for fifteen minutes, and then after the funeral service her voice went back out. Now it's gotten a lot stronger and her voice is coming back. So evidently the strength of my mother working through God has rubbed off on my sister."

Wade Boggs was stricken. For the first time in his life, he didn't care about hitting. He didn't fly into a rage when he made a few outs. He didn't curse inanimate objects. "Baseball became secondary," he admits. "I really didn't want to be out there. I didn't care and that's not me, the perfectionist. Even when I made outs I didn't care."

Going into the '86 season, Boggs's .351 career average was the seventh-best ever for all players after four years. His 240 hits in 1985 was eleventh best, and he tied a major league record by hitting safely in 135 games. He was considered the most likely candidate to hit .400, which hadn't been done since Ted Williams's .406 in 1941. Boggs actually did hit .400—over the course of 162 games in the second half of 1985 and the first half of '86.

Boggs has a pushbroom mustache and usually a wad of tobacco in his cheek. He has fiery hazel eyes and brown hair with more than a touch of crimson. Boggs definitely has the complexion and temperament of a redhead. He can be disagreeable and will snap at what he considers offensive questions, but usually grants candid and thoughtful interviews. He isn't afraid to tell the truth, a rare quality in pro sports.

Not particularly close to any of his teammates—as the cocoon isn't something that can be shared—there isn't a writer or statistical maven who knows more Boggs stats than old Wade himself. Certain teammates may even consider Boggs selfish. Jim Rice fueled such speculation when he told a reporter, "He [Boggs] could hit twenty homers and still bat .300, but does he want to? He's got the power, but he's not going to use it. Why not? I don't know. Maybe he doesn't want to weaken his foundation. Maybe he doesn't want to go beyond the limits of what he can do."

One can be around Boggs for weeks without seeing him smile, but away from the on deck circle he has a lighter side. He likes to laugh, have a few beers with teammates, and have some fun.

Boggs enjoys publicity and takes criticism well, unless he believes its a cheap shot. *Globe* columnist Mike Barnicle hit a nerve in a spring training column when he wrote, "In four major league seasons Wade Boggs has never shared a cab, had a drink, or eaten a meal with anybody other than his bat."

Angry and hurt, Boggs said, "Tell Mike Barnicle I want to punch his lights out. That's weak shit. He doesn't know me and he doesn't know who I go to eat with."

George Brett is one of Boggs's favorite dinner companions. They admire each other's abilities and love to talk about hitting. Wade and Debbie had a daughter Meagann in 1978, and when Debbie learned she was carrying a baby boy in the summer of '86, they agreed to name the child Brett Boggs.

There's another side to Wade that gets little publicity. When the Red Sox held an auction at Winter Haven to raise money for cancer research, Boggs manned the microphone and auctioned baseball memorabilia for more than three hours. He sounded like Wolfman Jack by the time he was done, but didn't yield the floor until all the souvenirs had been exchanged for pledges. Wade has also filmed a commercial to raise money for multiple sclerosis among other kind acts.

The Red Sox, meanwhile, went back to the task of trying to stay on top of the American League East. They had won during a period in May without Rich Gedman when his father died, and they would win with Ed Romero playing third base in place of the AL batting champ.

Rookie Rob Woodward, who had already beaten forty-seven-year-old Phil Niekro, started against forty-one-year-old Joe Niekro on the night Boggs lost his mother. Boston KO'd young Joe with seven runs in three innings and took a 7–6 lead into the bottom of the ninth. The Yankees led off the inning with three straight hits and a walk, but failed to score thanks to an error in judgment by former Sox manager Don Zimmer, hired to coach third base for New York that same day.

Joe Sambito was on the mound for the Sox as Butch Wynegar led with a single and Willie Randolph followed with another. The lead-footed Wynegar took second on Randolph's hit and lumbered on toward third when Dale Berra singled to left. Zimmer was on the spot and he waved Wynegar around third. Rice's throw home was a little off the mark, but it was in plenty of time to nail Wynegar. Backing up the plate, Sambito saw a nickel in the grass. He picked it up and put it in his pocket. Though Rickey Henderson walked to load the bases, Sambito sawed Don Mattingly's bat with an

inside fastball and the 1985 MVP hit a shallow fly to
Dwight Evans in right. Evans had hit two home runs
and smelled of beer thanks to a rude fan who'd doused
him in the fourth inning. Zimmer had managed Evans
long enough to know that Willie Randolph wasn't going
anywhere; and twenty-four minutes before midnight
Sambito got Dave Winfield on a grounder to third. The
Sox had two straight over the Yankees. And New York
manager Lou Piniella ripped a shelf off his office wall
before meeting the press.

Wednesday was Don Baylor night at the Stadium.
With the bases loaded and one out in the ninth, Baylor
broke open a 2–2 game with a full-count, bases-clearing
double to left-center off right-hander Brian Fisher. It
was the ultimate in-your-face disgrace for Yankee owner
George Steinbrenner, who had traded Baylor because
he didn't think the veteran DH could hit right-handed
pitching anymore. At second base Baylor stood tall, like
a man who'd just gotten an honorary degree from a university that had rejected him because of low SAT scores.
He had made his statement before 41,841 witnesses.
Upstairs in his private box where he was entertaining
United States House Speaker Tip O'Neill, Steinbrenner
announced, "Baylor's bat will be dead by August."

Oil Can Boyd was the other hero in Boston's sweep.
The Can gassed the Yanks for 9 innings and earned an
audition for the next casting of *Fame*. "This breaks their
morale. When they come to Fenway, we'll beat 'em
again. But this breaks their spirit," he said.

The Orioles were the only team the Sox hadn't faced,
and Baltimore bashed Boston 14–3 Friday night. On
Saturday, June 22, Boston came back with its two un-
stoppable weapons: Roger Clemens and Ms. Luck. With
two on, two outs, and two strikes in the first, Baylor

whiffed at a Ken Dixon pitch, but the ball sailed past catcher Rick Dempsey who had lined up inside for a pitch that broke away from Baylor. The ball skipped to the backstop allowing Baylor to take first as Ed Romero scored. It was the beginning of a 4-run inning and a 7–2 victory, which inflated Clemens's record to 13–0.

This was the seventh time Clemens had won after a loss. "He's everything. He's won every game, so you can call him anything you want. You can call him Cy Young, you can call him a stopper, you can call him Rocket. It just seems like we're more relaxed when he pitches. We score a lot more runs," Bill Buckner observed.

Baylor tossed this verbal bouquet at Clemens's feet: "I went against Guidry in 1978 when he was absolutely overpowering, day in, day out. Guidry was 25–3, and when you're doing that, you're doing something. I went against Vida Blue in 1971, when he packed 'em in everywhere he went and won the Cy Young. I played with Nolan Ryan, Frank Tanana, Jim Palmer, Dave McNally, just go down the list of guys I played with and against, and Clemens stands alone on what he brings to the team on the day he pitches."

The Sox were 21 games over .500 and led New York by 6 when the Yankees came to Fenway on June 23. Though Boggs was back from his mother's funeral, the pitching staff was in shambles. Since Boyd was shelled (11 hits and 5 runs en route to an 11–3 loss) in the series opener, the Yankees started thinking sweep. "If we beat them three in a row, they'll fold," said center-fielder Rickey Henderson. "They'll come down to earth from that cloud they've been on."

But McNamara admitted, "the pitching injuries are beginning to hurt us."

New York also won the next game 8–1. Boston had now dropped 4 of 5, surrendered 39 runs in 5 games, and appeared to be panicking. After the second loss, McNamara ended three days of speculation and announced that Al Nipper would start the next night's game against the Yankees. Nipper hadn't pitched in over five weeks, since his right thigh was gored by Parrish. Nipper was the choice because Mike Brown had a swollen elbow and GM Lou Gorman was unable to make a trade. "This is what we planned to do," McNamara said, but he didn't sound very convincing.

Nipper was at his Audie Murphy best on the evening of June 25. He yielded hits to the first three batters and fell behind 2–0 while throwing 30 pitches in the first inning, but settled down after the Sox scored 5 off Doug Drabek in the bottom of the first. Nipper scattered 8 hits in 7 innings and saved the bullpen. Boston led, 5–4, when Sambito came on to pitch the eighth. It was Sambito's finest hour of 1986.

Sambito struck out 3 straight in the eighth, the first time he'd whiffed the side since he hurt his arm against the Cardinals in 1982. In the ninth he won a dramatic duel with Henderson, baseball's most feared base-stealer and run-scorer. Henderson reached on a one-out Romero error, then went into his Muhammad Ali routine at first base. Gold jewelry dangled from Henderson's neck as he took a big lead, gestured toward Sambito, and talked trash. "I got you worried, I got you worried," he taunted.

Sambito threw to Buckner six times as he worked the count to 0–2 on Ken Griffey. Henderson took one last lead as Sambito went to the stretch and lifted his right leg. Sambito was still uncommitted when Henderson broke for second, and the veteran lefty fired a strike to first. Henderson was trapped. He stopped and forced a run-down. Buckner looked like a wounded dog as he ran Henderson toward second. He tossed to Romero, then got a toss back from Romero as the elusive Henderson reversed himself. Buckner's next toss was to Marty Barrett and when Henderson broke for first one last time Gedman was covering. The catcher took Barrett's throw and tagged Henderson. The play was scored 1-3-6-3-4-2.

"He's a good player, but he's a hot dog," said Stanley.

Sambito got Griffey on a fly to center and the flustered Steinbrenner who, for reasons known only to him, ordered tapes of the game sent to the baseball commissioner's office.

While the Yankees cried in their Sam Adams beer, the Red Sox had won some converts. They'd thrown a rusty pitcher into the breach and rebuffed the Yankee sweep. "We had our seven-game lead and it dropped to four and there was concern that we were gonna fold," said Sambito. "But you've got to realize that there's only three guys left [Rice, Evans, Stanley] from the last time that happened ['78]. There's no negative thinking around here."

The Sox spent the final weekend of June in Baltimore and came away with a 3-game sweep, Clemens's fourteenth straight victory, and pitcher Tom Seaver.

Clemens won 5–3 Friday night. The Rocket Man, a certified drawing card by this time, attracted the second largest crowd (52,159) in the Orioles's regular season history. Clemens struck out 11 and walked only 1 in 8 innings, then conducted his post-game press briefing in front of the retired locker of Dave McNally, who went 15–0 in 1969. McNally was one of only four pitchers ever to enjoy a better start than Clemens in '86. The others were Rube Marquard (19–0 with the Giants in 1912), Johnny Allen (15–0 with the Phillies in 1937), and Elroy Face (17–0 with the Pirates in 1959). Clemens was almost halfway to thirty and Nipper put "McLain" over his locker after he won his fourteenth.

Oil Can took the Memorial Stadium mound the next day winning 7–3, to give Boston a 25–6 record in games started by Clemens and Boyd. The Can danced about the Baltimore sod like a black Mick Jagger, then announced, "I love this mound. I wish I could dig it up and take it home with me."

While the Can was praising the mound, Lou Gorman was running up Haywood Sullivan's phone bill. The Yankees had flubbed their final chance to get Tom Seaver and Chicago GM Ken "Hawk" Harrelson was prepared to take Steve Lyons in exchange for the man with the Cooperstown baggage tags. Baltimore reporter Tim Kurkjian immediately dubbed the deal, "Cy Young for Psycho."

This was excitement. The Sox already had a pitcher with a 14–0 record, a batter flirting with .400, two MVP candidates, and a realistic shot at their first AL East title in eleven years. Now they were getting Tom Seaver, the best pitcher of his generation. Boston sports fans were reminded of a similar exchange involving the Celtics and Los Angeles Clippers a year earlier. Venerable cigar-smoker Red Auerbach had acquired Bill Walton to provide some backup help in the front court. The unhappy aging superstar left his sorry team and came to Boston, where he happily filled a smaller role in a championship cause. Like Walton, Seaver effectively traded himself to the team of his choice. Could Tom Seaver do for the Sox what Bill Walton had done for the Celtics?

Seaver is a rare individual whose name is synonymous with his craft. Baryshnikov means dancer. Wyeth means painter. Rockefeller means money. Seaver means pitcher. Seaver wrote the book. Literally. Decades after Ted Williams wrote *The Science of Hitting*, Tom Seaver wrote *The Art of Pitching*. Williams was a scientist in the batter's box, Seaver an artist on the mound.

Seaver wasn't in Baltimore the day the trade was announced, but his name was on everyone's tongue. In the Oriole dugout Earl Weaver remembered facing the National League Cy Young winner in the 1969 World Series—the year Seaver was 25–7 with a 2.21 ERA, the year the Mets stunned the Orioles, 4–1, in the World Series. "I remember it," said Weaver. "I was sitting right here when Donnie Buford hit his first pitch in the first game for a homer. I said to myself, 'We're the greatest team ever. A week later I got on the bus in New York wondering what the fuck had happened. We beat him in that first game, but he came back and stuck it to us."

Several pitchers in the Sox clubhouse were reminded of their youth. When Seaver pitched for the championship Mets in 1969, Roger Clemens was a seven-year-old whose older brother was trying to sneak him into little league. Al Nipper said he'd read Seaver's book. Joe Sambito, a New Yorker, had worshipped Tom Terrific. "I did a term paper on the Amazing Mets in 1970, my senior year of high school," he recalled. "My teacher gave me a C-plus. I guess he just didn't want to read it. The paper didn't go into too much depth. But Seaver was the best thing to come along in New York in a long time. We tried to emulate him because it seemed like everything was textbook. A lot of kids would try to get their knee dirty when they threw. I couldn't do that, but I tried. I tried to drive that hard."

McNamara smiled all afternoon. The Sox were in the process of sweeping Baltimore and the Boston manager was going to be reunited with a pitcher he had grown close to in Cincinnati.

Don Baylor had the only complaint. The chief justice in the Kangaroo Court saw a lot of potential fine money walk out the door when Lyons left. "I may have to fine Lou Gorman one hundred dollars," said Baylor. "He's taken away our main source of income."

Lyons would last less than two months with the White Sox. He'd be shipped to Buffalo in late August and Chicago manager Jim Fregosi would say, "He's always looking around the stands, watching. His strong point is that he gives good TV interviews."

Seaver was in California with the White Sox when the deal was completed. He was struggling with a 2–6 record, a 4.38 ERA, and a bad ballclub. He had expressed a desire to play near his Greenwich, Connecticut, home and the White Sox had finally accommodated him. He was home in Connecticut on Monday and drove to Fenway for a press conference. "My teammates don't want a memory coming in and pitching for them," said Seaver. "They want somebody who can contribute and I just hope I can help them."

Boston embraced the legendary right-hander. It was as if Walter Cronkite had come to town to anchor the local news. Joe Sambito stood in front of his locker talking about his boyhood idol, retelling the story about his high school term paper. Fifteen feet to Sambito's left, Sambito's idol sat on a stool with a towel around his waist, smoking a cigar, and doing *The New York Times* crossword puzzle.

Seaver's first start was Tuesday, July 1, against Toronto and 32,729 filed into Fenway to see the legendary practitioner. They cheered him when he walked to the bullpen to warm up and Seaver tipped his cap. They cheered when he came in from the bullpen to start the game and Seaver once again obliged. He'd yet to throw a pitch for the Sox and he already had a 2–0 lead over Ted Williams in the cap-tipping department. He was the first 300-game winner to take the mound wearing a Boston uniform since Cy Young. Seaver's wife and daughters sat nearby in box seats and some of the Sox bullpen stayed in the dugout for the start of the game, a Kangaroo Court violation. "We'll probably get fined, but it's worth it," said Sambito.

Seaver surrendered a run in the first, then watched his teammates score seven times in three innings. Tom Seaver knew how to pitch with a 7–1 lead and lasted seven innings, scattering nine hits en route to a 9–7 victory, Boston's sixth straight. He was undressing in the clubhouse when Steve Crawford came in from the bullpen to start the eighth. Thirty-two thousand people chanted "Sea-Va, Sea-Va," while Crawford warmed up. The book on Tom Seaver was that he would keep his team in the game. He could contribute six or seven steady innings without getting in a hole. The Sox thought of him as a number five starter when they made the deal and Seaver's first Boston outing fulfilled all expectations.

One night after the grand master beat Toronto, the young prodigy saw his historic 14-game winning streak snapped. The Blue Jays beat Roger Clemens, 4–2, on a night when Clemens was particularly overpowering. He struck out 8 and gave up only 1 hit in the first 7 innings, and carried a 2–1 lead into the eighth. Clemens walked catcher Ernie Whitt to start the inning, then surrendered a single to Damaso Garcia on an 0–2 pitch. Pinch runner Ron Shepherd was wiped out at third on a bunt, but Rance Mulliniks hit the next pitch to left for a run-scoring double. McNamara came out of the dugout and pulled Clemens in favor of Bob Stanley, a somewhat surprising move considering Clemens's streak and Stanley's chronic Fenway ineffectiveness. Stanley wasted no time flushing away the streak as after an intentional walk, Stanley gave up an RBI single, a sac fly, and another walk. Clemens, a 4–2 loser, was disappointed with McNamara's quick hook but would not publicly second-guess his skipper. "They know what's best in the dugout," he said into his shirt.

Like Perry Mason and Man O' War, Clemens finally had a loss to go with all of his victories.

Boston still held a hefty 8 game lead in the American League East after going 10–6 in the crucial three-week set with the Yankees, Orioles, and Blue Jays. Together with Seaver, things were looking very good for the Sox when the Seattle Mariners came to Boston on Liberty Weekend to open a 28-game stretch of Western Division competition for the AL East leaders. Boston took 2 of 3 from Seattle as Seaver won his second straight (no earned runs in seven innings), then took 2 of 3 from Oakland, including a comeback 8–7 win over the A's on July 8, which improved Boyd's record to 11–6.

Stewart said, "We're going to drive Italian style. We're gonna tear off the rear-view mirror, never look back, and drive full speed ahead."

He should have thought to check the Oil Can first. The most trying period of Boston's season was just around the corner and it all started with the clubhouse eruption of Dennis Oil Can Boyd.

5

THE COMBUSTIBLE CAN
SPARKS A SUMMER SLUMP

THE The Red Sox led the American League East by
8 games when Oil Can Boyd blew up in the clubhouse on the night of July 10. Before the Can would
next pitch, Boston's lead would be down to 2½ games
and the Sox would have endured the most stressful
month of an otherwise magical season.

Roger Clemens was the only pitcher in the American
League with more victories than Boyd when the All Star
staff was announced July 10. Yet Boyd did not make the
team. It appeared that the Can was a victim of the selection system, the Sox rotation, and his personality:
1. All fourteen American League clubs had to be represented, and manager Dick Howser was unlikely to
take two pitchers from one team when he had to find
room for players from Milwaukee and Texas; 2. Boyd
was scheduled to pitch on Sunday and the American
League's obsession with winning the midsummer clas-

sic meant that any pitcher who could not pitch Tuesday would not be selected, no matter how deserving; 3. Boyd spoke out when he was overlooked by Sparky Anderson in 1985, and his mound antics made him less-than popular.

Boyd, who had some financial problems at the time, was counting on the $25,000 incentive bonus in his contract to fly members of his family from Mississippi to Houston for the interleague classic. Believing he had the team made, Boyd was calm and even jovial during television interviews speculating on his chances.

One inexplicable custom of the big leagues is that managers never explain anything to players. The lineup card goes up on the wall and either you're in or you're out, but don't ask why. Players orbit in uncertainty throughout their careers and can only get explanations of a sort through the press. Fully aware of his explosive temperament, the Sox still didn't bother to put a hand on Boyd's shoulder and explain the situation. Later, McNamara bristled when asked why he had not taken Boyd aside to explain why he hadn't made the team. So the childlike Can had his heart broken when he got the news from reporters.

Boyd appeared calm when he first got word sitting in the dugout before a night game with the Angels. But he was smoldering inside. He went into the clubhouse, stripped to his long johns, then made a quick trip to the trainer's room and reappeared in front of his stall. Reporters were across the room interviewing Tom Seaver when Boyd started yelling.

"God damn motherfucker. Get out of my fuckin' face."

There was no one near Boyd.

"Go ahead, motherfucker. Fine me. I don't give a Goddamn."

It got worse. Clothes flew around the room and the

same invective was fired at McNamara, team physician
Arthur Pappas, and Boyd's close friend Nipper whom
he called a redneck.

Vince Orlando, the Ayatollah Khomeini of AL clubhouse men, announced an opportune team meeting and
evicted the press from the flammable locker room. The
Can cleared out, too, and screeched from the player's
parking lot in a Chevrolet Monte Carlo he'd loaned to
roommate Rey Quinones. McNamara left word that
Boyd was not to be allowed back into the park until he
visited the manager's office.

The game was in progress when the Can drove back
to Fenway. The Sox were en route to one of their
strangest wins of the season. The Angels led 3–1 early,
but the Sox forced extra innings only to have California
come up with 3 runs in the top of the twelfth. With Boston trailing 7–4 and 2 out in the bottom of the twelfth,
Jim Rice crashed a 2-run homer to cut the lead to a run.
Then former Sox shortstop Rick Burleson dropped a
game-ending pop-up by Don Baylor. Dwight Evans
then walked on a close 3–2 pitch before Rich Gedman
singled to score Baylor with the tying run. Evans took
third on Gedman's hit and scored on a balk by Todd
Fischer.

At some point during this memorable evening, Dennis Ray Boyd tried to come back to his team but, on
McNamara's orders, was denied entry.

The Can didn't show the next night and there was
little compassion for him in the clubhouse.

"I thought I knew him," said Nipper. "We came up
through the minors together. But I never saw him like
this. I guess I don't know him anymore."

McNamara said Boyd had desecrated his uniform and
added, "It was the worst situation, the worst incident I

have ever seen in any clubhouse, major or minor leagues."

In the first of a series of terse statements, the Sox issued a release that said:

> The Boston Red Sox announce that effective today, Friday, July 11th, Dennis Oil Can Boyd has been suspended for a minimum of three days without pay.
>
> Boyd must also apologize to his Red Sox teammates before he can be reinstated to an active status.
>
> This action is taken as a result of his unprofessional conduct in Fenway Park prior to Thursday night's game against the California Angels.
>
> Rookie Jeff Sellers will start Sunday's game against the Angels in place of Boyd.

The Can Watch was officially underway and reporters raced to Boyd's Chelsea condominium. Boyd sulked all weekend while Boston battled the Angels. He was front page news every day and said, "I'm gone. I don't want to pitch where I'm not wanted. I'm driving home tomorrow. They have to understand why I did what I did, and accept it for what it was. I can pitch anyplace I want."

Rumors flew. Players talked of Boyd's financial troubles. He was behind in car and condo payments, and his phone had been disconnected because the bill wasn't paid. It was known that the Sox had tested him for drugs at least six times during the '86 season. Boyd always said his drug tests were negative, but the Sox never supported his claim, which led to further speculation. Boston's large liberal population insisted that Boyd was a victim of racism but Don Baylor, one of his most disappointed teammates, said, "If he were with some other ballclub, he would have either been released or out of the game."

While Reggie Jackson said, "If I were his manager, he'd have to pee in a paper cup before he'd play for me after that exhibition." Drug rumors walked with Boyd like a penny in his shoe.

Sunday, July 13, was the day before the All Star break and Boyd came to the park early, apologized to his teammates, then left. It was the third and final day of his suspension, which would cost him $6,450. A brief Sox statement said that Boyd was expected to fly to the west coast with the team on Wednesday. Baylor said that Boyd's apology meant "nothing."

Boston was bashed by the Angels 12–3 that Sunday (the game Boyd had been scheduled to pitch), then scattered for the three-day break.

The Red Sox had a large contingent in Houston for the All Star game. Boyd was a hot topic and Clemens, who'd been selected to start the game, showed no tolerance when the Can's name surfaced at a press conference. "Other good pitchers were left off, too," said Clemens, who would be named MVP for three perfect innings in a 3–2 victory.

Sox owner Haywood Sullivan was also in Houston, but on learning of a new incident involving Boyd, returned to Boston before the start of the classic. Boyd had been approached by two undercover narcotics detectives outside his Chelsea condominium. There was some pushing and shoving and the next day Boyd was charged with complaints of assault and battery on a police officer and disorderly conduct, charges that were later dropped.

The day these charges were filed Boyd was scheduled to fly to Seattle with the team. He arrived late for a voluntary workout at Fenway, managed to dodge dozens of reporters, and met in the trainer's room with Sullivan,

Gorman, and Dr. Pappas. A half hour later the Sox issued a vague statement saying only that Boyd would continue to be suspended. The club would not say whether he was being paid or explain why he was still off the team. Boyd left the park in a huff.

A day later the Sox issued a release stating "Dennis Boyd admitted himself to the UMass Medical Center in Worcester today, as mutually agreed upon, for a comprehensive evaluation, including drug testing."

McNamara held a press briefing in a small room under the stands in the Seattle Kingdome on the night Boyd entered the hospital. At the end of the session a reporter asked the beleaguered skipper if Boyd would pitch for him again.

McNamara stood, put his hands to his face and rubbed both sides of it, wheeled, spit some tobacco juice, then sat down. Several seconds later he said, "Yes—and get his life together and his priorities straight. Yes, he can pitch for me again, but he is in control of his own destiny. I can forgive and forget."

Dennis Ray Boyd was born in Meridian, Mississippi, on October 6, 1959, the youngest of eight children (six boys and two girls) of Willie and Sweetie Boyd. Dennis was born a year after his parents bought their small white house at the corner of 16th Avenue and 20th Street. Sweetie, the daughter of a Meridian minister, was married at fifteen. Willie James Boyd was a landscaper by trade, but a pitcher by birthright. Like his father and grandfather, Willie grew up playing baseball at the Lake Erie Ballpark on 10th Avenue. He pitched with the semi-pro Meridian Braves and also had three brothers who played—K.T., Jake, and Goose. Jake was still playing on the sandlots of Detroit when he was forty-three. Willie James pitched to Henry Aaron and Willie Mays at the Lake Erie Ballpark, throwing the "dead red" fastball and the "yellow hammer" overhead curve. He threw "in-shooters" and "out-shooters," and pumped his fist when he struck out batters. But his career ended on a cold, wet night in Alabama when he hurt his shoulder throwing soggy lopsided balls.

Willie Boyd was animated on the mound and he taught his six sons to be the same way. Dennis Boyd's five older brothers all played baseball, but none made it to the big leagues. Willie, Jr., (Skeeter) was 19–1 for the Meridian White Sox, then became a singer. Brother Steven was a long-ball–hitting catcher, but he never played outside the neighborhood. Michael Boyd was 18–0 in high school and pitched for Florida A & M, but hurt his arm and also turned to singing. Though all the Boyd brothers could sing, Michael Boyd sounded more like Sam Cooke than Sam Cooke did. Don Boyd signed with the Cardinals in 1973, but then Willie and Sweetie Boyd separated and he came home when his mother got sick. (Sweetie Boyd's daughters had both married and moved to Virginia.) Neil went to Tuskegee in Alabama on a baseball scholarship after which he joined the Air Force. It was left to Dennis, the youngest son, to put the Boyd family in the major leagues.

He was always small and always emotional. He started his career playing Little League ball at the Jackson White Sox Park. Dennis threw a lot of tantrums, cried when he lost, and was seeing the school psychiatrist at twelve.

The tantrums didn't stop when he finished high school in 1977. By then his hometown friend Pat Blanks had nicknamed him "Oil Can" because of his fondness for beer. The Can went to Jackson State where he pitched for former major leaguer Scipio Spinks. Boston drafted Boyd in the sixteenth round of the 1980 draft and he sailed through their minor league system, going 35–17 in three summers before the Sox called him up in the fall of '82. He split the '83 season between Pawtucket and Boston, then went 12–12 in the majors in 1984. The proud people of Meridian, who had been Dodger fans since Brooklyn brought Jackie Robinson to the majors, became Red Sox fans. The Can was Boston's winningest pitcher in 1985 when he posted a 15–13 record with a 3.70 ERA in 272.1 innings for the most wins by any Sox pitcher since Dennis Eckersley won 17 in 1979. He threw harder than any thin man since Ron Guidry (circa 1978), and he had incredible control for someone whose life away from the park seemed forever chaotic.

Oil Can Boyd is animated and childlike with an infectious way of talking about himself in the third person. ("The Can, he don't like to lose, no sir.") He loves "old timey" baseball. Like Dizzy Dean and his idol, Satchel Paige, he tends to exaggerate and color stories. He once said he had seven brothers and six sisters (denied by Sweetie Boyd who should know). He said his father played for the Homestead Greys (he played against the Greys, but never left his eastern Mississippi hometown). In many ways the Can is a latter-day Paige, born late enough to take his talents to the limit. On days he pitches, Boyd wears low-cut socks and all-black shoes. "I am a little superstitious about the way I want to go out there and my dress code," he admits. "I try and feel relaxed. There is an old timey feeling that happens to me and kind of possesses me and takes me back to the thirties and forties as though I am Satchel or somebody. When

I first came up from double-A, I felt like I was drifting back again like an old timey ballplayer with the baggy uniforms. Where I come from deep in the south, he [Paige] was born in Mobile, Alabama, and grew up in Hattiesburg, Mississippi. I threw on the same mound when I was thirteen or fourteen years old. I know a lot about him. My parents talked a lot about him and people in town talked about him. He was like a folk hero. I grew up to throw a lot like him and have some of the same mechanics. I threw the ball fairly hard. Coming up I thought a lot of him. It was a thrill to see him pitch on film because my old man said he was awesome. The year I was drafted in 1980 in Hattesburg, Mississippi, I got to go down there with my pitching coach and a couple of my teammates. I got to sit there and talk to him for a little while and visit about the old days. At that time I was just getting out of college in my junior year and I told him how important it was for me to make the big leagues. He gave me a lot of inspirational things and told me just keep the ball down, move the ball in and out, and drop that yellow hammer and I would be okay."

The Can has close-cropped hair, a small head, and big brown eyes. A stranger in the Sox clubhouse would figure Boyd for an attendant or batboy (in fact, the visitor's batboy in Baltimore looked remarkably like Boyd and became known as Oil Can around the league). The Can's facial expressions while on the mound should be seen. He furrows his brow like the late Louis Armstrong and carries a pained look when he is in a jam.

He smokes cigarettes, wears casual shirts with the collar turned up, and owns a variety of hats. He is the only hurler who does not dress on "pitcher's row" as he asked for his locker to be in a corner on the other side of the room, nearest the door to the field and almost directly under the clubhouse clock.

There were plenty of nights when Boyd's stall was empty less than an hour before he was supposed to pitch, but McNamara and the rest of the team usually covered for the Can. "He's not late," the manager would say. "He called me and we know where he is." Eventually the Can would appear at the doorway wearing sneakers and jeans and swigging Orange Crush from a two-liter bottle. The Can's locker was cluttered like the third-floor attic of a house in which seven children were raised. He had an autographed—"To Dennis Boyd"—photograph of Ronald Reagan and explained, "A friend of mine is one of his security guards and had him sign it for me. He wanted to sign it to 'The Can,' but they're formal there at the White House. Along with the photograph of the President, Boyd's locker contained about twenty pairs of baseball shoes, two pairs of dark glasses, a stale box of Crackerjacks, a can of snuff, a photo of Clemens's 20-strikeout game, an oil can, an old-time baseball glove, and a black and white photo of Satchel Paige in a Monarchs uniform.

McNamara knew that many players resented Boyd. Pitchers Bob Stanley and Steve Crawford were particularly harsh on the Can, and when things went wrong on the mound, Boyd would cry that his teammates wouldn't "Let the Can be the Can." When the Sox were on the road, McNamara had more than one late-night phone call from a weeping Boyd. The manager tried to be patient, but he began to think that Boyd was using his emotions to excuse an occasional poor outing. There was still residual bitterness from Boyd's altercation with

Rice after a defeat in August 1985. Boyd threatened Rice at that time and went AWOL for a night.

As the team tried to stay afloat on the west coast without the headline-grabbing Can after the All-Star break, there was considerable doubt whether Boyd would ever be back. Crawford said, "You can't prove yourself just by words. You've got to prove yourself in a game with your teammates. He can't go back to the same old crap."

Gedman added, "I'm an easy-going guy. People can burn me, burn me, burn me, and I'll give them another chance. But he doesn't need to be babied anymore, that's for sure. Here I am talking like his pal—what about people who didn't like him from the start? They say, 'Get rid of him.' I don't know what his problems are, but it can't be just that he didn't make the All Star team. I didn't see much of his tantrum that night, but if he'd come on to me like he did to some of the other guys, I probably wouldn't want him back either."

The Sox dropped three of four in Seattle, winning only when Clemens pitched. It was indicative of the way the trip was going to go. Bruce Hurst, Sammy Stewart, Steve Crawford, and Tony Armas were on the disabled list and the Can was in the Worcester hospital. Nipper still hadn't fully recovered; Buckner was hobbling worse than ever, and Rice strained his right knee in the third game of the series. Desperate for pitching help, the Sox summoned Calvin Schiraldi from Pawtucket. Schiraldi had been converted to a short reliever and had 12 saves and a 2.86 ERA with 60 strikeouts in 44 triple-A innings. Schiraldi was the ninth Pawtucket player employed by Boston in the first three months of the season.

Sunday, July 20, in Seattle, the Sox had Don Baylor playing the outfield for the first time since May 11, 1984.

Mike Stenhouse was at first base. LaSchelle Tarver
(listed as Tarver LaSchelle in the program) was in center
while Jeff Sellers and Schiraldi pitched the first 7.1 innings of a 9–5 loss to the Mariners. "No question about
it, we're hurting right now," said McNamara.

A day later, in the lobby of the Oakland Edgewater
Hyatt, Sellers stood at a pay phone holding the receiver
two feet from his ear. "It's my mother," Sellers whis-
pered while placing his hand over the mouthpiece. "She
always yells at me when I do shitty." Sellers was a likeable Southern Californian who had a pierced left ear,
wore Ray-Bans, and answered to the nickname "Brain
dead." One day after talking to his mother, Sellers was
banished to the bullpen and replaced by Bruce Hurst,
who'd finally come off the disabled list. Hurst made his
first start in seven weeks Monday night in Oakland but
never had a chance. McNamara had the Bad News Bears
in the lineup again—the bottom four batters in Boston's
order—Dave Stapleton (.176), Rey Quinones (.242),
Marc Sullivan (.192), and Kevin Romine (.231). The A's
held the Sox to 3 hits and won, 5–2.

The young and improving A's took the Sox in straight
sets, 5–2, 4–2, 9–2, pushing Boston's losing streak to a
season-high four games. It marked the first time they
were swept in a series and Boston's 8-game lead had
been whittled to 3 in thirteen short days since *l'affaire*
Can. The sagging Sox had dropped seven of eight, and
eight of ten, and the Yankees were getting closer.
"We're going to catch them any second," Rickey Henderson said; and New York tabloids reported the news
of the Sox stumble under such splashy headlines as
"Timber!" "BoSox to Bomb" and "78 Again?"

The Sox were a mess. Baylor had only 2 homers in
six weeks, Quinones was erroring all over the place,

and Tarver and Kevin Romine were platooning in center and batting ninth, while the Sox waited for Armas (19 RBI in 193 at bats) to return from his latest hamstring pull. Rice did not play in Oakland and Boggs was in a sad stupor, en route to the worst month of his career. The battered Gedman was in a major defensive slump and wore paths to the backstops in Seattle and Oakland.

"We're not trying to do this bad," snapped Boggs. "We're not deliberately trying to lose."

"The key for us is not to panic," said Hurst. "Do not panic."

Hardball historians pointed out that the Sox had been in first place at some point after the break seven times in the previous fourteen years and had only one flag to show for it. A front page story in the *Globe* on July 24 reported, "Sox fans know better. They have seen this play before. The cast changes and new liberties are taken with an ancient script, but Hamlet always dies in the end." A *Sports Illustrated* piece was headlined, "Poised for another El Foldo?" and lowlighted Sox bellyflops of the previous fifteen years.

For the first time the 1986 Red Sox became aware of the weight of their uniforms: Sox uniforms are heavier than all others because leaded threads of haunting heartbreak are woven into the fabric. With the exception of veterans Rice, Evans, and Stanley (plus Gedman and Mark Sullivan who grew up near Boston), the players on the '86 team were unscarred by the sins of their predecessors. They didn't grow up in households where fathers who had been Sox fans for fifty years went to bed every night saying, "They'll blow it again." They didn't spend twelve months of the year in an area where Sox folds are as much a way of life as clam chowder, clapboard houses, and corrupt politicians. Big league ballplayers are hired soldiers with little attachment to the regions they represent. Roger Clemens was from Dayton and Houston, and had only known winning. Could he have been expected to answer questions about Mike Torrez's pitch to Bucky Dent in the 1978 playoff game? Wade Boggs was looking at his watch in Tampa, Florida, when Luis Aparicio fell rounding third base in the crucial season-ending series in Detroit in 1972. That was then. This was now. Boggs, like the others, did not understand the obsession with the past that tormented Boston fans. Like new owners of a haunted house, the players maintained that the past had nothing to do with them. Understandably they resented the negative reminders.

"I've had a hard time dealing with that," admitted Baylor, a veteran of successful and ghost-free organizations in Baltimore, Oakland, Anaheim, and New York. "I've had a hard time dealing with reporters. I don't care what happened in 1978. This club wants to win so bad. We haven't been swept in our division. And to have people telling you you're going to fail, that the same thing's going to happen that happened in 1978. . . . The fans believe the media and they see the same things. A lot of people see with their hearts instead of their eyes. But if they could see the things I see in this clubhouse, they'd see how this team is created."

"Everyone asks about seventy-eight," groaned Evans. "I don't care about it. It wasn't that great a team. We had a lot of talent, but we weren't together. The Yankees came back by playing .720 baseball. They were awesome. People say we choked, but we had to win twelve of fourteen just to tie them. I don't feel I have to answer for anything."

Cleveland outfielder Brett Butler also spoke to this:

"I was in Boston for three days and I couldn't believe it. Everybody was knocking the Red Sox. The fans think they're going to fail. I had dinner with some friends and they were talking about the Sox already being mathematically eliminated. 'You've got to be kidding me,' I told them. It's like everybody's expecting failure. If that's the way the media and the fans are going to be—not backing them like they should—then it's going to be tough. Cubs fans aren't like that. It's different. They always pull for their club, and if you say something about the Cubs, they say, 'Want to fight?'

"In *Gulliver's Travels* there's a character named Glug. He's never optimistic. He's pessimistic. That's what the Boston fans remind me of. They're saying, 'Oh, no, we're not going to win,' and 'Oh, no, Toronto's going to beat us.' Back your team. Come on."

Many members of the Red Sox thought the media were out to get them. Owner Haywood Sullivan had been a target of numerous shots since taking over the team with Buddy LeRoux and Jean Yawkey in 1978 and he encouraged writers to limit their stories to issues concerning "bat and ball." GM Lou Gorman kept handy a file of clippings in which the wisdom of his trades were questioned. "I'll be mailing these back to you when you see how well this works out," Gorman would say with a chuckle. When the team broke fast, public relations director Dick Bresciani took great delight in citing gloomy spring training stories filed from Winter Haven. Bresciani took it as a personal affront when the subject of former folds was raised during Boston's slump. "No other team has those things written about them," said the popular, but combative, publicist.

The Sox players used skepticism to their advantage. They turned their backs on history and laughed at the concept of predestination. The internal exertions and outside pressure made a closer, more confident team. There were never any skeptics in the clubhouse and these high, good spirits served them well in the final three months of the season.

"If we win, it'll screw up this whole town. They'll have to start thinking positive," said Sambito. Motioning toward a local writer he perceived as particularly negative, Sambito added, "You'll be out of a job—or else you'll have to change the way you write."

Boston is not the easiest place to make a living playing professional baseball. The Red Sox simply *mean* too much to the community. They are a regional institution, and they belong to everyone in six New England states. Summer tourists come to Boston to see the Freedom Trail, Harvard Yard, Hyannisport beaches, and Fenway Park bleachers. Members of the Red Sox are celebrity figures. Their smallest deeds take on large significance and they have ample opportunity to endorse products and pick up spare change on the speaking circuit. In exchange for fame and fortune they are stripped of some privacy and find little quiet time at the workplace. Fans want autographs, and writers and broadcasters want interviews—constantly. All this can become a nuisance and, if the coverage is negative or skeptical, even threatening. Playing for the Red Sox is not like working for the Texas Rangers where opening day is a big deal, then the Cowboys own the fans and sports pages for the rest of the season. There is no abject anonymity when a player wears a Boston uniform; his good days may knock the mayor off the front page of the *Globe*, but his failures may also put him on every dartboard from Groton to Greenwich. Fenway Park is like the *Cheers* bar— where everybody knows your name, even if it's Tim

Lollar or Rene Lachemann, and even if that's not what you want. Only in Boston would the Oil Can Boyd episode be covered like the Manson murders.

The standoff between players and media produces an underlying tension whenever the clubhouse doors swing open. There are few ugly scenes, although Nipper and *Hartford Courant* writer Steve Fainaru almost came to blows early in the year, and there have been minor scuffles in past years. Many players find it simplest to treat intrusive newspersons as if they are lampposts. McNamara takes care of his local writers and adroitly manipulates the rest, while the players can depend on clubhouse man Vinnie Orlando and trainer Charlie Moss. Orlando revels in overstepping his authority to usher the press out of the locker room and Moss is not above planting a false injury report.

Certain personalities thrive in Boston. Ken Harrelson was just another battle-weary, strikeout-prone slugger until he got to Boston in 1967 and became the flamboyant Hawk. The numbers suggest that George Scott's best years were in Milwaukee, but he's remembered for his seasons at Fenway when the oft-quoted Boomer was knocking 'taters over the wall. Bill Lee was the Spaceman when he won 17 games for the Sox in 3 straight years, but became simply lost in space when he left Fenway for Montreal.

Conversely there are players who are better off playing in towns where nobody cares. Fred Lynn was a great Sox performer, but he hated traffic rotaries, the media, and Fenway fervor. Lynn was a Southern California child of sand and surf, and baseball was a way to make a living. He never understood why the game meant so much to the paying public of New England.

The superbly gifted Jim Rice is another Sox star who

doesn't care for the extra attention. Rice wants to come to the park and play every day, even when he's hurt. But he doesn't like to answer questions about what pitch he hit nor does he wish to deal with any of the hype and hysteria that permeates his outdoor office. Rice would have been much better off hitting his home runs in Atlanta, a place with few baseball historians, no great expectations, and little public pressures.

It's no secret that Fenway Park can be a difficult environment for a black player. Sox crowds are 99 percent white and the city of Boston lacks a comfortable racial climate. The Bill Russell Celtics never knew the popularity of Larry Bird's team. Tommy Harper took the Red Sox to court attempting to prove that the Boston organization created an environment uncomfortable to blacks. (The Sox settled out of court, paying Harper approximately $400,000.)

On the other hand Luis Tiant and George Scott were loved at Fenway, and Baylor told Charley Rosen of *Inside Sports,* "I drive around Boston and I eat out everywhere, and I just don't find anything but respect. If a player believes that the Boston fans boo the black players and cheer the whites, I say that's just an excuse for his own shortcomings."

Less than an hour after the Sox extended their losing streak to 4 games in Oakland, it was learned that Oil Can had been arrested for having an outstanding speeding ticket. People wondered how the Can could be arrested while he was still in the hospital, until the Sox announced that Boyd was out on a pass to see an Eddie Murphy concert with his wife, Karen (whom Boyd frequently referred to as "my fiancée"). En route Karen was pulled over for speeding, and Boyd was riding in the passenger seat. A routine plate check found an outstanding warrant. The Sox front office handled this episode with all the skill and candor that matters related to Boyd seem to precipitate, first saying that he would be back at the hospital before daybreak, then saying he had an overnight pass, then saying he was getting his release from the hospital. On Thursday, July 24, a hospital spokesperson told reporters that Boyd was still in Worcester Center when he was actually at Wrentham District Court.

While the Sox were mimeographing their latest statement, Boyd issued one of his own that said, "I have been given medical clearance to return to baseball."

To which the Sox countered, "He remains suspended but will continue to engage in daily supervised workouts."

Three thousand miles away, the Sox staggered into Anaheim and turned to Roger Clemens once again. The Rocketman responded with a 2-hit masterpiece. Rich Gedman hit a grand slam in the fifth and Boston snapped their 4-game losing streak with an 8–1 victory. But the Angels came back to take the final 2 games of the series, and Boston's crash bottomed out at 2–8. Thirteen games after the night of Oil Can's tantrum, the Sox went 3–0 in games started by Clemens, 0–10 in all others. During the coast trip they batted .187 with men in scoring position, getting 17 runs in Clemens's two starts, and 17 in the other 8 games, all losses. McNamara was ejected from the finale in California as Don Sutton beat Tom Seaver in a rare matchup of 300-game winners.

On the way home, the Sox were able to refuel at Comiskey Park with a 3–1 victory over the White Sox, July 28. Baylor and Evans hit homers and Nipper went the route to give the Sox their first non-Clemens victory in nineteen days. The lowly White Sox rebounded with a 4–1 victory the next night and then beat Roger 7–2 in the trip finale. Clemens was leading 2–0 in the fifth inning when the game exploded in his face like one of Bill Veeck's scoreboards. After Chicago tied it up on 3 singles, a fielder's choice, and a sac fly, Harold Baines hit a 2-out grounder to Buckner at first base. Buckner fielded the ball and flipped to Clemens covering. Umpire Greg Kosc ruled that Clemens missed the bag with his foot and called Baines safe. Clemens, furious, inadvertently bumped Kosc and was thumbed out. When Clemens learned that he'd been ejected, his performance was positively Can-esque as he turned his hat around and went jaw to jaw with the ump before being carried away, horizontally, by strongmen Baylor and Rice. The Clemens tirade capped the trip in fitting fashion. Boston sans Boyd went 3–10 after the break, hit .211 in four cities, and returned to Fenway with a 3½ game lead.

Most of the Sox were still in bed after their red-eye flight home when the team announced that Oil Can would be reactivated before the next game and would receive full pay for his time on the suspended list (with the exception of the original three-day penalty). It did seem that Boyd might be coming back. He'd dumped agent Dennis Coleman and hired Jim Rice's agent, George Kalafatis. He'd moved out of his Chelsea condo (as had Quinones) and was living with his in-laws in East Providence, Rhode Island. Gorman said he'd never attempted to trade the Can and that Boyd would be placed in a counseling and support program for the balance of the season.

The Can kept the lid on when he returned and spoke little. One of his eventual interviews was with Ken

Picking of *USA Today*. Boyd not only trusted Picking but also knew his mother would see his words in Meridian. "I'm getting back to being me," he told Picking. "But I have to be careful. I've learned a lot of lessons this year, and I just don't want anything else to mess up what should be a season to remember for me and the Red Sox. I'm a temperamental individual. So's my dad, so's my dog. But that doesn't mean I'm on drugs and that doesn't mean the people I'm with are on drugs. I'm a good person and the people who really know me know that. It really bothers me to read how I'm portrayed as some sort of maniac. How would that make your family feel about you? All I want to do is play the game I love. Maybe I'm emotional, but I'm real and I just don't want people taking advantage of my emotions. I'm back to pitch. That's all I want to do."

The night the Can returned, Bruce Hurst won his first game in over two months, beating the Royals 5–3. Boston's bullpen blew up the next day. Tom Seaver walked off the mound with a 2–1 lead in the seventh, but torch twins Bob Stanley and Tim Lollar needed only 20 pitches to turn the 2–1 lead into a 9–2 deficit. The first twelve Royals reached base in the seventh and eleven scored. "I don't think we had our fielders in the right spots," said Lollar. "We couldn't put any out on the freeway."

Stanley did not stay to meet the press, but it was clear that something had to be done about the bullpen. Sambito was in a prolonged slump; Stanley was virtually useless, especially in Fenway, and Lollar should not have been on the team even with his $525,000 guaranteed contract. As of August 3, the Sox were 7–20 in games when Lollar was used. His presence was a sure sign that the team was hopelessly behind. A fan searching the radio dial needed only to hear "Lollar goes to the stretch," to know that the Sox were losing by a big margin.

The lead was now down to 3½ games with Boston preparing to play another round against the American League East. The Yankees, Orioles, Tigers, and Blue Jays were snapping at their heels and Boston was without a reliable closer.

McNamara turned to Schiraldi. The twenty-four-year-old Texan had pitched five times in long relief since he was recalled from Pawtucket July 18. In 14.2 innings Schiraldi had yielded only one run and 13 hits while striking out 15. Schiraldi had been used only once to save a game, but McNamara was out of options.

In the Fenway finale against the Royals, the Sox led 5–3 in the ninth when George Brett and Jorge Orta opened with singles off Al Nipper. McNamara hooked Nipper and looked to the pen. It was not a situation for Sambito because KC had two right-handed hitters coming up. And the sight of Stanley lumbering in from the pen might have set off a soccer-style riot. Schiraldi got the call. He blinded Frank White with five fastballs, fanning him on a 1–2 heater. He ran the count to 3–2 on Steve Balboni, then punched him out with another fastball. Balboni went down swinging and shook his head all the way back to the Royals' dugout. Schiraldi finished the job by getting KC rookie Mike Kingery on a first pitch grounder to Marty Barrett. McNamara bounded out of the dugout to shake the kid's hand. It was the birth of a bullpen stopper.

The White Sox came to town and took two straight, trimming Boston's lead to 2½ games, the smallest margin since June 1. On Clemens's twenty-fourth birthday the White Sox beat the Boston ace 1–0, scoring an unearned run in the eighth. The Can returned the next night, pitching 7.2 strong innings (108 pitches, 75 strikes) in a 3–1 defeat. The crowd chanted "Oy-el Can," and Boyd received numerous standing ovations from the 35,236. A plane flew overhead trailing the sign "Oil Can, Boston Loves You."

The Can was back, but the Sox were still unraveling. Boston had lost 5 of 7, and 11 of 15, scoring one run in its last 19 innings. The Sox also now ranked last in the American League infielding with 101 errors in 104 games.

"It gets exasperating," admitted McNamara. "But I know this is no time to panic. The race is still in front of us."

While all Boston heard footsteps from down under, McNamara was rewarded with a two-year contract extension August 6. Buoyed by this vote of confidence, the Sox manager shook up his lineup, moving Boggs into the leadoff spot and Barrett back to the number two spot. Bill Buckner, who'd been batting third, was dropped to sixth. Boggs was unhappy with the change. He was still bitter about his arbitration case that had knocked him for failing to drive in runs, which is a lot tougher to do batting leadoff. Boggs wanted to bat in the third spot, but the Chicken Man proved he could hit anywhere in the order and went 2–2 scoring 3 runs in his first night at leadoff. Buckner and Barrett each responded with three hits as well, and the Sox rode Hurst's 3-hitter to a 9–0 victory over Chicago. Four hundred miles to the southeast the Orioles hit 2 grand slams in one inning, then *lost* to the Texas Rangers. Baltimore dropped 3½ games back and Boston's lead never dipped below 3 games again. The Red Sox had endured a mid-season slump and were prepared to conquer every challenge in the final 2 months.

Boyd was now ready to win. "What's wrong with gettin' mad about somethin' you love, man? What's wrong with that?" the Can said. "It's just like there's a mark on me and it isn't going to go away this year or the next twenty years. What was written about me nearly destroyed me. I can be the way I want, I can be the way I am, I can only be me. There are things that everybody has to change, and I know what I got to do about me. I knew I was no fiend. I knew I was no madman. I was being misunderstood because I'm temperamental. I'm very emotional. So I sat down and what I told the team doctor was, 'Hey, I want to be tested. I want to go right now.' And it was the best thing that happened to me."

Brother Skeeter Boyd had one final piece of advice: "I told him that whenever he got in trouble, he should just reach back and grab a handful of grace and throw it across the plate."

6

CAPTAIN JIM AND COMPANY SHRED THE COMPETITION

A bolt of lightning struck the center field flagpole in Tiger Stadium late in the afternoon on Friday, August 8. At the time many of the Red Sox were in the visitors' dugout and others ran from the clubhouse to see the shredded and toasted Old Glory clinging to the pole. But the pre-game rains didn't dampen the spirits of 46,779 Michiganians who crowded the Chrysler and Ford freeways and turned their K Cars off Rosa Parks Boulevard to catch the big game. The Tigers were only twenty-two months removed from their championship and Sparky Anderson's veteran cast was first in line to topple the pretenders from Boston. The Yankees had failed to take advantage of Boston's summer slump, but the Tigers had roared back into the hunt. Detroit trailed by 14 games July 12, but sat a mere 4½ back when lightning struck in the Motor City. "No one imagined we could get back in the race this quickly," said Tiger

Tom Brookens. "They know now that we're around," added Detroit manager Sparky Anderson.

As always Sparky was talking a good game, but he stubbornly refused to change his pitching rotation to get ace Jack Morris into the series opener. Before the Sox got to town, Morris was used in a Thursday doubleheader and he beat Cleveland 15–1. That left the mortal Randy O'Neal to pitch the first game against Boston and pushed Morris out of the big 4-game set. Sparky said it was too early in the race to change his rotation for a specific series. O'Neal (1–6 at the time) would face Tom Seaver who led O'Neal in all-time victories, 308–8.

Anderson's strategy backfired when O'Neal walked six batters and gave up 5 runs in 2.2 innings. "He looked nervous," said Marty Barrett.

Seaver wasn't nervous. He went about his work like the village blacksmith. He was strong, steady, and precise, as he pitched his best game of 1986, holding the Tigers to 1 run on 5 hits and a walk while striking out 9 in 9 full innings. He threw 122 pitches and the Red Sox were 6–1 winners.

"I knew after the third inning that the party was over," said Anderson, who like McNamara had managed Seaver in Cincinnati. "I knew after the third that he was gonna win. That was a cakewalk and I enjoyed watching Seaver pitch. It was all him tonight. It's nice to see a forty-one-year-old guy pitch like that."

The victory pushed Seaver ahead of Old Hoss Radbourn on the all-time victory list. Old Hoss went 60–12 with Providence in 1884, compiling a 1.38 ERA with 441 strikeouts in 678.2 innings. After going only 49–25 in 1883, Radbourn must have been a candidate for comeback of the year when he won sixty in '84.

Seaver seemed fit for the role of clubhouse legend-in-residence. He was quiet, kept to himself, and rarely participated in the juvenile pranks that the younger men enjoyed. He'd done all that decades ago. He liked his cigars, his crossword puzzles, and a mug of beer after he pitched. The consummate pro was ready to pitch every fifth day. He didn't apportion blame when the Sox scored only 5 runs for him in a stretch of 5 starts, and he didn't push himself on the younger pitchers.

The Sox beat the Tigers again Saturday, 8–7, as Calvin Schiraldi picked up his second save. Boggs, still grumbling about his new leadoff role, made McNamara look like a genius in a game where if the first man up in an inning reaches, he has a 50 percent chance of scoring. (This drops to 14 percent if there is one out.) The Chicken Man slapped 4 hits, walked twice, and scored 3 runs. Since moving into the number one spot in the order, Boggs had reached base 15 times in 16 plate appearances (9–10 with six walks). The Tigers rallied with 3 in the seventh and 3 more in the eighth, but Schiraldi had the outfielders running down 440-foot fly balls in the ninth and saved it for Al Nipper.

Sunday in rainy, rusty Motown furnished more good omens for the year. Clemens was knocked from the mound and the Sox blew a 4–0 lead to trail 6–4 in the eighth. But Don Baylor homered with 1 out in the eighth, and with 2 outs Rey Quinones kept the inning alive by taking a pitch on the elbow that loaded the bases. Rich Gedman capped the comeback with a pinch grand slam off Tiger lefty Willie Hernandez. "If they can't be deflated after this one, they'll never be, but they've got to be. They knocked Roger Clemens out and had things the way they wanted, but then we took it back," said Barrett.

"A week ago the way we were playing we would have

been dead in the eighth. Now, though, we're playing the way we can play. We're back," added Gedman.

The Red Sox catcher was a homegrown product, just like his predecessor, but similarity ended there. Carlton Fisk was an upcountry woodsman, tall, strapping, and graceful. Gedman was a product of the grimy milltown of Worcester. He was a blue-collar kid with thick glasses and a thick body. Fisk earned the nickname "pudge" in his youth, but Gedman was a white whale of 260 pounds when he pitched and played first base for St. Peter's of Worcester. He was league MVP for the St. Peter's state championship team in his senior season (1977), but nobody drafted the overweight adolescent with the strong arm. He certainly didn't look like a young man capable of becoming Worcester's greatest gift to Boston since Bob Cousy and Tom Heinsohn left Holy Cross to join the Celtics.

Gedman could hit and throw, but he didn't have a big league pitching arm or big league speed. Red Sox scout Bill Enos had a better idea; he saw Gedman and thought "catcher," and so Boston signed the chubby seventeen-year-old on August 5. (Little League parents take note: the fastest way to get your son into professional baseball is to train him to be a switch-hitting catcher.)

It was too late for Gedman to play in the rookie league, so the Sox invited him to work out with their Pawtucket team in August and September. For the rest of his summer Gedman drove down Route 146 every day the PawSox were home and worked with the triple-A team, then watched the games. He went from there to the Florida Instructional League to practice catching.

"I was brutal," Gedman recalled. "My first week I

didn't catch a ball in the pocket of my glove. Everything was off the sides of it. I was clutching and sprawling all over the place. I felt like a cast-iron man with balls being dropped off a wall at me."

Gedman was a quick study. On his twenty-first birthday, three years after he was fitted for his first catcher's mitt, he caught Dennis Eckersley's 1-hitter in Toronto. In 1981 Gedman hit .288 with Boston and was named AL Rookie of the Year by the *Sporting News*. In 1985 he caught 139 games, hit .295 with 18 homers and 80 RBIs, and played in his first All Star game.

By 1986 Gedman was a rock-hard 205 pounds and wore contact lenses. He was a source of strength and security to all of his teammates. His father's illness and death made it Gedman's toughest season, but he kept playing through his sorrow, just as he played through the pain of foul tips, homeplate collisions, and chronic back discomfort.

"He's one tough son-of-a-bitch," said former catcher John McNamara.

Gedman eschewed publicity. He spoke softly and bashfully, blinking his heavy-lidded pale blue eyes under the glare of television lights. Most of the time Gedman projected the vacant stare of a college senior who'd been up for seventy-two straight hours drinking coffee and studying for finals. He majored in self-deprecation. "Don't ask me any cultural questions," he'd say. "I have enough on my mind with simple baseball questions. What do you want me to say? I'm not a word man. I'm not going to get out of character."

Gedman's day-off grand slam drove a stake through the eye of the Tigers and lifted the Sox to unexpected heights. In retrospect the trip to Detroit did for the 1986 Red Sox what the 1960 West Virginia primary did for presidential candidate John F. Kennedy. Boston's first place lead of 2½ games on Tuesday, August 5, was up to 6 games by Sunday night and Boston had at least 8 fewer losses than any other team in their division. In the first late-season *big* series, the Sox had snatched 3 straight on Detroit's home turf.

Anderson never admitted his mistake, but Sunday it was announced that Eric Steven King had a sore forearm and would not be able to start Monday. Jack Morris was named to pitch the series finale. Morris blanked Boston on 3 hits, then said, "How can it be a big game? We're nine hundred games out of first place."

A whopping 179,383 fans clicked the Detroit turnstiles to see the Sox and Tigers and when the showdown series was finally over Anderson said, "This series showed me one thing—they're not better than us. They are leading, but they're not better."

The statement rang hollow. Sparky had said it was too early to shuffle his pitching rotation, but by the time he got Morris into battle, it was too late. Boston had won the duel and carried new confidence the rest of the way.

The Sox went to Kansas City from Detroit and split 4 games with the defending World Champs. Seaver won his 310th and Schiraldi bagged his fourth save of the 8-game, 5–3 roadtrip. The man who would give Calvinism a whole new meaning had pitched 21.1 consecutive scoreless innings, had an ERA of 0.40, and hadn't allowed a run in 10 straight appearances. The Sox were hoping he could do for them what Tom Henke did for the Blue Jays in 1985.

Farm director Ed Kenney was the man who first suggested bullpen duty for Schiraldi when the former Met prospect was shipped to Pawtucket in the spring. "He seems to like it," observed Kenney. "It isn't something we pushed on him. I think he's more valuable doing what he's doing."

"I'll do whatever they want," said Schiraldi. "It takes a different mentality coming out of the pen. You have to go right in and throw strikes. There's no time to finesse the hitters."

Back for a mini-homestand Boston took two of three from Detroit, again losing only the game Morris pitched. Clemens won his eighteenth Friday night; and Sunday, August 17, Schiraldi bagged the first American League win of his career, pitching 3.2 innings in a come-from-behind, 7–5 victory. Boston now led the Yankees by 5 and the third-place Tigers by seven. The Orioles were tumbling out of sight.

The Sox, home less than sixty hours, were already set to embark on a ten-day road trip through Cleveland; Minneapolis; and Arlington, Texas—three garden spots on the American League tour. Players' sons helped them pack as daughters and wives waited in the parking lot. The trucks were loading up and equipment czar Orlando was barking orders and steamrolling any unfortunate soul in his path.

No one noticed Lou Gorman stroll into McNamara's office just before departure time. The door was closed, and it was assumed that the Boston brass was discussing the ten-game trip.

In fact Gorman was close to completing a deal that would send Quinones, Mike Brown, Mike Trujillo, and John Christensen to the Mariners for shortstop Spike Owen and outfielder Dave Henderson. This was the day the final pieces of the 1986 Red Sox were snapped into place.

Sunday a rumor circulated that the team had rejected Seattle's offer of Owen, Henderson, and pitcher Karl Best for Brown, Trujillo, and outfielder prospects Mike Greenwell and Ellis Burks. Quinones's name hadn't been mentioned. Gorman talked to the twenty-two-year-old shortstop early Sunday and told him that he might be dealt. But Quinones was unfazed. He was joshing with his teammates as they readied for the flight to Minnesota. Dressed in a bright red blazer and a short, squared tie, he looked like a young Lionel Richie.

McNamara presumed the deal was done when he boarded the Sox charter for the Twin Cities, but no announcement had been made because Owen and Henderson were still playing for the Mariners against the Twins in Seattle. When the Sox arrived at their Minneapolis hotel, Bill Buckner heard about the trade in his hotel room and it was he who told the rookie about the swap. Quinones was in New York City the next day to join his new team.

When Gorman announced the trade in Boston, he said, "We're going for broke." The deal was greeted with much celebration. The Sox had plugged their two remaining holes—shortstop and outfield depth. Yankee owner George Steinbrenner called it "The deal of the century. . . . My front office people were asleep at the wheel."

The five ten, 170 pound, switch-hitting Owen was, at first, a comforting sight. A Texas native (whose mother's maiden name is Spikes), Owen had played at the University of Texas with Clemens and Schiraldi. A superior gloveman, he led American League shortstops in assists, putouts, total chances, and doubleplays when the trade was made. He brought a modicum of speed to the Boston order and teamed with Barrett to form the Cabbage Patch Twins in the middle of the infield. As more members of the national media began trailing the Sox, they would ask Boston reporters, "Is that Barrett or Owen?" Sometimes it was Barrett, sometimes Owen, sometimes the batboy.

The twenty-eight-year-old Henderson was Tony Armas insurance. Armas had already gone down with hamstring pulls twice in 1986 and was just starting to find himself at the plate. Henderson had 14 homers for the Mariners, but fell into Dick Williams's vast doghouse and was considered expendable as Seattle committed to youth. "I know him really well," said Gorman, who was with Seattle when the Mariners drafted Henderson. "He gives us some power and depth in the outfield and he can play all three outfield positions."

Sox fans were comforted by the deal. Teams with a shot at a flag sometimes have to trade youth for experience during the stretch run and most pennant drives are fortified by mid-season moves. In 1967 Boston acquired Gary Bell from Cleveland for first baseman Tony Horton and outfielder Don Demeter. Bell stepped into the rotation and finished with a 12–8 record and a 3.15 ERA. The Bell deal was made two days after Boston traded pitcher Don McMahon and Rob Snow to Chicago for invaluable utility infielder Jerry Adair. The '67 Sox also added veteran catcher Elston Howard in August and signed Ken Harrelson at the end of August. In 1975 the pennant-bound team picked up Denny Doyle from the Angels on June 14. Three weeks later the Sox called for relief pitcher Jim Willoughby from St. Louis. Willoughby was the player-to-be-named later in a deal that had sent Mario Guerrero to St. Louis in April. Boston's mid-August deal with the Mariners was applauded. The trade torch had been passed from Adair to Doyle to Owen.

There was considerable confusion late Monday afternoon as the Sox prepared to play the Twins in the Metrodome. Owen and Henderson were scheduled to land at the Minneapolis–St. Paul Airport at 4:30, but their flight was delayed. Meanwhile Boggs's back was bothering him and he was not in McNamara's lineup. Mac had Owen playing short and batting leadoff and Romero playing third. The manager was not aware that League officials had discovered a problem with the trade Monday afternoon. Gorman had failed to ask for waivers on Brown and Trujillo. Though only a technicality, the Sox GM had illegally traded two players and the deal was put on hold until it could be restructured to the satisfaction of the League office and both parties. In Minnesota McNamara still had no idea of the situation forty-five minutes before game time. When reporters got wind of the confusion, they asked McNamara if Owen would still hit leadoff.

"Yes," said the manager. "If there was any problem, I'm sure I'd know about it."

Owen and Henderson made it to the ballpark on time, only to be told they could not play. McNamara finally got word from Gorman a half hour before the game. Sox fans listening to the game back home were reminded of a night in Oakland ten years earlier when Boston bought Rollie Fingers and Joe Rudi from the A's during a Charlie Finley fire sale. The Sox were in Oakland for their first game after the trade and issued uniforms to the newly-acquired stars. Manager Darrell Johnson elected not to use Rudi and Fingers on the night they were eligible, then Commissioner Bowie Kuhn intervened and the deal was killed three days later.

The Owen-Henderson deal was never in such danger. Gorman and Seattle GM Dick Balderson restructured the trade the next day (Trujillo and Brown were pulled out and claimed on waivers by the Mariners), and Owen was in the lineup against the Twins August 19. Two nights later Owen became only the second player in League history to score 6 runs in a game as the Sox bludgeoned the Indians, 24–5.

The Lake Erie slaughter indicated that the Red Sox were finally starting to polish their hitting shoes. Clemens got 9 runs a day earlier in Minnesota and said, "People forget what this team can do offensively. I've heard Dave Winfield say that the Yankees haven't had their hot streak yet. Well, neither have we."

Clemens's Texas pal Greg Swindell was one of the unfortunate Indian hurlers in the 24–5 game. With only 18 innings of pro ball (all in A Ball) under his belt, Swindell was called up just before he was scheduled to make his first major league start. An injury to knuckleballer Phil Niekro forced the decision at the start of a crucial weekend set with Boston.

The Sox had a 6–1 lead when Swindell left, then erupted for 12 runs in the sixth for their biggest inning of the year. Eleven of the runs were scored after 2 outs, including four on Armas's first grand slam of the season. Boggs and Baylor were both hitless, but Buckner had 5 hits. Armas drove in a career-high 6 runs, and Dave Stapleton had his first hit since June 4. "It was clutch," said Stapleton. "I came through for the team. I was way down below the Mendoza line, I was all the way down to the Can line."

The Mendoza Line is a handle invented by George Brett in honor of light-hitting Mario Mendoza. Mendoza was usually hovering near the .200 mark and when Brett looked at the Sunday averages, he would announce which players had fallen below the Mendoza Line. Stapleton was hitting .100 (3–30) at the time.

Before Owen, Red Sox shortstop Johnny Pesky was the only other American Leaguer to score 6 runs in a single game (1946). The 24 runs tied for second in Sox history. Boston scored 29 against the St. Louis Browns in 1950. "My feet got kind of tired from going around the bases," said Owen, a cheerful man with a young face and thinning hair. The doughboy shortstop in a Boston uniform for only 3 games had already done something that Ted Williams and Carl Yastrzemski never had.

"Spike Owen is the type of ballplayer that fits right into a ballclub. He fits into the chemistry of this ballclub. He and Barrett are going to work well together. They complement each other," McNamara said. McNamara had started to say that Owen fit into the Sox system better than Quinones, but stopped himself short.

The rise and fall of Rey Quinones was swift. Gorman raved about the young Puerto Rican in spring training and Ted Williams fell in love with his swing, calling him "a pup out of Frank Robinson" (Robinson scoffed when told he'd been compared to a skinny shortstop). Quinones helped the Sox win some games when Hoffman was disabled and Romero faltered, but he wasn't ready for the big leagues. McNamara didn't like the rookie's work habits and Quinones hurt his case by choosing to live with Oil Can.

The core of the team seemed to agree with McNamara. When Baylor was asked about working with indefatigable batting coach Walter Hriniak, the judge went out of his way to take a subtle shot at Quinones. "You never know all there is to know about hitting," said Baylor. "But Rey, he told Walter, 'I'll let you know when I need you.'"

His first game with the Mariners Quinones batted leadoff in Yankee Stadium and went 2–4, knocked in two runs, and made a sparkling defensive play in Seattle's victory over New York. He was more than a thousand miles from his former teammates and he was still helping them. There was some fear in the Sox camp that Quinones might develop into the next Dave Conception, but Earl Weaver shook his head and said, "In five years, he'll be the same player he is now."

There was one more memorable play before Boston left Cleveland in late August. On Saturday, August 23rd, the Sox trailed the Indians, 4–3, in the top of the ninth when Boggs came to the plate with 1 out and Romero at third. Indian reliever Ernie Comacho was throwing hard and Boggs, who'd already homered earlier in the game, looked at ball 1. The Chicken Man lofted the next pitch high and far down the line in left. The ball sailed into foul territory, but was still catchable near the Indians' bullpen. Otis Nixon, who'd been inserted for defensive purposes, drifted into foul territory and caught the ball. Romero scored easily to tie the game, 4–4.

Should Nixon have caught the ball in that situation or let it drop? By letting the ball drop, the Tribe would have preserved its lead and taken its chances pitching to Boggs with a 1–1 count. By catching the ball, the Indians forced themselves into a tie ballgame. Postgame queries produced a split decision. Cleveland manager Pat Corrales backed his outfielder, and McNamara agreed that he'd want the ball caught. But Red Sox coaches Joe Morgan and Rene Lachmann said they'd have wanted the ball dropped and Barrett agreed. Boggs said he'd have caught the ball, then asked, "What if their bullpen guys had tackled him to keep him from catching the ball?" The question was put to homeplate umpire Al Clark, who answered, "That's a good question. I think I'd have called him out and scored the run.

I don't know if there's any rule to back me up, but that's what I'd have done."

It was a moot point when Cleveland scored a run off Bob Stanley in the bottom of the ninth. Cleveland's winning rally was aided when Evans, Buckner, and Barrett converged on a lazy fly to shallow right with two on and 1 out. Evans called for it and was camped under the ball when Buckner came crashing through. The ball glanced off Buckner's glove, everybody was safe, and the next batter, Andre Thornton, won the game with a pinch single. Evans and Barrett said Buckner couldn't hear over the crowd noise (40,246). Buckner masterfully demonstrated his dilemma by answering questions from the whirlpool in the trainer's room: As he explained that he couldn't hear Evans over the crowd noise, reporters couldn't hear Buckner over the sound of the whirlpool.

For Sox fans still on the edge, waiting for another fold, this kindled thoughts of another folly fly that landed in the middle of five Sox players when the Yankees beat the Red Sox on September 9, 1978. Utility infielder Frank Duffy had been the closest player to the '78 pop and earned a place in Boston sports lore.

The Saturday loss in Cleveland was to be the first of three. On Monday, August 25, Clemens took a 2-hitter and a 2–0 lead into the eighth in Arlington, Texas, but Geno Petralli (whose cousin is married to McNamara's brother) cranked a first-pitch, pinch-hit, 2-run homer over the 330-foot sign in right to tie the game. Though going for his twentieth win, Clemens didn't come out to pitch the ninth and his Texas frat brother, Schiraldi, surrendered a 2-out, 2-run game winning blast to Ruben Sierra. *Dallas Morning News* columnist Randy Galloway called it "The biggest victory in Ranger club history, period."

The Sox won the next night when Boyd pitched a 4-hit, 10-strikeout masterpiece in an 8–1 victory over Texas. The final night in Texas produced a 4–1 loss and the Sox never looked more tired. They'd been on the road for 31 out of 40 games since the All Star break. Most important they'd survived the stretch without losing significant ground. Boston led the AL East by 7 games at the break and staggered home from Texas still with a 5-game lead.

The Sox were looking at the Indians when they finally set foot back in Fenway. Cleveland had come directly from Canada where the fading Tribe dropped three straight to the surging Blue Jays. It was Labor Day weekend and Boston had finally identified the enemy. It wasn't the Yankees who were reeling from a brutal homestand and now faced a 14-game trip. The Orioles were stumbling toward the basement and also faced the cruel coast. The Tigers hadn't recovered from their losses to Boston, and the Brewers and Indians had double digit deficits in the loss column. One rival remained: the defending division champion Blue Jays.

Toronto had been wallowing all season: 1. They missed manager Bobby Cox, who had left to take over as General Manager of Ted Turner's Atlanta Braves. Rookie skipper Jimy (he changed his name from Jimmy to Jimy as a school prank) Williams was too soft on the defending champs. 2. The Jays never fully recovered from blowing their 3–1 playoff lead against the Royals in '85. 3. Toronto fell victim to the dreaded repeat syndrome. No American League East team had repeated since the 1980–81 Yankees, and Toronto's players didn't have the maturity or fortitude to overcome the inevitable complacency that accompanies defending champs. 4. Dave Stieb, one of baseball's best pitchers in the 1980s, suddenly lost everything in the first five months of the 1986 season. He had a sore arm, stopped pitching inside, and had perhaps thrown too many sliders. His ERA topped the charts for most of the season and he had won only 4 games. Stieb was 4–11 with a 5.37 ERA on September first.

The Jays were further discouraged when Doyle Alexander and Jim Acker were shipped to Atlanta during the summer. Alexander was involved in an ugly contract dispute and was set to become a free agent at the end of the season. When he and Acker were reunited with Cox in Atlanta, it was taken as a sign that the Blue Jays had given up.

Not quite. Toronto had the best shortstop in the League in Tony Fernandez, and their outfield of Jesse Barfield, Lloyd Moseby, and George Bell was best in baseball. (Incidentally, they were all born within fifteen days of one another in 1959.) Barfield and Bell were assembling MVP numbers by late August as it got warm north of the border. Toronto started winning games in the late innings. The Jays would stay close, bring in rookie reliever Mark Eichhorn or Tom Henke, then wait for Barfield or Bell to tag one. The formula worked through Labor Day as the Jays swept Minnesota and closed to within 3½ of Boston. It was a remarkable comeback, considering that Toronto had been in last place on June 3 and 12 games out on June 15.

The Red Sox were watching the scoreboard on Labor Day weekend and they watched the Blue Jays. Boston lost its Friday night game, but Roger Clemens won number 20 in the Saturday afternoon special. Clemens became the Sox first 20-game winner since Dennis Eckersley's 20–8 in 1978 and won for the twelfth time after a Boston loss. He was solidifying his case for MVP.

Clemens's twentieth proved to be the start of Boston's finest stretch of baseball and the Sox reeled off 11 in a row, including 9 come-from-behind victories. The lead, which had been down to 3 games early in the home-stand, swelled to 6½ (7 in the loss column) before the Sox left Fenway, and ballooned to 8½ before the streak ended. During this stretch Captain Jim Rice carried the ballclub—just as he had in the old days.

As the fall fun started at Fenway, more believers were filing out of the park every day. After a zany Sunday win against Cleveland, the Sox swept 3 straight from the Rangers and Twins to wrap up their schedule against the American League West. All 3 victories against Texas were comebacks, none more typical of the '86 season than the 4–3 series finale played on Wednesday, September 3.

A gutty performance by Seaver (2 runs, no walks, 7 hits, 4 strikeouts in 8 innings) kept the Sox close throughout. The locals led 3–2 when Stanley came in to pitch the ninth. The once-feared Steamer was a local laughing stock by now—Boston's fool on the hill—and every one of his Fenway appearances was greeted with a chorus of boos. Stanley was endorsing a car phone company and a north shore scribe had implored the Sox in the *Herald*'s Letters About Bob Stanley collection to keep him away from Fenway. After reading the rip, Stanley confronted a writer from the paper and said, "I'm going to cancel my prescription."

Standing in the visitor's dugout, listening to the chorus of boos raining down on Stanley, Texas pitching coach Tom House was reminded of his short tenure in Boston. "I never heard my last name the whole time I pitched here. I'd hear, 'Now pitching for the Red Sox, Tom Boooooooo.'" Now it was Stanley's turn.

After the usual reception, Stanley squandered Seaver's lead. The Steamer was greeted with a couple of groundball singles, then mishandled what should have been a doubleplay ball, and watched Texas Cleveland score the tying run as the mob screamed for blood. Stanley's teammates remedied the situation in the bottom of the ninth. Rookie Mike Greenwell led with a pinch single and LaSchelle Tarver ran for Greenwell. Tarver, part of the Bobby Ojeda swap with the Mets, had just been called up from Pawtucket the day before. After Owen struck out, Boggs, who had already homered off Charlie Hough, drilled a 3–2 Dale Mahorcic pitch into the small gap in left-center. The ball was perfectly placed between Texas outfielders Gary Ward and Oddibie McDowell. Boggs could not have thrown the ball into a better spot. Tarver was running on the pitch and never stopped. He scored easily from first as Boggs loped into second with his game-winning hit.

Jim-Rice Weekend followed, a 3-day stretch when the Blue Jays lost twice to the White Sox and Boston rode their captain's big shoulders to 3 more wins and a 6½ game lead. Rice went 7–12 with 10 RBIs in the 3-game set, hitting a pair of grand slams. He hadn't hit a home run with more than 1 runner aboard in almost 15 calendar months (June 10, 1985, off Rollie Fingers) but broke out dramatically. He also played the left field wall like a young Carl Yastrzemski, holding Minnesota hitters to long singles and making strong throws to the infield.

Rice was unusually expansive after his weekend binge. There'd been an invisible mine field around his locker since he joined the team in 1974 and reporters rarely invaded his space. Casual conversation with Rice seemed difficult for those who weren't teammates or friends. He reacted to every question and comment as if he'd been challenged. One was careful not to say, "Nice day, huh, Jim?" out of fear that he'd snap, "Hey, I'm no meteorologist."

Rice started to thaw as the leaves began to turn. In the twelfth year of a truly brilliant career, he was on the verge of playing in his first championship series. He'd taken a bone-cracking Vern Ruhle pitch off the wrist late in the 1975 season and watched the epic World Series from the bench. His only post-season game was the 1978 playoff loss.

"I'm not really concerned about myself this year, it's the team," Rice said after his weekend grand slam binge. "This year we've acquired Don Baylor and that has made me do some of the things that I used to do back in '75 and '78. Things like hitting behind the runner. I also enjoy hitting balls to the right side because I've seen holes over there you could drive two trucks through. Whereas last year I had those holes there, but I wasn't seeing them. But this year I'm seeing the holes and I'm working my way over. If guys are on first and third or first and second, you've got to get those guys over, and if you don't, it's going to cost you five dollars. That's what's changed everything. Don Baylor's Kangaroo Court."

James Edward Rice was born in Anderson, South Carolina, on March 8, 1953, the fourth of nine children born to Julia May Rice. He grew up on Reed Street in the small town (pop. 30,000) in the western corner of the state where his father, Roger Edward, was a supervisor for a company that made CB radios. Young Jim Ed could always hit a baseball farther than anybody his age. He was a starter on the Westside High School team when he was a fourteen-year-old eighth grader, and he played for the local Legion Post 14. He was shy and sometimes reluctant to devote himself to baseball. His legion coach, Olan Saylors, remembers when Rice failed to show for practice. Saylors had to track Rice down at a local variety store and implore him to return to the team. Rice told Saylors he wasn't going to waste his time playing baseball; he was going to get a job and buy some clothes. Saylors had seen Jim Ed Rice hit a baseball and he told the kid, "You stick with baseball and some-day you'll be wearing silk underwear."

Rice also quit on his school coach John Moore, and Moore chased Jim Ed off the premises when he tried to come back the next year as Moore wanted to make sure the youngster was serious about baseball. Rice also played football, basketball, and track and he was so good that city officials allegedly altered the local desegre-gation line to move Rice into the predominantly white high school for his senior year. Though the coach at Hanna claimed there was no collusion to get Rice, he wound up being one of only two blacks on the team. Rice hit .457 and turned down football scholarship offers from Clemson, North Carolina, and Nebraska to sign for a $45,000 bonus when the Red Sox drafted him in the first round in 1971. For one whose spending money had been made loading boxes for the Carolina Produce Company, the bonus was a strong inducement. Eigh-teen-year-old Jim Rice left home and took his bat to the minors for a 4-year climb to the big leagues.

The Red Sox called up Rice for 24 games at the end of the 1974 season and the next year he won a job in spring training and came north with another rookie named Fred Lynn. The Sox won the American League pennant in '75 and Rice and Lynn were the Gold Dust Twins, each hitting over .300 with more than 20 homers and 100 RBIs. No baseball team ever had a comparable pair of rookies and it seemed the two would solidify the middle of the Boston batting order for years to come.

Rice gave the impression that he felt slighted by the recognition Lynn received in their rookie seasons. Lynn won Rookie of the Year Award and MVP, and was able to showcase his grace and skills in one of the best World Series ever. Rice, who trailed Lynn in all the post-season voting, missed the Series with a broken left hand. Fred Lynn was a white superstar in a town that loves white superstars. Jim Rice was a quiet, moody, black slugger. Boston was not his element.

Lynn gave the Sox five more solid seasons, but Rice became the League's premier power hitter. From 1977 to '79 Rice had at least 200 hits and 35 homers in three consecutive seasons, a feat never before accomplished. He was the AL Most Valuable Player when he hit .315 with 46 homers and 139 RBI in 1978. He was also the first American Leaguer to compile 400 total bases (406) since 1937.

No one ever doubted Rice's ability or his pain threshold. He came to play every day, even hurt, and always put numbers on the board. He did nothing to disgrace himself or his sport and he never complained. He was every manager's dream. Despite all of this, Jim Rice was not able to win Boston's heart. He was appreciated and respected, but never loved. He received courtesy ovations, but few endorsement opportunities. When he finally landed one, $225,000 for 3 years from Colonial Provisions, he was fired because he was allegedly uncooperative and in violation of his contract. As valuable as the slugger was to the Sox franchise, fans chided him for grounding into doubleplays and maligned him because they thought he was a late-game rally killer. When Rice signed a long-term, $2 million per year contract, talk shows spread silly trade rumors.

Rice has never been embraced the way Ted Williams, Carl Yastrzemski, and Luis Tiant eventually would be. It might well have been different if Rice had played somewhere else. After eighteen years in Anderson, South Carolina, the Boston of 1974 must have seemed like Mars to him. Rice's first days north, coinciding as they did with the violent start of forced busing in Boston public schools, must have been an eye-opener for the shy young man from South Carolina. He had to notice that there were few black faces in the Sox organization and in the Boston clubhouse, and there were almost no black faces in the stands at Fenway Park. The thirsty media posed another hurdle for the taciturn rookie.

"He don't like northern states," his father said ten years later. "But his job calls for it."

Rice withdrew. He sat in stoney silence and glared at people he didn't know. He grew bitter and arrogant. He could be a clubhouse cut-up and sometimes was even loud when joshing with teammates on bus rides, but he would not let outsiders get to know him. Even some former friends felt excluded. Back in Anderson, one of his childhood mentors was upset when Rice said on national television that he owed thanks to no one. Rice's photograph came down off the wall, and visitors to Anderson have noticed a conspicuous dearth of Jim Ed Rice memorabilia.

Despite such obstacles, an image of Jim Rice off-the-field has slowly surfaced. He is married to Corrine Gilliard and they live in the northern suburb of Peabody with son Chauncy and daughter Carissa. Rice loves golf and he can hit a Titlist farther than most touring pros (according to the 1986 Red Sox yearbook, Rice's favorite magazine is *Golf Digest*). He doesn't smoke and never has a beer in the clubhouse after a game. He often wears glasses when he isn't on the field, and in 1986 started wearing a contact lens in his right eye during games. He is movie-star handsome with a Billy Dee Williams mustache and perfect teeth. He is a smart and tasteful dresser and has his suits made—better to fit his huge muscular thighs and triangular torso. Cars are a passion. He collects antique autos and has six '55 Chevys, two '56 Chevys, and one '57 Chevy. His closest friend on the club this past year was former teammate Bob Montgomery, a color commentator for Sox telecasts, with whom he usually sat on team bus rides.

Rice is defensive about his defense. He worked hard to make himself an average outfielder. He has limited range and plays very deep, much to the dismay of some Sox pitchers who watch fly balls drop for hits in front of the tentative Rice. But he knows how to play left in Fenway; 12 years with his back to the wall has made Rice a geometric genius when opponents scrape Fenway's green monster. In 1986 he threw out 16 baserunners.

His penchant for grounding into doubleplays was a source of embarrassment. In 1984 an impatient Rice grounded into a major league record thirty-six of them, and in '85 he turned the trick thirty-five more times. Fans were chanting "6–4–3" when he came to bat. In '86 he made a conscious effort to wait for his pitch and cut down on his grounders to the left side. He hit the ball where it was pitched and choked-up on the bat when the count ran to 2 strikes; the result was 16 fewer doubleplays, 41 more hits, a higher batting average (.291 to .324), and only 7 fewer home runs.

Batting champ Wade Boggs greets catcher Rich Gedman at the start of spring training in Winter Haven, Florida.
The Boston Globe

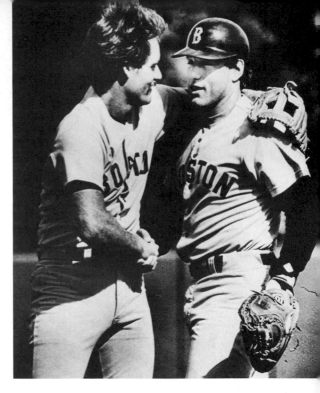

Utility man Steve Lyons, who spent much of his tenure with the Sox in John McNamara's doghouse, appears happy enough here as he walks away from a spring training chat with the skipper.
The Boston Globe

Six months after shoulder surgery, Roger Clemens works out in Winter Haven under the watchful eye of team physician Dr. Arthur Pappas. *The Boston Globe*

Bill Buckner bats on
opening day.
Bruce L. Schwartzman

Bruce Hurst, Jim Rice, Al Nipper, and Tony Armas follow the action on a
cold night in Boston. *The Boston Globe*

Dennis "Oil Can" Boyd posts an early season victory at home.
Bruce L. Schwartzman

Clemens records an early season win at Fenway.
Bruce L. Schwartzman

Tom Seaver's second start and second win for the Sox came on Sunday, July 6, in a 7–3 game against Seattle.
Bruce L. Schwartzman

Don Baylor and Wade Boggs
wait behind manager John
McNamara to hit.
The Boston Globe

Sox pitcher Al Nipper after his collision with Larry Parrish of the Rangers
on May 18. *UPI/Bettmann Newsphotos*

McNamara directs play on the field. *The Boston Globe*

Boyd, Ed Romero, Rey Quinones, Clemens, and Armas watch from the dugout as Seaver pitches against Seattle. *Bruce L. Schwartzman*

Rice belts second grand slam during his big weekend against the Twins. This came in the third inning of Boston's 9–0 win by Hurst on Sunday, September 7. *UPI/Bettmann Newsphotos*

New York's MVP Don Mattingly scores over Rob Woodward as the Yankees sweep the Sox in the final series of the regular season. *The Boston Globe*

Joe Sambito of Brooklyn and Boston. *Bruce L. Schwartzman*

On Sunday, September 28, Oil Can went the distance as Boston clinched the American League East championship with a decisive 12–3 win over Toronto. After the final out, he was joined on the mound by a few friends. *The Boston Globe*

Dave Stapleton jumps in ecstasy after grabbing Brian Downing's pop up to end Game Five of the ALCS—an eleven inning, 7–6 miracle for Boston. *AP/Wide World Photos*

The Can is restrained by umpires after a controversial play at the plate on October 10 during the American League Championship Series in Anaheim.
The Boston Globe

Centerfielder Dave Henderson has the long fly ball hit by Angel Bobby Grich in his glove. Then, as he strikes the fence, the ball pops out and goes over for a home run. *UPI/Bettmann Newsphotos*

Steve Crawford, after going 0–2 in the regular season, won two post season games.
Bruce L. Schwartzman

Henderson is greeted at home plate by Dave Stapleton and Bill Buckner after smashing a two run homer against the Angels in the top of the ninth to save the Sox from elimination on October 12. *UPI/Bettmann Newsphotos*

Spike Owen erases Rick Burleson at second and throws to first to complete this double play against the Angels at Fenway.
The Boston Globe

A rally by the Sox in Game Six of the ALCS stirs the Boston dugout. Left to right: Marty Barrett, Hurst, Clemens, Bob Stanley, Boggs, Nipper, Buckner, and Boyd.
The Boston Globe

Teammates rush to congratulate relief pitcher Calvin Schiraldi after he struck out the side in the ninth to end Game Seven of the ALCS.
The Boston Globe

Jim Rice scores the only run in Boston's 1–0 win over New York in the first game of the World Series, as Gary Carter takes the late throw following Tim Teufel's error.
UPI/Bettmann Newsphotos

Wade Boggs unleashed his glove to make a few fielding gems in the second game of the World Series won by the Sox 9–3.
UPI/Bettmann Newsphotos

Dwight Evans steps back from the plate. *The Boston Globe*

Bill Buckner crawls after Dwight Gooden's pop bunt in Game Two at Shea. *UPI/Bettmann Newsphotos*

Carter is safe at second with a double as the Series moved to Fenway for Game Three won by the Mets 7–1. *The Boston Globe*

Dejected reliever Bob Stanley stands by as Kevin Mitchell scores the tying run in Game Six. Stanley's wild pitch to Mookie Wilson on a 2–2 count enabled Mitchell to cross the plate. New York won the game 6–5 in ten innings. *The Boston Globe*

Rice hates talking about himself, but as he has learned to trust a few people in the media, it gradually has come out that Rice is unusual in another aspect: he doesn't make excuses or hide from his mistakes. He explains his errors or failures with more patience than when he is asked about his home runs. But most writers who don't know him find it impossible to have a normal conversation with the slugger. Rice's answers are usually short and terse and he *never* looks at the questioner. When a reporter mentioned to Rice that he'd be visiting Anderson to do a profile on the slugger's early days, Rice snarled, "What are you doing that for? It's not necessary."

"I'm used to Boston," Rice told another writer in the spring of 1986. "What people think of me comes with the job. It bothers me. Of course, it bothers me because it'd bother everyone. But there's nothing you can do about. . . . I'm a left fielder. Williams, he was misunderstood. Yaz, he was misunderstood: and now me. Hey, what the heck. It bothers you. You pick up the paper, and you're so used to goin' out and bustin' your butt and the guy plays hurt and the guy does this and the guy does that, but all of a sudden, because the guy is not a talkative guy, he's a bad guy because he's not talkative."

It's said that Rice is not misunderstood so much as he simply fails to employ common courtesy much of the time. But disagreeable and rude people usually have a few friends who claim, "He's a good guy if you really get to know him." And there are those who will defend Rice. Still, a man who won't smile can't expect smiles in return. Rice is a great ballplayer with a poor image, and he has worked hard and deserves both distinctions.

There was a new buoyancy about the Sox when they arrived in Baltimore. They were starting a final stretch of 26 games against the American League East and fully expected to wrap up the division before the 4-game final weekend series at Fenway against New York.

The team paying rent at Memorial Stadium provided a striking contrast. The Orioles, who'd been 2½ games out on August 5, had dropped 22 of 30 games and manager Earl Weaver was ready to announce that he'd retire for the second time after the '86 season. It was a classic role reversal. The Sox had always been the folders and Weaver had benefited from and played a part in several Boston stranglings. In 1974 Weaver's Orioles won 28 of their last 34 contests to shatter a Sox lead. Boston was 8 games ahead of Baltimore on August 29 and wound up finishing third, *seven* games behind the Orioles. The crushing blow was a Labor Day doubleheader defeat by bookend scores of 1–0 and 1–0. A year later, before the Sox finally won the American League East, Weaver brought his proud team into Fenway in mid-September and proceeded to spook the town. Baltimore was 4½ games off the pace when Weaver announced, "We've crawled out of more coffins than Bella Lugosi." Sox fans, remembering 1974, cringed.

Though Baltimore only managed to split the series, Weaver kept the pressure on: "Well, if we win the rest of our games, they still have to play .600 ball to win this thing and it's awfully difficult to play .600 ball." There was no mention of how difficult it would be for the Orioles to win *all* of their games. This leap of logic assured that the pressure was still on Boston, and many simply accepted that as fact.

The Earl of Baltimore had reason to be cocky in earlier years. In 15 seasons his Orioles played .624 (301–

181) baseball in September and October regular season games. But in the fall of 1986 Weaver was a beaten man with a tired team. "We're in the pennant race for the next four days," he said with a sigh when it was pointed out that his team trailed by 15 games with 26 to play. "I don't think Boston is worried about us anymore." Weaver's demise was not without its rewards. He'd made $1 million dollars for roughly three hundred days' work since being talked out of retirement by persuasive owner Edward Bennett Williams. "I look at it this way," said Weaver. "There's this giant pile of shit. But in the middle, there's all these green guys with presidents' pictures on 'em. And all of a sudden, this pile of shit doesn't seem so bad."

The Sox took the first game in Baltimore, 9–3 in 11 innings. Boston scored 6 in the eleventh. Gedman was supposed to have the night off but came in for the last 2 innings. Gedman batted twice, first hitting a vicious ground rule double off Eddie Murray into the Sox dugout, then crushing a 3-home homer in the 6-run eleventh. Boggs rang out 4 hits and reached base 5 times. Evans homered and drove in 4 runs. Buckner broke it open with a key double in the eleventh, and Calvin Schiraldi picked up the win after blowing Seaver's 3–1 lead in the ninth. It was Boston's ninth straight win, the lead was up to 7 games, and when the press entered the winner's clubhouse, Sambito leaped from his stall, pointed at the door, and exclaimed, "That's why we're going to win it."

The Sox fell behind 4–1 the next night, but Evans hit a pair of homers, Marty Barrett delivered a 2-run double, and Boston scored 5 times in the final 3 innings to take a 7–5 win. The streak had now reached double figures and eight of the last nine had been comeback victories.

"They look pretty solid to me," the beaten Weaver said.

"It's been a different guy each night," said winner Al Nipper. "And tomorrow we got Rocket going and you know how that story goes."

It was easy to be prophetic with Clemens. The Sox extended their streak to 11 games the following night by 9–4 over the increasingly hapless Orioles. Clemens struggled through 6 innings, but had plenty of offensive support. "We're trying to catch the Mets, now," joked Buckner. "That's our new goal."

The Sox were hitting home runs again, like the Crunch Bunch Gang of the late seventies. Boston ranked eleventh in league homers for most of the season, but hit 32 in 20 games in this August-September stretch, including 10 on their visit to Baltimore. Rice went 18 for 46 with 5 during the winning streak. He was up to 18, but bristled when asked if he was finally trying to hit the long ball. "I never tried to hit homers," snapped the slugger. "That's the worst thing you can do. You take what comes, that's all. Look at all the doubles I hit off the wall in Fenway. Those would be homers in other parks and I'd have twenty-five by now. No one can try to hit home runs. You just take what comes."

Weaver thought otherwise: "Rice is going for homers now that he knows he's going to hit 300."

Clemens was unusually cheerful after victory number 22. He'd spent part of the day at the White House visiting President Reagan with teammates Baylor, Sambito, Nipper, and Greenwell plus broadcasters Ken Coleman and Joe Castiglione as well as traveling secretary Jack Rogers.

"I was in awe," said Clemens. "I gave him one of my twenty-strikeout balls and he talked about that movie he was in, when he was a pitcher [*The Winning Season* with Reagan as Grover Cleveland Alexander]. We also got to meet George Bush and Donald Regan. It was exciting. It kind of makes baseball seem small. The day took a lot out of me and made me real tired, but I'd do it again. I might never get another chance to do something like that. I met a President."

Baylor presented Reagan with a Red Sox cap and jacket, and said the President promised no audits for 1986. Sambito got Reagan to sign some balls. Nipper was going around telling everyone that Reagan said, "Win one for the Nipper." And the players were all fascinated with the secret service briefcase that doubles as an automatic weapon. "They showed us how it works," said Clemens. "The thing fires six shots a second."

Baylor was less awed than his teammates. He had seen Richard Nixon frequently stalk Anaheim Stadium in the late seventies. Nixon attended the 1979 Baltimore-California playoff games in Anaheim and hung a "Never Give Up" banner from his upstairs box. Midway through the fourth and deciding game, a lopsided Oriole victory, somebody removed the banner.

Because of their proximity, the Orioles had plenty of experience with Chief Executives. Memorial Stadium is only an hour's drive from Washington and Reagan spent the first inning of Baltimore's 1986 opener in the Orioles' dugout. President Jimmy Carter attended the final game of the 1979 World Series between the Orioles and Pirates. After Baltimore's 4–1 defeat Carter visited both managers and delivered praise. Nixon was in office when Weaver's Orioles were at their best, 1969–71, and Weaver still has a photograph of himself with Nixon, Johnny Bench, and Gil Hodges taken at the 1970 All

Star game. "I kept it because of Hodges and Bench," said Weaver.

In the Baltimore finale the Orioles finally beat Boston, snapping the Sox 11-game streak. Bill Buckner hit 2 homers and Oil Can had a 5–2 lead in the fourth, but the Orioles rallied to an 8–6 win. Boston's streak was the longest in the American League in 1986 and matched the Mets's for the longest in baseball. Only once had Boston won more than 10 in a row since 1948 when Williams led the Sox to 13 straight. Boston's club record was 15 straight, set in the 100-win season of 1946.

Incredibly the Sox managed to gain more ground the night their streak ended as New York took 2 from the Blue Jays. Boston's lead swelled to 9 games, with 22 to play. Even when they lost, they won. The AL East race was a bed of ashes by the time the Sox reached New York for a weekend series with the Yankees. New York was 10 games behind and all hopes of a Yankee surge were wiped out when Bruce Hurst beat them 7–2 on Friday night, September 12. Buckner hit another pair of homers (giving him 5 in 3 games) and the Sox did what they had done so often—won the first game of a series against a division foe.

Saturday, September 13, was a cool, crisp, sunny day in New York City. The game was scheduled for 3:20 P.M. because of network television. The Sox's chartered bus was parked outside the Grand Hyatt early in the afternoon and a nattily attired Jim Rice was one of the first players to walk from the hotel toward the bus. A star athlete boarding a team bus in New York is usually interrupted by a few professional autograph collectors. The people seeking signatures aren't wide-eyed kids who happen to be in the neighborhood; they are tradesmen, equipped with felt-tip pens, three-inch scrapbooks, and sophisticated filing systems. Rice rushed past the small group, saying "Not today." When he got on the bus, the driver struck up a conversation.

"We see those same four guys every game, it doesn't matter what team is in town," said the driver.

Rice and the driver chatted. This was the relaxed Rice the media never saw. The bus driver and the baseball player talked about autograph collectors. Rice said MVP balls were popular, collectors tried to get as many former MVP's as they could on one ball (Rice won the AL MVP in 1978). They talked about Donald Trump's new tower. The driver said it would be 119 stories and that they had special teams of guys who worked on the highest floors. The driver said the high floor specialists pulled down over $50 an hour. Rice, a man who makes $2 million a year playing baseball, said, "That still ain't enough." The driver said he had twelve more years of driving, then he'd retire to some land he owned in South Carolina. Rice, a South Carolina native, was interested in the location of the property. The driver said New York was okay, but he wanted to spend his retirement someplace else.

Rice looked outside the bus, turned back to the driver, and said, "As far as I'm concerned you can take an atom bomb to this place and I wouldn't miss it a bit."

Approximately five hours later, in the eighth inning of a nationally televised game, Rice charged into the Yankee Stadium stands in search of his cap and a fan who'd hurled racial slurs at him. Rice was followed by most of the Red Sox team.

The Yankees had an 11–6 lead in the eighth when Dan Pasqua lofted a soft fly down the line in left. Rice came in and Sox shortstop Spike Owen ran back. Both players and the ball arrived at the same instant. Rice caught the pop and simultaneously bounced Owen into the short padded wall by the lower boxes. Rice held the ball as both players sprawled near the foul line. Owen was motionless for a few moments, and trainer Charlie Moss bolted from the dugout. When NBC-TV replayed the collision, a fan could be seen leaning out over the rail and reaching for Rice's hat with a gloved hand. Owen finally got to his feet and walked off as Ed Romero came in to replace him. As Rice, meanwhile, was looking for his hat, fans pointed to the culprit. Rice offered the fan a replacement hat, but wanted his "gamer" returned. The fan resisted, swore at Rice, stuffed the hat down his trousers, and took off. Rice was over the wall, and the stands parted as Boston's strongman took after him. Ironically this was the day the Yankees had honored their one hundred millionth fan, selected at random. The lucky fan was Ralph Urban. The unlucky fan was being pursued by Jim Rice.

Rice was followed by Don Baylor, Oil Can Boyd, Al Nipper, Wade Boggs, Roger Clemens, John McNamara, coach Rene Lachemann, a helmeted Marc Sullivan, a bat-toting LaSchelle Tarver, and most of the other Red Sox uniformed personnel. Sambito was tossing some warm-up pitches, went into his motion, looked toward the plate, and held the ball when he noticed his catcher was missing. Rich Gedman was on his way. Marty Barrett stayed behind, citing old-timer Eddie Popowski's line: "Somebody's got to watch the gloves." Lachemann got into a shoving match with a fan. Another grabbed Oil Can's hat, but McNamara and Baylor succeeded in getting it back. Rice returned with his cap but dodged debris for the rest of the game.

The Sox lost the game, but as Baylor proudly said, "The old story about the Boston Red Sox always has been that they needed twenty-four cabs for twenty-four players. Well, you saw everyone moving in one direction today. That was a team."

7

A CLINCH PARTY

THE 4–3 trip through Baltimore and New York had a curious impact back in Boston. The sky-is-falling mentality vanished and was replaced by a strange, unsettling security. Sox fans, scribes, and talk show hosts no longer spoke of collapse. It seemed that no one really knew how to feel about this unusual team. Every autumn since 1946 the Red Sox had either been hopelessly out of the race, close to first, or tentatively holding on to a narrow lead. The '86 Sox went into the final 3 weeks with a fat 9-game margin and virtually no chance of failure.

Post-game awards became a hot topic. Clemens had already clinched the Cy Young trophy and he and Rice were being touted as MVP candidates, although Rice said he wasn't having an MVP year. Clemens said he didn't think about things that far in advance. Baylor was

161

honest and said he thought Rice deserved the award. Evans said he wouldn't be outraged if the trophy went to Clemens. There was much talk about the California Angels, and, as always, the Mets. The American League East division had been won and there would be no suspense in the final three weeks. It was time to think about Roger Clemens vs. Angel ace Mike Witt or Clemens vs. Gooden. Procurement of playoff and Series tickets was a daily story. The pennant race had been vaporized and fans were thinking about October.

The Sox, meanwhile, were still thinking about September. McNamara would not discuss his post-season pitching plans "until we have a bigger lead than the number of games we have left."

While the stubborn and superstitious manager refused to admit victory, the Sox swept 4 from the Brewers without breaking a sweat. Boston outscored Milwaukee 22–6 at Fenway and left town with a 10½ game lead and 15 to play, the largest lead any Red Sox team had held since the '46 flag winners finished the season 12 games ahead.

A large media contingent accompanied the team to Toronto for the start of the final regular season road trip. Boston's Magic Number was down to 6 and the Sox would have a chance to clinch before returning home from Milwaukee the following week. North of the border the Sox–Blue Jays series had lost much of its lustre because the Jays had fallen to 10½ back. Toronto, 3½ back of the Sox on September 1, had added another 7 in 18 short days.

The Blue Jays, who drew crowds of 40,494, 43,713, and 44,197 for the 3-game Boston set, won the first 2 games. The Sox suffered a double loss in game 1 en route to a 6–4 defeat as Tom Seaver "felt something pop" in his right knee while throwing a pitch to Blue Jay second baseman Manny Lee with 2 out in the fourth. Seaver came out after the inning and was examined by Blue Jay physician Ron Taylor. Ironically he was a teammate of Seaver's on the 1969 Mets. Taylor detected no tear and there was little swelling around the knee, but Seaver made plans to go home to see Arthur Pappas the next day. The forty-one-year-old righty didn't seem too nervous as he rode the bus back to the hotel that night. He reminisced about his triple-A days in Toronto when he pitched against a Boston minor league squad managed by Dick Williams. He also kidded coach Bill Fischer, telling the baseball-lifer that he ought to stroll into a Toronto museum during the weekend. "You'd enjoy it Fish," said Seaver. "There's a lot of sculptures by Henry Moore. You know Henry Moore, don't you?" Fischer wouldn't know Henry Moore from Mary Tyler Moore.

Seaver flew out of Toronto the next afternoon and Dr. Pappas said he'd miss one or two starts. In fact Seaver was through for 1986 with a slight tear in the ligament of his right knee, and the Sox had left one of their most important weapons on the artificial turf of Exhibition Stadium. Tom Seaver would be missed.

Meanwhile, back in Molson Country, Boston dropped their second straight to the Jays, prompting outfielder Jesse Barfield to remark, "It would take a miracle to beat these guys now, but I'm one of those people who believes in miracles."

Prior to the Saturday afternoon game in Toronto, someone phoned the Sox clubhouse claiming a bomb was going to go off during the game. When a second call said the bomb would explode in 90 seconds, Clemens and Company were flushed from the locker room.

McNamara first became aware that something was wrong when he saw Nipper sitting on the dugout bench in his underwear. Nipper had been knocked out earlier and was undressing for his shower when the second threat forced immediate clubhouse evacuation. To try and prevent considerable panic, Blue Jay fans were not advised of the situation. Long-time Sox watchers couldn't help but be reminded of an incident in Bloomington, Minnesota, years earlier. Security officials at the old Metropolitan Stadium were advised by the Bloomington police while a Sox-Twins game was in progress that a bomb threat had been reported. PA announcer Bob Casey, asked to clear the ballpark, boomed this frightening message: "Ladies and gentlemen. We have just been informed by the Bloomington Police that in fifteen minutes there will be an explosion." Nothing happened either time.

As it became apparent they weren't going to clinch the division on the road, Sox players started talking about the possibility of an ugly scene at Fenway. When the Mets clinched at home September 17, six thousand unruly spectators vaulted the rails at Shea Stadium and ripped up yards of sod and everything else not nailed down. Pitcher Rick Aguilera sustained a shoulder injury, and Gary Carter's catcher's mask was ripped from his strong right hand. Several Met players described the scene as scary and the Sox had hoped to avert a similar situation by winning on the road. "I'm glad to see the New York papers starting to get on the fans there," said native New Yorker Joe Sambito. "It's been going on for too many years and people have to realize it's a dangerous situation. Fenway isn't big enough for them to use mounted police like the Phillies did in 1980, but attack dogs would be okay and they could just announce that anyone going on the field would be at risk of being bitten by an attack dog."

After Seaver and Nipper were hammered and hurt Friday and Saturday, the Sox again turned to their stopper. Boston hadn't been swept by a division rival all season and Clemens had won thirteen times after a Sox defeat.

The Rocket Man did the job once again, beating the Jays 3–2 with 8 innings of 7-hit, no walk baseball. He threw 102 pitches (71 strikes) while effectively clinching Boston's first division flag in eleven years. It was Clemens's seventh straight victory, moved him to 20 games over .500 lifetime, and gave him 24 wins for the year. The last Boston pitcher to finish a season with exactly 24 wins was Babe Ruth (1917).

"I was keyed up," admitted Clemens. "I've had a lot of games with a lot of pressure and I like that. This was a big game. We had to have one here." There was nothing easy about it. The Blue Jays were the team that snapped his 14-game winning streak in July, and they led the American League in runs in 1986.

"I don't think my fastball was moving as much as it usually does," he admitted. "But I got ticked off a little and started reaching back and throwing the ball. The main thing was getting my breaking ball over."

Nursing his 3–2 margin in the eighth, Clemens issued a leadoff single to Fernandez. McNamara might have yanked another pitcher at that juncture, but not Clemens, not in 1986. At least not this time. After Rance Mulliniks bunted Fernandez to second, Clemens retired Moseby on a hot grounder to third, then faced the highly unpopular George Bell, Toronto's multi-talented MVP candidate. Clemens started Bell with a slider for a strike, then threw a ball that Clemens thought was a strike.

Umpire Tim Welke called it a ball and Clemens grimaced. Bell fouled one back, then fanned on a high heater. It was Clemens's fifth strikeout and it came on Clemens's final pitch of the day. "That was one of the critical at bats," he admitted. "I wanted to keep him off balance and I tried to get the ball in on him. If the game's close, I've expressed that I want to be in there. I still had good stuff."

Sox reliever Sammy Stewart shook his head in admiration as he dressed after the game. "I've been on teams with Steve Stone [25–7 in 1980] and Mike Flanagan [23–9 in '79]," said Stewart. "But he's just come through with the consistency. Roger Clemens has come right on time for us every time." Across the room Clemens refused to entertain thoughts of future autumnal highlights. "I'm not thinking about all the stuff that's going to happen later," he said. "We still got a lot of work to do. We're going to put some numbers up before we're through with this thing."

The lead was 9½ games with 12 to play and the magic number was down to 4, when the Sox flew to Milwaukee for their final 2 regular season road games. Though still hoping to clinch before returning to Boston, that possibility was eliminated when they dropped the opener at County Stadium.

Meanwhile Boggs's quest to retain his 1985 batting title was receiving little attention. It was a complete reversal from the final days of the 1985 season when The Boggs Watch was the only reason to follow the Sox. Red Sox hitters had won 18 batting crowns. Ted Williams won 6, and Carney Lansford, Fred Lynn, Pete Runnels (2), Carl Yastrzemski (3), Billy Goodman, Jimmie Foxx, Dale Alexander, and Boggs (2) had won the rest, but Yaz ('67) was the only silver batsman who played for a pennant winner.

Boggs suffered through a 1–12 weekend in Toronto as he had his 20-game hitting streak snapped and struggled for 3 straight games. "When I go to Toronto, I really don't feel like I can get a hit," Boggs said. "I don't know what it is about the park. I just have a negative feeling." Boston's Toronto hotel headquarters also gave Boggs bad vibes. It was in Toronto in June that he cracked a rib while taking off his cowboy boots.

Yankee first baseman Don Mattingly led Boggs .351–.346 with 12 games to play, when Boggs slapped 4 singles in the first game at Milwaukee to tie Mattingly (1–5 in Baltimore) at .350. Boggs's .350 was actually higher than Mattingly's. Technically, Boggs was at .3501805 (194–554) while Mattingly was .3496835 (221–632).

When it was pointed out to Boggs that back in Boston the Clinch Watch had pushed the batting race into the shadows, he snapped, "That's where it's going to stay. As far as I'm concerned, my main objective is the pennant."

In New York Mattingly's push to the top was receiving considerable attention. It was the only drama the Yankees had left. New York's radio team regularly phoned Boston's broadcast booth during Sox games to get Boggs's updates. Billy Martin predicted that Mattingly would prevail. And Yankee owner George Steinbrenner might have ordered an investigation if he'd seen Boggs bat in the ninth inning at Milwaukee September 23. With 1 on and no outs, Boggs faced former teammate Mark Clear and appeared to ground out to first. However, Clear had been called for a balk before the pitch and Boggs had another chance. "The third base ump [Tim McClelland] called it," said Lachemann. "They couldn't hear it at home plate."

Boggs took advantage, hitting a rocket to Rob Deer in right. Deer collapsed in a heap as the ball went in and out of his glove. It was ruled a base hit. "When I get a second life, that's a bonus," said Boggs. "As it turned out, I hit it into the lights and he lost it."

"That's a bad spot out there," added Lach. "I saw Davey Lopes get hit right between the eyes in that spot when I managed here." This was the sixth time in 1986 that Boggs had 4 or more hits in a game.

The Magic Number was 3 when Boston and Toronto squared off for a 3-game weekend set back in Boston. The first 2 games of the series were tight and well-played. Placed in a final weekend do-or-die pennant race, they would have been remembered as classics. Friday night was a scoreless duel between Roger Clemens and Jimmy Key. Key came out in the eighth and Clemens left after the ninth, but neither team scored until the twelfth when Toronto's Jesse Barfield led with a solo homer off Schiraldi. A few hours later on a splendid, crisp autumn afternoon, the Red Sox answered with a 2–0 shutout victory hurled by Bruce Hurst. The Fenway crowd stood for the final inning. Hurst fanned Barfield for the last out and leaped off the mound with fists raised. The Magic Number was 1.

Oil Can Boyd spent Saturday night at the Sheraton Boston. After a strange summer in Chelsea and a calming month at his in-laws' home in Rhode Island, Boyd decided to take shelter in a hotel room on the eve of his magic moment. There was no clock in the room, but Boyd went to bed early and was at the park early. "I had a dream with myself," he said later.

Nineteen years earlier Sox right-hander Jim Lonborg had spent the most nervous night of his life in the Sheraton Boston. Lonborg was already a 20-game winner but needed to beat the Minnesota Twins on the final Sunday of the season to clinch at least a tie for the American

League pennant. Gentleman Jim was a bachelor at the time and had a Back Bay apartment with fellow pitcher Dennis Bennett and a third roommate. "We had a lot of fun in those days," recalled Lonborg. "I felt I had to get away to be with myself and my thoughts. I think it's good that he [Boyd] thought enough of the game to get away like that. I'm sure it was as important for him as it was for me back then."

Sunday, September 28, 1986, was yet another perfect fall day in New England. The trees were already bleeding red, orange, and yellow in northern Maine, but the water was still tolerable for swimmers on Nantucket. Though a beautiful day to be outside, the only important activity was taking place at 24 Yawkey Way, Boston. A crowd of 32,929 baseball worshippers filled Fenway in anticipation of seeing the Sox clinch their first division title since 1975.

There were no small security preparations for this game. The Sox teamed with the Boston police to make sure the Fenway sod remained intact and one hundred patrolmen, plus sixty police academy cadets were re-cruited to protect the city's most famous lawn. Fans witnessed a show of force when they arrived at the ball-park. Two hours before game time the stern-looking ca-dets stood in formation and fifteen mounted police pep-pered the perimeter of the ancient green stadium.

At 12:31 P.M. Boyd and pitching coach Bill Fischer strolled from the dugout to the Red Sox bullpen. The Can was wildly cheered as he made his way to the prac-tice mound. Boyd rang up a pair of strikeouts in the first 2 innings, and the Sox blew it open with 5 runs in the second. After two noble weekend efforts the Blue Jays finally surrendered the flag. Manager Jimy Williams tried six pitchers, but there was no saving the Canadian

Club on this afternoon. The Jays kicked more balls than the Toronto Argonauts as they staggered toward a 12–3 defeat. The game, lasting 3:09, certainly lacked drama but Sox fans savored the anticipation of celebration. The Can almost didn't make it to the end. Leading 10–3, he issued a 1-out single and a walk in the sixth. McNamara bolted from the dugout with all the purpose of Ralph Nader at a Corvair convention. His message to Boyd: throw strikes.

The Can settled down after the firestorm chat. He gave up an infield single, then retired 11 straight to end it. Before the start of the seventh, the large garage door opened in center field and mounted police galloped around the warning track. Someone cracked that there was already too much horseshit in the Sox bullpen. The police ponies returned to the trojan horse underneath the bleachers before play resumed, but the message was clear. Uniformed officers lined the rail around foul territory throughout the ninth.

At 4:17 Blue Jay infielder Kelly Gruber lofted a high pop to the right side of the infield. Buckner camped under the ball and smothered it as the Can leaped into the arms of Rich Gedman. In a rare demonstration of compliance and common sense, few fans attempted to join the celebration. The polite customers stayed in their place as the ecstatic Red Sox executed the traditional tribal rites of a team that's just won a division title. At one point Clemens hoisted the 205 Gedman as if the Sox catcher were a hamburger bun. Bad back and all Gedman didn't seem to mind. The celebration moved inside where Sox lockers had been covered with plastic to prevent damage from the beverage of choice. The kids said they were happy for the veterans and the veterans said they were happy for the kids.

Everyone was happy for Dwight Evans, the thoughtful veteran who'd been wearing a Boston uniform longer than any other member of the 1986 team. Evans was only twenty years old when he was thrust into his first pennant race in 1972 and he'd been a guest at the heartbreak hotel for most of his fifteen big league seasons. Evans had played on eight teams that made it to first place after the All Star break, but this was only the second time he'd tasted champagne.

Evans was always a joy to watch in Fenway's spacious right field. He broke back on balls as well as anyone ever had and his arm was legendary. By 1986 he was no longer the best right-fielder in the league, but no one was more commanding or graceful.

He was an ardent student of batting instructor Walter Hriniak. When possible, Evans watched films of himself after every at bat, and talked to Hriniak before going up to the plate. When Hriniak had been a bullpen coach, Evans would call the pen for counseling. After years of tinkering with his stance, he had settled on a workable routine, one that Ted Williams disdained. Williams never liked the way Hriniak had Sox hitters bow their heads and take their top hands off the bat at the end of their swings. Hriniak stressed contact hitting and hitting the ball to the opposite field. Williams looked at Evans's raw power potential, spit, and said, "Dewey Evans pretty near makes me vomit the way he swings."

Evans was born in Santa Monica, California, on November 3, 1951. He spent some of his early years living in Hawaii, but played Little League, Colt, Pony, and Connie Mack ball in Northridge, California. One of his teammates was Doug DeCinces, and DeCinces's dad was usually the coach. Evans, not DeCinces, was the third baseman in those days and Ted DeCinces recalled, "He had a temper. I had to sit him down every once in a while because he could be difficult to control." He was MVP at Chatsworth High School and was Boston's fifth round selection in 1969. Evans was playing in a pennant race 3 years later.

Carl Yastrzemski was Evans's mentor and friend. They dressed next to each other and talked hitting, fishing, and food. In his early years Evans talked hitting with Yaz, his mailman, grocer, and butcher. He became confused and discouraged and often looked foolish at the plate.

Things got worse when he was beaned by a Mike Paul pitch in 1973. Evans was unconscious for a couple of minutes after the hit. When he recovered, the emotional scars remained; and in 1978 he was seriously beaned again. The pitching book on Evans was never rewritten. In 1986 the Baltimore Orioles official index card stipulating how to pitch Evans started with, "Back him off the plate on the first pitch."

Evans developed a glare that offended many pitchers, as he would stare hard at them, especially after striking out. Big leaguers call this "stylin' " and Evans did more stylin' than most. He flipped his bat and helmet with style, removed his batting glove with style, and trotted to his position with style. A handsome member of Boston's mustache club, like television's Dick Clark, Evans never seemed to look older.

He was a perfect physical specimen for baseball, six three, 204 pounds, with good speed, a great arm, and longball power. He could hit the ball out of any park in the league and *never* hit a cheap home run. Despite this, many years passed before Dwight Evans was emotionally equipped to deal with the pressures of playing right field for the Sox. He was bothered by trade rumors and carried an additional burden that most young men don't have to worry about: a sick child.

In 1975 it was discovered that his two-year-old son, Timothy, had neurofibromatosis, a rare genetic disorder that required lengthy hospitalization and would call for ten operations in the next three years. The Evanses had two other children, a daughter Kirstin and a son Justin. In 1982 doctors found that Justin had a brain tumor. Somehow, Dwight and Susan managed to cope. Gradually things got better for Timothy. Then Justin stunned everyone with a miraculous return to good health. His tumor had dissolved.

Evans signed a long-term contract and welcomed the arrival of Boston's new manager, Ralph Houk. Dewey had struggled under the squinty glare of Zimmer, who always suspected that Evans wasn't quite tough enough. Fans weren't altogether kind either, but few were aware of the personal ordeal Evans was living through.

In Houk's lineup Evans became an offensive force. He led the team in scoring four times in six years and was one of only five men (Babe Ruth, Jimmie Foxx, Ted Williams, and Mickey Mantle are the others) to lead the American League in walks and total bases. In 1984 he hit .295 with 32 homers and 104 RBI. By 1986 he was considered a stabilizing presence and a Sox lifer. When Roger Clemens talked about winning it for the older players, he always mentioned "winning for D-wight."

Clemens owed Evans a favor. If not for D-wight's 3-run home run on April 29, Clemens would have been a 1–0 loser in his 20-strikeout game. Evans chuckled at the thought because he'd been a footnote in other great games. Evans's ninth-inning homer off Rawley Eastwick tied the third game of the 1975 Series, but the blast was forgotten when Ed Armbrister and Carlton Fisk danced at homeplate in the tenth inning. And it was Evans's dramatic eleventh-inning catch off a Joe Morgan blast that enabled Mr. Fisk to become a folk hero in the twelfth. Red manager Sparky Anderson told people he thought Evans might be better than Lynn or Rice after that series. It was just another prediction that Evans struggled to live up to.

Evans was the only member of the 1986 Sox who'd played in Boston's last championship series. Rice was a rookie member of the '75 team, but sat out the post-season with a broken hand.

As the Red Sox celebrated in their clubhouse, the crowd called out for more and owner Haywood Sullivan led some of the players back out to the field. Few of the well-mannered fans had left. At the urging of Rice, Clemens got up on one of the police horses—Boston's knight in shining armor. The horse bucked slightly, but the Sox owner had no fear of losing his meal ticket. "He was born on a horse," said Sullivan, forgetting that Texan Clemens spent the first eleven years of his life in Dayton, Ohio. "There's nothing in his contract that says he can't ride horses—only motorcycles."

The daylight ride of Roger Clemens was the highlight of a wholesome celebration. The lowlight came a few hours later when Rob Woodward's genitals were featured on the local six o'clock news. While sports reporter Mike Dowling interviewed Baylor and Rice live from the Sox clubhouse, Woodward, the shy rookie pitcher from West Lebanon, New Hampshire, was making his first appearance since being recalled from Pawtucket and the naked truth caused some embarrassment. WCVB's telephone switchboard lit up, but not every caller was outraged: One woman phoned to ask if the Woodward tape would be repeated at 11 o'clock.

Many Sox players moved the celebration to Jason's, a local restaurant and dance club. Boggs, Nipper, and Clemens made late-night live appearances on the news and the last two manufactured a degree of silliness by butting heads before signing off.

Rich Gedman wasn't celebrating, however. His sister had died Sunday morning and the family waited until after the game to give him the news. For Gedman, who had already lost his father earlier in the season, 1986 would be a year without happy memories.

Seven meaningless games remained to be played before the start of the playoffs. Baltimore followed Toronto to Boston and the Orioles were en route to their first last-place finish in franchise history. The team that had pulled to within 2½ games of the top spot on August 6 now, on September 29, trailed the Sox by a whopping 22 games. Earl Weaver, experiencing his first losing season since he managed at Fitzgerald, Georgia, in 1957, was in no mood to toss bouquets at the BoSox in the final meaningless week of the regular season. Instead Weaver and Sox first baseman Bill Buckner got into a hot dispute—the kind that can only happen late in the year when all else has been decided. Buckner carried a 17-game hitting streak into the Baltimore series. McNamara was intent on resting most of his troops that final week, but the gimpy Buckner wanted to keep his streak going. Buckner was 0–3 when he came to the plate in the eighth inning with the Sox leading 6–5. Weaver ordered a walk, and Buckner didn't like it. Buckner grabbed his crotch when he got to first base and Weaver exploded. The fiesty Oriole manager pointed to his head and cut loose with an intemperate diatribe. The Earl of Baltimore has a tongue that would make Eddie Murphy blush and he let Buckner have it. A day later Weaver was still hot. "We're trying to win a game," said the retiring manager. "I don't care about his fucking hitting streak and he shouldn't either. All he has to do is send his runners back to second and first, then I'll pitch to him. That's what they do in the Instructional League. If you want to work on something, they let you send a guy back to first after he steals second so you can work on your throw to second." Weaver denied threatening to throw at Buckner, but Buckner did not play in either of the next two games against Baltimore.

Buckner needed rest as his body had totally broken down. His season got off to a painful start when he needed three cortisone shots to numb tendinitis in his throwing elbow. He had a bruised right knee and a sore left hamstring, which required ice every day. But the real problem was the junkyard of bone chips and other floating matter in his left foot and ankle. X-rays showed bone grinding against bone. Buckner's chronic ankle injury made him walk like a movie star—Nick Nolte in *North Dallas Forty* or Dustin Hoffman in *Midnight Cowboy*. Buckner first injured the ankle in a steal attempt when he was playing for the Dodgers against the Giants on April 18, 1975. He got a good lead off John Montefusco and slid into second where he caught his left foot on the bag, tearing ligaments and severely spraining the ankle. He needed two operations to remove a tendon, then chips.

"I was pretty fast before then," he says. "I wasn't lightning or anything, but I was a lot better than I am

now. I absolutely hate to run now, but I used to run.
Back at USC Bobby Valentine and I would sprint to
classes. I could frolic and everything. Now some days
I feel like I can run really fast, but other days I feel like
I have a piano on my back. I don't run. I wouldn't call
what I do running. I'd call it moving. Somewhere between jogging and walking. That's what I do."

He took anti-inflammatory drugs for over ten years
and needed nine cortisone shots to get through the 1986
season. He talks of having the ankle fused or possibly
having a plastic ankle implanted someday.

Buckner grew up in Napa Valley, California, where
he and his brothers, Bob and Jim, were all good hitters.
Bill could run then, and Stanford football coach Dick
Vermeil recruited him as a wide receiver. The Dodgers
made Buckner their number two pick in the 1968 draft
and sent him to their rookie league team in Ogden,
Utah. Tom Lasorda was the Ogden manager and Buckner roomed with the speedy Valentine. In 1968 Buckner
led the rookie league with a .344 average. He also
smashed a lot of helmets and made a lot of enemies.
The usually mild-mannered Buckner turned into a
madman on a baseball field. He slid into bases with his
spikes high and he did not go gently into the night after
going 0–3 in the afternoon. Teammates thought he was
selfish. They said that Billy Buck loved doubles so much
that he'd slow down near second even if he could have
taken third on a gap hit.

Nothing changed at the big league level. Buckner hit;
Buckner broke things, and Buckner made enemies. He
helped the Dodgers win the National League pennant
in 1974 batting .314, but he always had a poor relationship with Dodger GM Al Campanis and was traded to
the Cubs in 1977. Dodgers are trained to think they are

superior and Buckner learned his lessons well. He tried to fight his own manager, Lee Elia, in Chicago and engaged in a classic brawl with Expos catcher Gary Carter in 1980. Chicago GM Dallas Green wanted no part of Buckner and the Cubs sent him to Boston for Dennis Eckersley in 1984. Buckner still has fond memories of his chaotic Chicago years. When the Sox had a day off in Milwaukee late in the '86 season, he rented a car and drove one hundred miles to Chicago to catch the Cubs in an afternoon contest.

Buckner found an untapped power source when Boston batting coach Walt Hriniak taught him to shift his weight. He settled into a home in Andover with wife Jody and daughters Brittany and Christen, and continued his icing rituals at home and on the road. Ice was Buckner's fix. It kept him going. The meltdown from Buckner's 1986 ice packs would have filled the Quabbin Reservoir. While other players requested suites or single rooms on the road, Buckner asked for a room near the ice machine. It was not unusual, at any hour, to see Buckner limping down a hotel corridor, filling his wastebasket with ice, and limping back to his room. "It's the first thing I look for when I get to my room," he admitted. "In the hotel in Philadelphia, when I played in the National League, they didn't have ice machines. You had to call room service and they charged you four dollars. I ran up some big bills in that hotel."

Like many of the veterans in the Sox clubhouse, Buckner was somewhat of a loner. He had friends and relatives in a lot of cities and was often seen limping off to dinner with one of his brothers. He is a player of average size by major league standards, six one and a trim 180 pounds. He has an Eddie Munster hairline and his bushy black mustache and eyebrows give him a sinister appearance. Buckner would have worn the black hat in a Wyatt Earp episode.

Buckner was on the bench when the Sox got a big scare in the final game of the Baltimore series. Pitching to Oriole catcher John Stefero in the second inning, Clemens was struck on the right elbow by a liner back to the mound. Boston's Cy Young stopper saw the shot coming and turned his back toward the ball, but couldn't escape Stefero's laser. The ball deflected off Clemens's pitching elbow and flew out into shallow right field. The Sox didn't take any chances with The Franchise: accompanied by his wife, Debbie, and Nipper, Clemens was rushed to Children's Hospital in an ambulance. X rays were negative, but there were still some anxious moments on the night of the incident. Clemens was injured the same day that President Reagan and Soviet leader Gorbachev agreed to a summit meeting. When Bostonians switched on the local evening news Wednesday, October 1, most deemed the bruised right elbow of a twenty-four-year-old Katy, Texas, resident more important than a summit meeting between leaders from the two most powerful nations in the world.

Injuries plagued the Sox through the final weekend of the regular season. Four days before the start of the playoffs, Gedman was hit on the right shoulder by a foul tip and took the same Clemens shortcut to Children's Hospital. In 1982 Gedman had suffered a broken right clavicle. "Any time I get hit there, I wonder if it's broken," Gedman said. "I didn't think it was this time, but they wanted to get me right out of there to be sure. It'll take a lot to keep me out of the playoffs."

Seaver was not as fortunate as Gedman. He never pitched after injuring his knee in Toronto September 19 and on Saturday, October 4, the national and local media assembled in the Red Sox dugout at 11:30 A.M. for a hastily called press conference involving Seaver, McNamara, and Dr. Pappas. Seaver opened the session, saying, "Unfortunately, I have to tell you I won't be able to pitch in the championship series." His knee was not strong enough. The Sox weren't sure whether it was torn cartilage or a strained tendon, but the forty-one-year-old pitcher hadn't been able to move the knee laterally and it was impossible for him to perform in the post-season. There was considerable speculation that Seaver was through. Seaver spoke of pitching in the World Series, but admitted the hope was "slight." The Red Sox had an option to renew his contract for the 1987 season, but were not interested in paying $1,125,000 for the forty-two-year-old. It seemed possible that Seaver had thrown his last major league pitch when he retired Toronto's Tony Fernandez on a fly to right in the fourth inning of a 6–4 loss on Friday, September 19, 1986.

When Rice was asked to compare Seaver's shelf status with his during the 1975 post season, he said, "It's different. He probably could pitch, but he's worried about the effects it would have on his injury. In seventy-five, my injury forced me not to play, I had no choice."

Wade Boggs was the other wounded star on Boston's roster in the final week, and there was considerable speculation about the convenience of his hamstring tear. Early in the week Boggs said, "Mac wants me to rest, and I want to be as strong as I can before the playoffs. I don't want to go into the playoffs dragging. I think it's an unfortunate thing that the Yankees are playing the last four games here, but I don't have anything to do with that. Naturally if we weren't in the playoffs, I wouldn't rest."

Boggs led Mattingly by 4 points when he made that comment, and, when it was repeated to Weaver, the Oriole manager snapped, "If he goes 0–6 tonight and Mattingly goes 5–6, he won't rest. But how can he go 0–6 against us?" Weaver proved prophetic as Boggs rattled 4 hits against the Orioles and took a 9 point lead (.358 to .349) with 5 games remaining. Boggs's final game of the season was against Baltimore. He went 1–4 to finish at .357. The next day it was announced that Boggs had suffered a slight hamstring tear in his right leg prior to the clincher. He had aggravated the injury while running to third against Baltimore and would sit out the 4-game set with the Yankees.

The decision to rest Boggs was greeted with considerable skepticism in New York. *The Daily News* headlined a story "Chicken" and Yankee announcers Phil Rizzutto and Bill White questioned the severity of the injury. Mattingly was batting .350 to Boggs's .357 when the Yankees got to town and needed to go 9–12 to overtake an idle Boggs.

Baseball history is peppered with late-season batting race chicanery, including a couple of incidents involving Boggs. In 1980 he lost the International League batting title by .0007 in bizarre fashion. Boggs had a lead over Toledo's Dave Engle going into the ninth inning of the final game of the season, but a Toledo rally forced Boggs to hit one last time. Boggs still led Toledo's rightfielder, but jeopardized his lead by going to the plate. With 2 outs and Boggs in the on-deck circle, Toledo's pitcher issued an intentional walk to bring Boggs up. The Pawtucket baserunner stole second, then third, and didn't draw a throw. When he broke for home, the Toledo pitcher fired the ball to the backstop. "He should have just kept on going after they walked him," Boggs said later. "He could have walked all the way to right field and shaken Engle's hand and said, 'Congratulations, Wade Boggs just won the batting title.' He would have been automatically out for abandoning first base. I was ahead and if I didn't bat, I'd win. Joe [former Pawtucket manager Joe Morgan] asked me if I wanted to hit and I said, 'yeah.' "

"I never rooted harder for anybody to get a base hit," Morgan remembers. "It was a travesty and I still regret not pinch-hitting for him."

Boggs grounded to first and lost the crown. A year later Boggs was in a race with Charleston's Brett Butler, who had already been called up by the Atlanta Braves. On the next to last day of the International League season Boggs got a hit to move ahead of Butler with a .335 average. He never batted again, as Morgan later lifted Boggs for a pinch hitter and then did not play him in the final game of the season. "He got a basehit and I got him out of there," said Morgan. "The GM at Charleston was ripped."

Sox fans will never forget the 1970 silver bat chase between Carl Yastrzemski and California's Alex Johnson. On the final day of the season Johnson went 2–3 to inflate his average to .3290. Yaz had finished his season a day earlier at .3286. Johnson never batted after he overtook Yaz on October 1, 1970; he left the lineup for a pinch-hitter in the fifth inning as seven thousand cheered in Anaheim.

The 1956 batting race was very similar to the Boggs-Mattingly contest. In '56 Mickey Mantle had a .354–.350 lead over Ted Williams prior to the final three games of the season against Boston. He went 1–4 in the first game, but didn't start the final two due to a groin pull. The Yanks were preparing for the World Series and Mantle needed to rest. Mantle pinch hit in the final two games, going 1–5 over the weekend. He finished at .353, winning the triple crown. Williams played in all three games, went 1–10, and finished at .345.

Mattingly put on an incredible show that final weekend in Boston. He went 3–5 in the first game of a Saturday doubleheader, then homered in game two. The homer was his thirtieth, making him the first American League player in history to get 30 homers, 100 RBI, and 230 hits in a season. The home run, however, was Mattingly's only hit in the second game of the doubleheader and his 1–5 dropped him to .351 going into game three. Mattingly needed a 6–6 day in the finale to overtake Boggs, and Yankee manager Lou Piniella inserted him into the leadoff spot to give him every opportunity. Mattingly homered off Jeff Sellers in his first at bat, but flied to left on his next trip and effectively bowed out of the race. He finished 2–5 with a walk and batted .352 to Boggs's .357.

The final numbers were on the board and the postseason award ballots were in the mail. Boggs won the batting title and Clemens would win the Cy Young and MVP, while McNamara would cop Manager of the Year honors. Rice would finish third in MVP voting (behind Mattingly) and Lou Gorman second in voting for Executive of the Year.

But there was only one award that mattered to the Red Sox on October 5: They wanted to wear championship rings.

8

THE PLAYOFFS

BASEBALL officials insist on calling the pre–World Series tournaments the championship series, but these games will always be known to most simply as the playoffs. The baseball playoffs were born in 1969 when the American and National Leagues expanded from ten to twelve teams. The owners didn't want twelve-team pennant races and so created a five-game bake-off to qualify for the World Series. This meant more money, more coveted television time, and more fan interest. There was now less chance of a runaway race that would economically drain eleven other cities.

The creation of the championship series was considered somewhat artificial, but baseball was still far removed from pro basketball and hockey, where qualifying for the playoffs was like getting one's name in the telephone book. Four finalists in a twenty-four-team derby (later twenty-six teams) did not seem like an effort to extend happy hour by watering the whiskey. The greatest fear, shared by Commissioner Bowie Kuhn and most team owners, was that a strong club might be upset by a weak one in a short series. Imagine the 1927 Yankees (110–44) losing a fluky 5-game playoff to the Washington Senators and being denied a chance to make their case as the greatest team ever?

Oriole manager Earl Weaver felt the heat when his Birds won 109 games in 1969, then had to face the Western-division winners from Minnesota. "It was a traumatic experience," Weaver later admitted. "To win one hundred nine games and then to have to put it on the line for three more wasn't too good. You say to yourself, 'If this was last year, we'd be American League champs.'"

Weaver's Orioles swept the first three American League Championship Series, winning 9 straight playoff games. In the National League, the Mets, Reds, and Pirates went 9–1 in '69, '70, and '71. The playoffs, it seemed, were a bore.

No more. Since the mid-seventies, some of baseball's most dramatic moments have come during these games. Chris Chambliss's pennant-clinching homer in 1976 was far more exciting than anything that happened later between the Reds and Yankees (Cincinnati, 4–0). The pressure of a short playoff after a 162 game series is enormous. Teams were disappointed when they lost the World Series, but they were devastated when they checked out in the playoffs. Series losers retained nobility, while playoff losers were quickly forgotten. When Baltimore won the '83 playoffs and World Series, who remembered that the 1983 Chicago White Sox had won more games than any team in baseball and had captured

186 ◇ *One Strike Away*

the American League West by 20 games? As the years passed, the real pressure was in the playoffs, and the best games often preceded the World Series. Teams played on the edge in the playoffs, then relaxed in the Series.

The 1986 Boston Red Sox and California Angel franchises had limited playoff experience. The Sox had made one prior trip to the ALCS to beat the A's in three straight in 1975. The Angels had lost to the Orioles in four games in 1979 and dropped a 5-game heartbreaker to the Brewers in 1982. The '82 Angels, managed by Gene Mauch, were the only team in playoff history to have lost a 5-game series after winning the first 2 games.

The Red Sox and Angel rosters were loaded with veteran players who'd encountered playoff pressure. The bi-coastal rivalry also presented a lot of interesting overlaps. Mauch had played for the Red Sox, and McNamara had managed the Angels. Baylor had been MVP of the '79 Angels, while California infielder Rick Burleson had been an All Star shortstop with the Red Sox. The fathers of Angel shortstop Dick Schofield (Ducky Schofield) and catcher Bob Boone both had played for the Red Sox. Boone's father, Ray Boone, was still a Boston scout. Red Sox third-base coach Rene Lachemann and California pitching coach Marcel Lachemann were brothers. Sox right-fielder Dwight Evans and California third baseman Doug DeCinces were teammates in Pony League and Colt League. The teams were owned by a pair of Jeans, Boston's Jean Yawkey heading a troika with the estranged duo of Haywood Sullivan and Buddy LeRoux, and Gene Autry, the singing cowboy who owned the Angels.

Mauch was *the* central figure of the Series. He'd managed almost four thousand games in twenty-five years without winning a pennant. No baseball manager ever managed longer without raising a flag and Mauch seemed destined to carry the folds of the '64 Phillies and the '82 Angels to his grave. His '64 Phillies led the National League by 6½ games with 12 to play, but finished second. Mauch was blamed for panicking and using Chris Short and Jim Bunning with insufficient rest during the stretch dive. In 1982 the Angels led the Brewers, 2–0, but Mauch rushed Tommy John into Game Four, pulling Ken Forsch from the rotation. John and the Angels lost Game Four, then dropped Game Five after leading, 3–1.

"I want this team to win this championship," Mauch said before Game One in Boston. "I'd rather do that than eat when I'm hungry. I want to win, not because I haven't been there, but simply because it's the thing to do. Years ago people said I was pretty hot stuff. I might have had a tendency to believe them. I might have had a tendency to take a lot of credit. But it doesn't take long to find out that players carry managers to championships. This will be the highlight of my baseball life."

A handsome man with silver hair, Mauch took long walks around the warning track before each game. He needed his quiet time to replay the last game and to prepare for the present one. Mauch was the image of a frustrated, paranoid man rolling marbles in his hand and mumbling about "the strawberry incident." At his worst, he was icy and aloof. At his best, he was brilliant, affable, and charming.

The 1986 Angels were an aging team with fourteen players over the age of thirty. Don Sutton was born when FDR was still President and ten Angels had been eligible for student deferments during the Vietnam War.

California boasted four solid starting pitchers—Mike Witt, Kirk McCaskill, John Candelaria, and Sutton. Mauch tinkered with his lineup every day, but each combination assured a potent offense and a sure-handed defense.

There was grumbling in the California camp. Eight free agents wondered about their contract status and Angel GM Mike Port intentionally ignored them. Veterans Reggie Jackson, Doug DeCinces, Brian Downing, Bobby Grich, Bob Boone, and Rick Burleson (among others) were playing to extend their careers and Port thought they'd play harder if the future was uncertain. "It's been a distraction for us, but this is not the last roundup," said DeCinces.

Mauch was particularly unpopular with his veterans. Burleson blasted the manager late in the season and DeCinces was always whining about how he'd been used. "We'll win this thing—in spite of the manager," Jackson said.

The Angels beat the Sox seven times in twelve meetings during the regular season, outscoring them 32–19 in 6 Fenway games. Boston scored fewer runs against California than against any other American League team. Sox pitchers had an ERA of 4.46 against the Angels, while California's mound men posted a 2.98 ERA against Boston.

McNamara had Roger Clemens slated for Game One and announced lefty Bruce Hurst as his Game Two starter. Pitching a southpaw in Fenway was considered a gamble, but Hurst had been Boston's best hurler over the last month (5–0, 1.07 ERA in September) and his stuff was considered as tough on right-handed batters as it was on lefties. Boyd would pitch Game Three in Anaheim, but McNamara refused to name his Game

Four starter. Tom Seaver was out and Clemens hadn't pitched on three days' rest all season, except at the All Star game when he threw 3 innings on two days' rest. Throughout the '86 season Clemens's effectiveness depended on his rest: He was 8–0 with a 2.13 ERA and 78 strikeouts in 72 innings when he pitched with five or six days' rest.

The Red Sox had another, more substantial, pitching problem. Standing in the press box, holding a Boston stat sheet during the final week of the regular season, Oriole General Manager Hank Peters noted, "The Red Sox seem to have a lot of pitchers they don't want to use."

It was true. By the time the playoffs rolled around, McNamara had confidence in only four pitchers: Clemens, Hurst, Boyd, and Schiraldi. The other six pitchers on the post-season roster were Sammy Stewart, Tim Lollar, Al Nipper, Joe Sambito, Bob Stanley, and Steve Crawford. In 1986 this motley crew had compiled an aggregate ERA of 4.96, yielding a whopping 533 hits, 186 walks, and 9 hit batters in 450 innings, which added up to an eye-popping 728 baserunners in 450 innings. Against the Angels, the six gave up 23 runs in 33 innings.

McNamara was asked if there were certain pitchers he was afraid to go to.

"If they're there and it's a situation, they've got to be used," he said, not sounding very confident.

The manager was carrying two pitchers he simply would not use. Lollar and Stewart didn't know it, but they were already through for the season. The Sox finished 9–23 in games where Lollar appeared. Meanwhile Stewart was in the doghouse, Nipper remained highly flammable, and Sambito had used up his arm in the spring. As Stanley admitted, "I hope they don't have to go to us at all. If I'm in the game, that means we're losing and we don't want that."

"You'll see a whole different staff in the playoffs," promised Crawford, who was on the disabled list from July 18 to September 1.

The 1986 playoffs started in Fenway due to baseball's generous concession to the NFL. Since most National League West teams played in parks used by the NFL, football commissioner Pete Rozelle asked baseball czar Peter Ueberroth to keep the Astrodome available for Sunday, October 12, when the Oilers were playing host to the Chicago Bears. In order to do that baseball reverted to the 1985 playoff format, which meant starting in the NL West and the AL East.

The '86 playoffs were the second set since the '84 switch from best-of-five to best-of-seven series. The 1985 Royals benefited from the format, coming back from a 3–1 deficit against Toronto. There would be another 3–1 comeback in 1986.

Captain Jim Rice, a casual student of the game, apparently didn't know the playoffs had been expanded to seven games and went on local television predicting, "The way Clemens and Boyd are pitching, if we go with a rotation of Clemens, Boyd, and Clemens, we might be able to take care of 'em in three straight."

The Sox were favored to beat the Angels. American League East teams were routinely stronger and deeper and the Sox had the home-field advantage, plus a 24–4 stopper.

There was no shortage of hype and hoopla preceding the 1986 American League playoffs. *The Boston Globe* went to its forty-man roster and trotted out such well known sportswriters as John Updike, George Will, Robert Parker, Stephen King, David Halberstam, Doris Kearns Goodwin, and other literati for a special Red Sox section. The *Herald*, meanwhile, enlisted the services of Messrs. Rice and Clemens for daily commentary. Local radio stations played the latest assortment of Sox songs, including "McNamara's Team" and "The Green Monster Mash."

No detail was too small to merit a headline. It was news when Wade Boggs announced that he'd eat barbecue chicken before Game One because he'd had four 4-hit games after eating the sloppy dish in 1986. The Brothers Lachemann got as much ink as the Brothers Karamazov. Sox GM Lou Gorman talked of getting ticket requests from Cardinals (not Vince Coleman or Whitey Herzog Cardinals), and Oil Can told the national media that he planned to return to Jackson State to get a degree in sociology (he minored in art). Boston rookie Mike Greenwell did a few interviews with strangers who thought he was Spike Owen, and Kirk McCaskill spilled thousands of words concerning his cameo appearance on *Days of Our Lives* as well as his hockey career at the University of Vermont.

The Angels had nine players with World Series experience, but the California franchise had never made it to the classic. The Red Sox were seeking to win their fourth pennant since 1918, the year they won their last world championship. Mauch was like a bucking bronco trying to throw a stubborn rider who'd been digging spurs into his butt for twenty-five years, while the '86 Sox edition was committed to proving that it was different from those Boston ballclubs that folded at the finish.

Boston had one additional incentive. If they beat the Angels, John McNamara would manage the American League All Star team in 1987 and would be able to control the tears and fears of Dennis Oil Can Boyd in the summer of '87.

Game One (CALIFORNIA 8, BOSTON 1)

It was 0–0 when Roger Clemens struck out the first 2 batters of the second inning. Rob Wilfong and Dick Schofield looked overmatched. Then Clemens blew up. With 2 outs and no one on base, he walked the number 8 and 9 batters (Bob Boone and Gary Pettis), then surrendered 3 straight singles and fell behind, 4–0. It was only the second time in 1986 that Clemens had given up 4 runs in a single inning. The turning point came when Clemens appeared to fan Brian Downing on a 1–2 pitch with 2 on and 2 runs already in. Homeplate ump Larry Barnett didn't give him the call ("to be truthful, it was too close to take," Downing admitted), and Downing cracked a 3–2 pitch to left for a 2-run single. A Spike Owen error and 2 more hits gave the Angels a 5–0 third-inning lead in quiet Fenway.

California's Mike Witt knew what to do with a 5–0 lead. He retired 17 straight batters, took a no-hitter into the sixth, and shut down the Sox in 9 economical innings, throwing only 116 pitches and giving up only 5 hits. He dedicated the game to his day-old son, Justin Michael. Sox manager John McNamara, who managed Witt in 1984, was asked if he'd ever seen Witt pitch a better game.

"I saw him pitch a perfect game at the end of the '84 season," deadpanned McNamara. "You can't get any better than perfect."

Second-guessing managerial moves and nonmoves became the national pastime for the next three weeks and after Game One of the ALCS McNamara was taken to task for leaving Clemens in to throw 134 pitches. It was clear that the Sox weren't going to win the game after the first three innings and McNamara perhaps should have been thinking about having Clemens rested for his next start. McNamara spoke in his defense: "The man hadn't pitched in two weeks. He was well-rested and we're only down five to one after the second inning [it was 5–1 after the sixth]. He pitched very well after that and five runs is not that big a deficit in this park. What am I gonna do? Throw in the towel? Are we out of a game, down five to one? No, we had chances. To me that is quitting."

DeCinces made an enemy when he questioned Boggs's hamstring injury after watching Boggs beat out a hit in the sixth. "I thought that man was supposed to have a groin pull," said the Angel third baseman. "If I was Don Mattingly and I saw him do that, I'd be pissed."

Though a dull game, California had beaten Boston's ace and stripped the Sox of their home-field advantage.

Game Two (BOSTON 9, CALIFORNIA 2)

The Angels staged a tribute to former Commissioner Kuhn on the afternoon of October 8, 1986. Kuhn was the man who brought night baseball to the post-season in 1971, and the Angels proved beyond the shadow of a shadow that ballplayers had forgotton how to play the game in October's orange daylight. Less than forty-eight hours after Mauch proclaimed, "We won't beat ourselves," the Angels did just that throughout a 9-inning slopfest against the opportunistic Sox. How strange that a team from California would have so much trouble playing in the sunshine.

The game started at 3:30 and players noted that the

sun was low, the sky was high, and the field was rock
hard. The Angels were credited with only 3 errors, but
official scorers can't penalize players for mental blunders and untouched pop ups. "They don't judge us for
style points," said Owen, Boston's nervous Nellie
shortstop.

Boggs started things in the first with a shot off the
wall in center. California roadrunner Gary Pettis let the
carom bounce over his head and Boggs had a triple.
Marty Barrett followed with a double to right but ran
into an out when Jim Rice hit a 1-out grounder to short.
When Don Baylor followed with a single off the fall,
fans groaned, figuring Barrett would have scored from
second on the hit. Wrong.

This fallacious logic was labeled "the fallacy of the
predestined hit" by Baltimore sportswriter Ken Nigro.
Just because Barrett was on second and Baylor hit a single off the wall after Barrett was erased doesn't mean
that the Sox would have scored on Baylor's hit. It is not
certain that Baylor would have gotten a hit if Barrett
was still on second. Every occurrence in a game directly
alters what happens next. The pitcher might throw a
different pitch, the manager might use a new pitcher,
the hitter might attempt to put the ball in another spot
in the park. Everything changes. A man involved in a
car accident can't look back to two minutes before the
crash and say, "If only I hadn't stopped to let that old
lady cross the street, I wouldn't have been in this spot
at this time to get hit broadside."

Owen dropped a foul pop up in the second. The Sox
were unharmed by the non-error, but some paused to
wonder why Owen suddenly was playing shortstop like
a man with two bags of groceries trying to pass through
a subway turnstile.

When the Sox came to bat in the second, Owen's doubleplay grounder took a hop over the head of Schofield. Boggs followed with a high bouncer in front of the mound, but McCaskill lost the ball in the sun and the Chicken Man had another hit. A Barrett single made it 2–0.

It was Boston's turn to blunder in the fourth. Boggs's 1-out error enabled the Angels to load the bases, then Owen hesitated with a Schofield grounder allowing Downing to score. With 1 out in the fifth, Angel rookie Wally Joyner lofted a high fly toward the Sox bullpen. "We never saw it," remembered Nipper. "Somebody yelled, 'Incoming!' and then there it was bouncing around in the pen."

"I knew where it was going," said Hurst, who was on the mound.

In the fifth with the score tied at 2–2, Dwight Evans hit a 2-on, 2-out pop behind second base. Veteran Bobby Grich lost the ball in the sun and it landed for a double. The Sox led 3–2. With Grich on second and 1 out in the sixth, Boone singled to left. Grich roared into third, saw nothing from coach Moose Stubing, rounded the bag, and then saw he was a dead Angel. After being tagged out by Owen at third, Grich took time on his way to the dugout to yell at Stubing, spike his helmet, and raise his hands in the air in a rather complete display of anger and disgust. While Grich stewed in the dugout, the pitiful Stubing was left naked in the third base coach's box. "It was not a class act, it was just an emotional act," Grich admitted later.

There were more California follies. After a Grich error helped load the bases, DeCinces failed to handle a shot by Evans and the Sox had a 3-run inning in the seventh. Boston added 3 more in the eighth and Hurst had no trouble going the distance. Barrett made the final put-out and lobbed the ball into the stands as he came off the field.

DeCinces was defensive in the clubhouse.

"Doug, about the grounder. . .' started one questioner.

"Grounder?" challenged the Angels' third baseman. "You mean that rocket?"

Reggie Jackson, who did not play, said, "The first three or four innings, it looked like I was playing defense."

Veteran Don Sutton added, "The last time I saw a gem like this our coach wouldn't take us to Tastee-Freeze for a milkshake afterward."

Mauch listened to three questions, gave three goofy answers, then stormed out of the post-game interview room.

Ironically Game Two was played on the thirtieth anniversary of Don Larsen's perfect game.

Red Sox travelling secretary Jack Rogers had a chartered DC-10 waiting for the team at Logan Airport four hours after the game ended. The Sox owners were taking players' wives and most members of the front office with their spouses to California for the 3-game set in Anaheim. Ted Williams and Boston Mayor Ray Flynn joined the entourage. After takeoff the Sox were able to watch most of Game One of the National League play-offs between the Astros and Mets, then saw *Ferris Bueller's Day Off.*

Ignoring the game and the movie, a pregnant Debbie Boggs (carrying little Brett Boggs) sat on the floor near the back of the plane and played cards with Tracy Greenwell and the Schiraldis.

Wade Boggs was in a good mood and kidded Dave Henderson, a man with a sizeable gap between his front teeth. "Hey, Hendu," yelled Boggs. "I got some rope here in my back pocket. Want to floss your teeth?"

Henderson laughed and went to the telephone. "Calling Domino's?" asked Boggs. "Let's see 'em deliver up here."

Henderson used the new-fangled air-phone for a few minutes. No one on the plane would have guessed that the bench-splintered outfielder was less than one hundred hours away from Boston sports immortality.

The Sox dined on selections of steak, seafood, and chicken, slept through *Ferris Bueller,* and took the one hour bus ride from Los Angeles to Anaheim after they touched down in LA. Dairy farmers, mothers of infant twins, and those working the graveyard shift were the only New Englanders awake when the Sox finally straggled into the lobby of the Hotel California. Hotel employees saw a lot of loosened ties and Marty Feldman eyes.

When the Sox went to Anaheim Stadium for their off-day workout, McNamara and PR director Dick Bresciani orchestrated a seven-minute press conference with Game Three starter Oil Can Boyd. The Can was figuratively bound and gagged, and projected all the candor and spontaneity of a stewardess doing the seat belt routine on the Eastern Air Shuttle. Bresciani ended Boyd's press conference with an abrupt, Ron Ziegler-esque, "Thank you, gentlemen."

More noteworthy was McNamara's announcement that Clemens would pitch the fourth game. "We came up with it ten days ago."

It was typical of McNamara to project that kind of control when, in fact, the Sox were scratching their heads about their Game Four starter right up until Clemens lost Game One. If they planned on Clemens to pitch Games One, Four, and Seven, why didn't they announce it prior to the Series? If they planned it ten days before Game Three, why was Nipper so upset to learn he wasn't pitching Game Four, and why was Hurst surprised to learn he'd have to pitch Game Five on three days' rest? For some reason, perhaps his obsession with control, McNamara never wanted any suspicion that he was letting events dictate his moves—that would smack of panic and leave him open to second-guessing. While all the agonizing decisions were being made, he'd say nothing had been settled, then he'd come on like John Wayne and announce that it was all decided ten days ago. This paranoid fear of showing that he wasn't on top of everything would get McNamara into trouble in the ensuing weeks. The 1986 post-season categorically proved that baseball events are beyond the control of any manager, owner, player, or fan.

Game Three (CALIFORNIA 5, BOSTON 3)

The early evening rumor was that Oil Can Boyd was in a car accident and would not be able to pitch. Eighty minutes before gametime McNamara emerged from the Sox clubhouse (closed prior to post-season games) and said, "He will be here. He was not involved in any accident whatsoever and whoever started that story is—" McNamara looked around, presumably to see who was in earshot. Tom Singer, of *The Los Angeles Herald Examiner,* gave McNamara clearance saying, "It's okay, you can say it." Instead McNamara wheeled on Singer and said, "And you're an asshole, too," and then walked away from the pack.

"Nice talking to you, Mac," said a Boston reporter.

"Nice talking to you, gentlemen," said McNamara.

The Sox manager was upset with Singer's printed

suggestion that Mauch would have been flogged for
moving Witt up the way McNamara had moved Clemens.

Across the way DeCinces was discussing the relative
merits of the Boston and Anaheim infields. Dubbed
"California Whine" by Baltimore scribes who covered
him in the late seventies, DeCinces was always making
excuses and never felt he should be charged with an
error. He was still steamed over the call on Evans's ball
in Game Two and said, "This infield here is probably
the slowest in the big leagues. The Rams play here, but
my problem isn't what the football team does to it. It's
the cheerleaders. They don't play football over by third
base, but all those cheerleaders with their high heel
boots are always discoing around here. That's the problem I have."

Sammy Davis, Jr., required 2:09 to get through the
anthem, then John Candelaria threw his first pitch to
Boggs.

The Sox struck early when Jim Rice scored on a Rich
Gedman single in the second. The rally was aborted
when Baylor was picked off first base for the first time
in eleven years. The judge faced a heavy fine for that
one.

The Angels almost tied the game in the fourth, but
lost a run and their manager on one of the strangest plays
in years. With 2 on and 2 out, DeCinces hit a spinning
roller down the first base line. Bill Buckner, showcasing
some of the immobility that would make him a national
celebrity two weeks later, froze behind the bag and
waited for the ball, which was alternating between foul
and fair territory. Finally it bounced off the base, then
off the Can, and into the hand of Buckner. Joyner was
on second when the ball was hit, but rounded third as

the ball rattled off the bag and Boyd. Buckner threw home to Gedman. Joyner stepped on Gedman's foot and the plate but did not slide. Gedman tagged Joyner. Homeplate umpire Terry Cooney was still way down the first base line where he'd been following De-Cinces's grounder. Gedman obscured Cooney's view of the play, and Cooney called Joyner safe. Chaos reigned as McNamara bolted from the dugout, Barrett and Gedman reasoned with the umps, and Cooney consulted his third base colleague Rich Garcia. Meanwhile Oil Can shifted into his Wild Man of Borneo–Joaquin Andujar mode and miraculously escaped ejection. When Garcia said he saw Gedman tag Joyner, Cooney changed his call. Then it was Mauch's turn to become heated; and he was ejected by umpire Nick Bremigan. (Interestingly, the volatile Weaver managed to survive six tournaments without a single ejection.) Mauch went into the clubhouse and managed from the television. The Can also left the field for a smoke and to calm down.

Reggie Jackson singled home a run in the sixth and in the seventh the Can was knocked from the hill by sluggers Dick Schofield and Gary Pettis—not exactly a Mantle-Maris tandem. Schofield had 28 homers in four seasons, Pettis 12 in 5. Schofield cracked a 2-out first-pitch solo homer off Boyd, and Boone followed with a single. Boyd had little left, but the Sox feared their bullpen and the Can was left to face one more batter, Pettis. Pettis knocked a high screwball over the fence in right to make it 4–1, and the happy hands on the giant Big A scoreboard instructed 64,206 to make noise. Orange County's happy faces instantly complied.

American League public relations director Phyllis Merhige may have had the toughest job of the playoffs. She conducted the post-game press conferences and had to deal with the temperamental Mauch and the easily baited McNamara. Mauch had stormed out of the Game Two briefing and McNamara wasn't much more cooperative after losing Game Three. A writer asked the Boston manager, "Can you assess your situation, trailing 2–1, with Roger pitching tomorrow?"

Convinced the questioner was second-guessing him for rushing Clemens, McNamara snapped, "I'm trying to be patient. I'm really trying to be patient. He is pitching tomorrow. I'm really trying to be patient."

No one paid much attention when Joyner complained of a mysterious malady. The All Star rookie said, "When I was playing in the second game, I thought someone must have stepped on me. Thursday, I discussed it with our trainers and we treated it as if it were a bruise. That night, I was sick all night with a 102 degree fever. I thought I had the flu. When I mentioned it to the trainers, they decided that I must have been bitten by something that caused an allergic reaction. So they treated me for an insect bite."

California's superb first baseman was born during the golden age of sluggers, and of Wallys. When Joyner was born in the summer of 1962, 8 of the 13 major league 500-homer hitters were active, and Wallys were newsmakers across the land; Wally Moon was knocking them out for the Dodgers, Wally Schirra was one of America's seven "right stuff" astronauts, Wally Cox was on the *Ed Sullivan Show*, and Wally Cleaver was escorting Mary Ellen Rodgers to the junior prom.

Wally Joyner had remarkable poise for a rookie. Mauch noted, "It seems there are a lot of younger guys born in that era who are like that now, and I don't know why."

California's medical team didn't know why Joyner

had a staph infection, but the American League Rookie of the Year was through for the year and it was going to cost the Angels in the next four games.

Game Four (CALIFORNIA 4, BOSTON 3)

In 648 post-season games no team had ever taken a 3-run, or greater, lead into the ninth inning and lost.

The three days' rest controversy was finally put to the test and Clemens threw gas for 8 innings as old-timers nodded sagely and scoffed at the way modern pitchers were coddled. After all when men were men and our fathers walked ten miles through four-foot snowdrifts to get to school every day Christy Mathewson hurled three World Series shutouts in six days. Latter day saints Bob Gibson and Mickey Lolich pitched on three days' rest in the World Series and asked, "Is that all there is?" How many twenty-four-year-old kids need seventy-two hours of R & R between work days?

Clemens struck out 6 Angels in the first 3 innings, including Reggie Jackson on a 95 MPH fastball. With 2 outs in the seventh Clemens pumped his fist in a Can-like gesture after making the bothersome Pettis look at 3 straight strikes. It was Clemens's most animated moment since butting heads with Nipper on clinch night in Boston. Ruppert Jones led the eighth with a double, but expired at second when Clemens retired Grich, Downing, and Jackson in order.

Sutton had the ice age to go with Clemens's great balls of fire. California's cool right-hander blanked the Sox with infuriating ease and boring precision as he allowed but 1 hit and 0 walks in the first 5 innings.

Struggling Bill Buckner broke up the scoreless duel in the sixth, scoring Tony Armas with a 2-out double to right. This was the last run Armas would score in a Boston uniform and it would have been a 2-run double if not for the Lach Factor. Sox third base coach Rene Lachemann was in the final month of a tough year in the third base coach's box. Third base coaches are like air traffic controllers; you only notice them when they make mistakes. The position is a highly visible one, which requires knowledge of opponents and game situations plus the ability to make important decisions instantly. Lachemann had been in a season-long slump. A popular and brilliant young baseball man (he'd managed the Mariners and Brewers), Lach seemed to make the wrong choices with alarming regularity in 1986. He held runners that could have scored and, with Lach in the third base coach's box, the 1986 Sox had 10 runners thrown out at home while attempting to score from second, 9 thrown out going from first to third, 3 erased on sac fly attempts, and 8 baserunners wiped out at the plate on unforced putouts. Marty Barrett could have scored easily on Buckner's double off Sutton, as Jones's throw from right reached for the stars, but he was held at third by Lachemann.

Boston padded things with 2 more in the eighth; and Clemens took a 5-hit, 3–0 lead into the ninth. No Angel had reached third base. DeCinces then led with a homer to center and, with 1 out, Schofield and Boone hit singles (Boone on an 0–2 pitch). McNamara came out to get Clemens and inserted Calvin Schiraldi, a man with less than 95 innings of big league experience. Schiraldi did his job as Pettis drove a routine fly ball to left field, but Rice lost the ball in the lights. He broke in, then over, and, finally, back. Pettis's shot landed behind Rice on the grass in front of the warning track. Rice compounded his error of judgment with one of carelessness. He retrieved the ball, whirled, and tossed a foolish high heave over two cutoff men, allowing a confused Schofield and pinch runner Devon White to escape a rundown. It was now 3–2 and the Angels had runners on second and third with one out. Jones was walked intentionally and Schiraldi showed remarkable composure, fanning Grich for the second out. The game was winnable again and, when Schiraldi worked the count to 0–2 on Downing, it looked like the Sox were set to even the series. But on a 1–2 pitch, Schiraldi tried a backdoor slider and it slipped off his fingers. The slow pitch sailed toward a stunned Downing and slapped his left side as Schiraldi jumped off the mound in disgust. It was 3–3.

The Sox made Doug Corbett look like their own former relief artist Dick Radatz in the next 2 innings and Grich won it, scoring plowhorse Jerry Narron with a 1-out single off Schiraldi in the eleventh. The young Texan cried in the dugout as Baylor and Henderson formed a human apron to shield him from intrusive cameras. When Schiraldi regained his composure, he sat in front of his stall, head down, and answered questions for more than a half hour. It was a magnificent display of strength from the twenty-four-year-old hurler who'd just seen a pro career flash before his eyes. "It was the stupidest pitch of my life," he admitted. "I tried to throw the perfect pitch and choked it."

There were tears on pillows all over New England where the midnight horror show was reviewed harshly by Sox fans who'd promised not to be fooled again. After the jubilant joyride of 1986 Boston was melting on the west coast. The Sox trailed 1–3, had lost both games started by Clemens, and Game One wizard Mike Witt was slated to pitch in another fifteen hours. Schiraldi and Rice had earned plaques in the Sox Hall of Shame. Would other teammates gain first-ballot admission in the Sunday finale? Oft-burned Bostonians could only wonder what ghastly form the final death would take.

When the Sox team bus rolled back to the Anaheim Marriott, players' wives and forgiving fans were waiting in the lobby to console their disappointed champs. It looked like the magic season was going to end just a few miles down the road from the Magic Kingdom. Schiraldi was comforted by his wife, Debbie. Gedman and his wife, Sherri, went to a Mexican restaurant with two friends. Rice met with old pal Luis Tiant and tried to forget his troubles in the hotel disco. McNamara promised no Knute Rockne speeches on Sunday.

"I'm going to think positive," said Clemens. "I'm going to go back to work tomorrow and get ready to pitch Game Seven."

Game Five (BOSTON 7, CALIFORNIA 6)

Dave Henderson turned and raced for the fence. Bobby Grich's high shot was bound for the warning track, if not beyond. Henderson had only been in the game for one inning, subbing for Tony Armas who had sprained his ankle chasing a DeCinces's double in the second. Armas would not have caught up with Grich's thunderbolt. The regular Boston center fielder had lost a couple of steps in the last few years and would have watched the ball hit the top of the fence. Armas could probably have held Grich to a double.

Henderson had a shot. He was like a man on a motorcycle with a butterfly net and he timed his leap perfectly, cradling the ball in the pocket of his left-handed glove while bracing himself with his right hand on the fence. But his momentum carried him into the green padding with considerable force and his left elbow crashed against the top of the wall, jarring the baseball out of his glove and, worse, over the wall.

So *this was how* it was going to happen.The final page was written. This time the Sox were going to lose because a good outfielder, making an extra effort, accidentally carried a ball over the wall. Grich's shot would have been a game-tying double if Armas had still been in the game, but the cruel baseball gods put Henderson in center and penalized the Sox for extra effort. California now had a 3–2 lead. Only the Red Sox could lose in this fashion. Would the Celtics lose because John Havlicek put the ball in the wrong basket? Would the Bruins lose because Bobby Orr put the puck in the wrong net? No, but the Sox were going to lose because their center fielder with the best of intentions inadvertently scored for the other team.

Dave Henderson was an all-American high school football player who had an uncle who played major league baseball. Henderson was big and fast, a linebacker and a running back at Dos Palos High in southern California. Nebraska and USC were among the NCAA football powers who recruited him and Henderson loved the courtship. USC recruiter Marvin Goux shoved four Rose Bowl rings in Henderson's face and said, "Kid, you want one of these?" With friend Freeman McNeil, Henderson took as many recruiting visits as the NCAA allowed before he agreed to play football at Fresno State. Then the infant Seattle Mariners made

him their first draft choice on the recommendation of
assistant GM Lou Gorman. Uncle Joe Henderson rec-
ommended baseball and Dave listened. He signed with
the Mariners and made it to the majors in four years. In
1983 he hit .269 with 17 homers and 55 RBI in 137
games. He could play all three outfield positions, hit
for power, and run. He bought a house in Bellevue,
Washington, married a pretty girl named Loni and they
had a son, David Chase. Life in the Pacific Northwest
wasn't bad.

Henderson was a fixture in the Seattle outfield until
Dick Williams took over for Chuck Cottier early in the
1986 season. Williams didn't see any future in a twenty-
eight-year-old outfielder with a .253 lifetime average
and 100-strikeout potential. And besides, Henderson
wasn't serious enough for Williams, a man given to
laughter only during tapings for Lite Beer commercials.
Henderson didn't like playing behind John Moses and
said of Williams, "He treats people like they're not people."

He was traded to Boston a few weeks later. Henderson was delighted, and when he first met Haywood
Sullivan acted like an inmate who'd just been pardoned
by the governor. The big outfielder pumped the tri-
owner's huge hand, saying, "Thank you, thank you,
thank you."

He didn't play many games after the trade, but said,
"I could digest it better sitting behind Tony Armas, Jim
Rice, and Dwight Evans instead of Bradley and Moses
in Seattle."

The misplay seemed unfair. Henderson was a well-
liked sub who'd played virtually no part in the saga of
the '86 Sox and now he was going to be forever cursed
for an extraordinary effort. He sat alone in the dugout

between innings. Clemens was the only teammate who bothered to console him. "I had a few guys come to me and say they were ready to hang me," Henderson remembered later.

Bruce Hurst struck out Reggie Jackson after Grich's homer, but the big lefty had nothing more to give. Like Clemens, Hurst hadn't pitched on three days' rest all season and 101 pitches in 6 innings was all he had. Between innings Hurst got a congratulatory handshake from Clemens.

"It's been a fun year," Hurst told Clemens. "I'm going to work real hard during the off season and get ready to come back because I learned a lot this year."

Clemens stopped him. "Bruce, I agree that hard work pays off, but I just got a funny feeling we're not done yet. I'm not ready to pack my bags."

When Bob Stanley came out for the seventh and the Angels bled him for 2 cheap runs, the sand was indeed running out on the season. Barrett popped up to end the eighth and figured it was over.

Witt had a 6-hitter and a 5–2 lead as Buckner loosened up to lead off the ninth. Baylor, who had been at the park since 8:15 A.M., turned to his teammates in the dugout and said, "We have to have quality swings. If we're going to make outs, they have to be quality outs. I don't want to make the last out. Do any of you want to make the last out?"

Evans shouted, "We've got more baseball to play."

Somewhat more quietly, Gedman added, "This is it, fellas. We either do it or we don't."

Buckner cracked a prototype one-armed single up the middle. Rice stepped to the plate and, looking like a man who wished he were someplace else, was called out on strikes. There was champagne in the Angels' clubhouse. Security guards gathered the equipment in the Sox bullpen and prepared to drive it to the Boston clubhouse. Hats and gloves were swept from the Angel dugout as 64,223 Californians braced for their first pennant-clinching celebration.

Proud Don Baylor fell behind on the count, then drove a 3–2 Witt curveball over the fence in left-center to cut the Angel lead to 5–4. Sox numerologists groaned. Just another barrel of pain. Five-four was the final score of Boston's 1978 playoff loss to the Yankees. When Evans's popped up for the second out, the end was at hand.

Gedman was coming to the plate and Boston's lionhearted catcher already had a home run, a double, and a single in three tries against Witt. A decision had to be made. Mauch had spent a lifetime making moves like this and he never maneuvered to please his critics or to cover his hide. He made the decisions he felt he had to make and at this moment he felt he should lift Witt (121 pitches) and summon lefty Gary Lucas to face Boston's left-hand-hitting catcher. Lucas had struck out Gedman Saturday night. Mauch later said he'd never seen Gedman do anything but strike out against Lucas. Witt walked off in stunned silence and went into the clubhouse.

Gedman stepped out of the box as Lucas looked homeward and pointed to center—not in any Ruthesque manner, he simply wanted the "Another Boston Choke" banner removed. It was distracting to the eye and the soul. The errand carried out, Lucas threw one pitch and hit Gedman in the hand. Lucas hadn't hit a batter in 322 innings since May 3, 1982. The Sox were still breathing.

Donnie "Gas Can" Moore was called in to face Henderson. Moore was California's most reliable reliever (he signed a three-year, $3 million contract after saving 31 games in 1985), but shoulder and rib problems were causing him difficulties by the time the 1986 post-season rolled around.

Henderson had fanned on 4 pitches in the seventh and would have had little hope of success if Witt were still in the game. Moore was slightly more vulnerable but looked in control as he ran the count to 2–2 on Boston's outfield sub. Members of the Sox bullpen crew immediately began their inexplicable hat ritual when, with the count 2–2 and 2 outs, they take off their caps and hold them out in a begging position. Henderson fouled off a pitch, then stepped out to gather his thoughts. He looked particularly inept fouling back the next pitch on a wild swing. Henderson now assumed his emergency stance, feet spread wide, as if he were playing pepper in front of the backstop. In the Sox clubhouse Oil Can Boyd, Wes Gardner, Clemens, and Stanley watched the television set, refusing to change chairs because it might bring bad luck. On the bench Dave Stapleton was dubious. "I didn't think he had a chance, man," Stapleton said later. "The way he looked on the first two swings, it was like a monkey playing football." McNamara looked across the field and saw Reggie Jackson remove his hat and sunglasses. Jackson was hugging Gene Mauch. In the Angel clubhouse Witt and Ruppert Jones looked at the television monitor and agreed that Moore could get Henderson with any pitch except a forkball.

There is no logical explanation for what happened next. Moore threw a forkball low and away. In the Angel clubhouse Witt and Jones shrieked as soon as the pitch left Witt's hand. Henderson, who later admitted he "didn't have a clue," uncoiled from his stance, lunged over the plate, and got the fat part of his bat on the ball.

There was little doubt where it was going. Henderson was a strong man with a big swing. It didn't matter that he hit only 1 homer with 3 RBI in his short season with the Sox. He'd knocked one ball over the fence with his glove, now it was his bat's turn. He caught up with Moore's slowhand serve and spiked it over the fence in left-center. Running down the first base line, Henderson leaped and did a 360-degree pirouette in midair, a move that would have given Peggy Fleming a 6.0. Henderson, Boston's prince, wouldn't touch the ground again until October 27th.

It wasn't the first time a man named Henderson rescued a Boston sports franchise. In 1982 a work-release inmate named Mark Henderson cleared snow with a small plow in Foxboro, allowing Patriot kicker John Smith to boot a field goal, which helped New England beat the Miami Dolphins. In '84 Celtic guard Gerald Henderson stole a James Worthy pass and converted a layup in the closing seconds to rescue the Celtics from a sure defeat in the second game of the NBA finals against the Lakers. This time it was Dave Henderson saving a laudable season for the Red Sox.

Fiction is peppered with Dave Hendersons. Shoeless Joe Hardy sold his soul to the devil in exchange for a chance to beat those damn Yankees. Roy Hobbs wanted to walk down the street and have people say "There goes the best there ever was," and he got his wish late in life in *The Year the Yankees Lost the Pennant*. Henderson had no designs on everlasting fame but was granted immortality when he took Moore's changeup over the bridge. A phone call to Bobby Thomson would explain everything. A man's life changes and he spends the rest of his time on earth answering inquiries about a single moment.

"You try to explain that Donnie Moore thing and you

go bananas," Henderson said later. "He threw a good pitch. I wasn't supposed to hit it, and what the hell? He'll probably throw that pitch ten times and I'll miss it ten times. We are ballplayers and we fail most of the time."

Henderson said he didn't expect any endorsement opportunities. "What would I endorse, Dentyne?" he asked, flashing a gap-toothed smile. He also said he wasn't prepared to be a cult hero. "The only cult figure I ever heard of was Jim Jones, and I don't want to be like that guy."

But it was too late. Dave Henderson did something Ted Williams, Carl Yastrzemski, and Jim Rice never did. With the Red Sox one strike away from extinction, he saved the season and the pennant.

Henderson's former manager Lachemann said, "A lot of people were ready to go ahead and make him a goat for a ball nobody else would have gotten to. And for him to be able to come back like he did is great. Every time I see the tape of his homer, it still gives me a bunch of chills and I know it will for the rest of my life."

The Angels should have won it anyway. California tied the game in the bottom of the ninth and had the bases loaded with 1 out when clean-up man DeCinces came to the plate with a chance to do so. Little-used Steve Crawford was pitching for Boston and McNamara had the infield drawn in. DeCinces could have won the game with a high chopper, a hard grounder through the infield, a medium-range fly ball, a walk. A hit of any kind. But the California third baseman played right into Boston's hand, swinging at the first pitch and lofting a fly to shallow right. Evans made the catch and Wilfong had to hold. Not even Rene Lachemann would have sent a runner in that situation. Grich was next and he hit a soft liner back to Crawford to end the inning.

A prototypical double play grounder by Rice killed a Sox threat in the tenth, but Rice finally contributed by making a good catch at the wall to end the bottom of the inning. In the eleventh the Sox went to their secret weapon: Baylor was hit by a pitch leading off the inning.

Baylor trotted to first where he encountered former teammate and friend Bobby Grich. The veterans of thirty baseball summers slapped five in celebration of what they both agreed was the best game they'd ever played in. Evans followed with a single up the middle, then the heroic Gedman stunned DeCinces, plopping a bunt toward third. Gedman had his fourth hit and the Sox had the bases loaded. Henderson (who else?) came to the plate and smoked a liner to center, which scored Baylor easily. Boston almost blew it open when Ed Romero followed with a smash to left, but Brian Downing made a sensational catch and held the ball after crashing into the wall.

Schiraldi had his blinding date with redemption in the bottom of the eleventh. Tracing the tracks of his tears back to the Big A mound, he fanned Wilfong and Schofield to start the inning. He was pitching for the third straight day for the first time all year, but there would be no more silly off-speed stuff. Appropriately Downing—the player young Calvin had hit in Game Four—became the final batter as Schiraldi got the Angel outfielder to pop to Stapleton. The Sox were bringing it home.

Sounding like happy Little Leaguers with ice-cream treats, the 1986 Red Sox bounded up the ramp that leads from the visitors' dugout. Clemens yelled, " 'Bout time, we've been playing Santa Claus ever since we've been here."

Barrett hollered, "I can't believe Mauch took Witt out."

Henderson was the last man out of the tunnel and he wanted a beer. Crawford had his first win of the 1986 season; Stapleton had his second hit since August 21, and Henderson, Schiraldi, and Rice were redeemed. The final score was 7–6—the same as the Greatest Game Ever Played in 1975.

Down the hall Mauch kicked a suitcase and said, "I can't believe I have to pack that thing tonight." Then added, "I have no place to sleep tonight. I bet my house that Doug DeCinces would get Wilfong home."

Five hundred fans greeted the Sox at Fenway when the team buses pulled up on the morning of Monday, October 13. There were no scheduled workouts on the off day, but smoke detector Clemens was back at the park by mid-afternoon to do his throwing with coach Bill Fischer. The Can was down to pitch Game Six, and Clemens was still counting on pitching Game Seven.

Clemens told the Can, "Dennis, you get me the ball for the seventh game and I'll take it from there."

Game Six (BOSTON 10, CALIFORNIA 4)

The heat was off. The Sox were home for Games Six and Seven and suddenly it was as if they were preparing to face the Mariners in May, or the Tigers at Lakeland in March.

"There was no pressure, none," Marty Barrett recalls. "The fifth game was our seventh game. That was the way we felt. If we could beat Mike Witt in that game in California, we had a good chance to come back here and win the last two. After we won the fifth game, it was just like we were playing with the house's money."

The well-scrubbed second baseman was at the end of a starlit season. In 1986 Barrett hit .286 while striking out only 31 times in 713 plate appearances. He played in a career-high 158 games and led all American League second basemen in assists. A pillar of consistency his average never dipped below .280 after July 1, and he had 50 multi-hit games.

He was the sun belt's gift to Boston, a durable five ten, 176 pounder with the look of a stockbroker and the unassuming presence of a management trainee. Barrett had oft-cut, Brylcream hair, dressed conservatively, and carried a brief case. Passengers watching the Sox file through an airport terminal would have voted Barrett most-likely-to-install-a-car-phone. Barrett was born in Arcadia, California, but played his high school ball at Rancho High, Las Vegas, where he was also a football quarterback and basketball playmaker. His older brother Charlie pitched in the Dodger system for five years, and his younger brother Tom was an infield prospect with the Yankees. Marty Barrett played two years at Mesa Community College, then one year at Arizona State before he was selected by the Red Sox in the secondary phase of the June '79 draft. He hit .300 for Pawtucket in his fourth year of minor league ball and was hitting .345 when the Sox called him up for good on June 17, 1983. When Jerry Remy's knee gave out in '84, Barrett took over and hit .303 in 139 games while making only 9 errors. It was the highest average for a Sox second-baseman since Pete Runnels's .320 in 1960. He was also a master of deception, working hidden ball tricks, and forcing balks with heads-up baserunning. Teammates dubbed Barrett "The Deke Master."

In 1985 Barrett came to camp a little overweight and overconfident, and he had a disappointing season. His average dropped to .266; his strikeouts doubled; and there was considerable grumbling about his range.

Barrett silenced his critics in '86, arriving in great shape and having an excellent year. Sparky Anderson called him, "An Eddie Stankey with more ability." Twins manager Ray Miller said, "One guy I'm going to have to change my opinion of is Marty Barrett. I wasn't that impressed when I first saw him, but he's killed us this year and he's in the middle of everything for them."

Barrett's range wasn't any better, but he noted, "I do know how to play hitters, regardless of whether I have great range. Look at chances. If I have to go five feet for a ball and a guy with great range has to go fifteen feet, we still caught the same ball."

He also emerged as a media darling. Unfailingly cordial, candid, and articulate in a wasteland of athletes who'd rather stick needles in their eyes than talk to the press, Barrett shed his cloak of anonymity when the Sox moved into the pennant race. He did a regular spot on a local morning radio show, and his locker became an oasis for out of town reporters walking the path of least resistance.

As the playoffs progressed everyone saw that Barrett not only could talk, he could play. He had 8 hits in the first 5 games and gave the Sox an ideal contact hitter in the number two spot in the order.

Before Game Six Barrett had a scare. While watching the Mets-Astros game with his wife Robin, son Eric, and daughter Kathryn, he turned on the couch to avoid his onrushing daughter and hurt his neck and back. He walked around the house like Quasimodo for the rest of the day until his muscles gradually loosened, and he was cleared to play.

Barrett's back and neck weren't the only topics of dis-

cussion prior to Game Six. Doug Flutie and his shame-
less publicity-seeking agent, Bob Woolf, violated pro-
tocol and appeared on Fenway sod to formally announce
Flutie's move to the NFL. Ironically a day earlier John
McNamara had compared Henderson's Sunday shot
with Flutie's Hail Mary touchdown pass against the
University of Miami in 1984.

While Flutie and Woolf were being nudged off the
field, DeCinces was walking around gleefully showing
off his bat, which had a Chardonnay cork wedged into
the hollow end of the barrel. Evans had charged some
of the Angels with using corked bats and DeCinces was
attempting to show how relaxed he and his teammates
were. Whether the cork came from one of the champagne bottles that had been opened in the ninth inning
of Game Five he wouldn't say.

Bill Buckner was less relaxed when asked by a local
sportscaster if Boston's big bats were ready to go. "What
kind of a question is that?" snapped the man with a
robust .136 average. Buckner delivered a few more per-
functory answers, announced that he'd been offended,
then stalked off in mid-interview.

Print reporters could only smile. Ballplayers usually
wear halos during radio and television interviews so the
public rarely sees how rude and spoiled they can be.

The pertinent question was answered when Boston's
bats pounded 16 hits as the Sox claimed a 10–4 victory.
Buckner had 2 hits, Spike Owen was 4–4, and Barrett
had 3 hits in the cakewalk. Barrett was hitting .423 (11–
26) and was 7–9 with men in scoring position and was
being touted as a series MVP candidate.

The Can staggered through a 44-pitch first inning and
fell behind 2–0, but he settled down and left after 7
with an 8–3 lead. Stanley mopped up, and Henderson

(who else?) caught the final out to force a seventh game.

Mauch said, "The only people who feel pressure are those who don't know how to handle it."

McNamara said, "I don't think winning or losing will have anything to do with history. That jinx stuff is something made by you people."

Reporters noted that while Mauch hadn't won a pennant in his twenty-five years of managing, the Red Sox hadn't won a seventh game of any kind since 1918. Something had to give.

Game Seven (BOSTON 8, CALIFORNIA 1)

Early Wednesday a man bumped into Reggie Jackson as he was browsing in the Paperback Booksmith on Boylston Street in Boston's Back Bay.

"Hey, Reggie," said the stranger. "What's going to happen tonight?"

"We're gone, man," said Jackson.

And so they were.

For the first time in eleven years the Red Sox and the New England foliage peaked simultaneously. Under a hunter's moon and clear October skies the Sox pulverized the Angels, scoring 7 runs in the first 4 innings. They rode Roger Clemens's huge shoulders to an 8–1 win, good for the American League pennant.

A dizzy Clemens threw 93 pitches in 7 innings and allowed only 4 hits. He won for the first time since he'd ridden that police horse on clinch day, and he won despite a flu that made him weak and turned his skin from pale to bone white.

The Sox scored 3 times in the second with 2 runs

crossing after Wade Boggs's single smacked off second base. Jim Rice crashed a monstrous 3-run homer over the wall in the fourth, capping a 4-run inning and sending California starter John Candelaria to the showers.

Schiraldi pitched the last two innings and struck out 5, fanning Jerry Narron for the clincher. Narron was the man who crossed home plate and made Schiraldi cry Saturday night. "Saturday night I was as low as I could be," said Schiraldi. "Now I'm drinking champagne."

The Sox were the seventh team in major league history to overcome a 3–1 deficit in a post-season series.

"We've had so much magic this year," Boggs said. "Look at the ways we've won. Something weird's always happened when we needed it. Always. As soon as we got back to even, we knew we could win this thing. This is a team that's done everything it's had to do. No matter what the count. No matter what the situation. Magic."

Pitching coach Bill Fischer still had his pet rock, the lucky one that the eccentric old man gave him in Chicago in April and that Fischer carried in his warm-up jacket all season. "You want to know why it'd be one hundred twelve degrees in Kansas City and I'd still be wearing my warmup jacket?" Fischer said. "Because I had the rock in the pocket, that's why. Every game, right there in my warmup jacket. That crazy old geezer was right."

The taste should have been sweetest for Rice. After eleven years, 328 homers, and 1,001 abrupt interviews, the Sox captain was finally getting a shot at the World Series. "No doubt about it I've waited a long time," said the slugger. In his moment of glory Rice also took time to chide Sox critics. "We made believers of 'em," he said. "The guys that put us down, the guys that travel with us. They made us feel bad. Now we have something to look forward to."

The other clubhouse was also emotional. The Angels could have made excuses about the sudden, mysterious loss of Joyner, but they didn't. Grich announced his retirement, while Jackson asked, "What the hell happened to us?"

DeCinces—true to form—complained about a scoring decision that charged Gary Pettis with an error in the fourth inning. DeCinces had boasted California's defensive superiority prior to the series, but the Angels tied an ALCS record with eight errors. Mauch delivered this Nixonian remark: "My situation is something that a lot of the media obviously enjoys. So I'll let them take care of that. They can wonder what I'll do, wonder how I'll feel."

Playoff MVP Marty Barrett (.367, 39 chances, 0 errors) admitted, "The truth is, when I popped up in the eighth inning of the fifth game, I went back to the dugout thinking the game was over. I felt like we were dead and the pop-up didn't make any difference. Now I realize anything is possible and I will never have that dead feeling again as long as I live. I've seen that there's always a chance and I'll feel that way long after I've retired from baseball."

A few blocks from Fenway, way down the right field foul line, the Prudential Tower brightened the Boston skyline with a proud message. Select office lights had been left lit in eighteen floors near the top of the tower, creating a giant numeric one. The message was clear for all to see. The Red Sox had won their fourth pennant since 1918 and were going to New York to meet the Mets in the World Series.

9

THE WORLD SERIES

NEW York City had a response to Boston's Prudential proclamation. The top of the Empire State Building was bathed in Mets colors: orange and blue. In front of the old Treasury Building on Wall Street, the granite arms of George Washington held a sign that read: "God isn't dead. He's alive and playing for the Mets."

It was the first time Boston and New York had faced each other in a World Series since 1912, and Eastern and Pan American airlines joined NBC-TV as the happiest corporations in America. A Houston–California World Series would have scrapped thousands of shuttle passengers and millions of television viewers. Eastern added two more flights and reduced fares, while Pan Am gave away free Mets and Red Sox caps and offered bus service to Shea Stadium. NBC charged $260,000 for a thirty-second ad.

The matchup of Eastern corridor teams assured bets and fistfights in frat houses and high-rise dormitories from Orono, Maine, to Mays Landing, New Jersey, but there was none of the history and hatred of the Red Sox–Yankee tong wars. The Mets had been to Fenway Park only once—for a charity exhibition game in September—the Sox on the other hand had two years of experience in the ballpark near Archie Bunker's place when The House That Ruth Built was being renovated in 1974 and '75 and the Yankees borrowed Shea.

The 1986 Mets enjoyed one of the best regular seasons of modern times. After narrow misses in 1984 and '85 they decimated the NL East, winning 108 games and taking the title by a whopping 21½ games, the largest division-winning margin in league history. New York's 108–54 record tied the 1975 Reds for the best in modern National League history. The Mets led NL in pitching, hitting, scoring, arrogance, and book contracts. They were heavy pre-season favorites and stormed the NL East from wire to wire with young genius Davey Johnson (known as "dum-dum" when he played for the Orioles) keeping his foot on the accelerator from April to October.

New York had a starting quartet of Dwight Gooden, Ron Darling, Bobby Ojeda, and Sid Fernandez who went 63–22 during the 1986 season. They also had a solid lefty-righty combo of Jesse Orosco and Roger McDowell in the bullpen. First baseman Keith Hernandez and catcher Gary Carter were MVP candidates; Darryl Strawberry was touted as the next Ted Williams; Lenny Dykstra and Wally Backman were super-smurfs, and Ray Knight (Mr. Nancy Lopez) had proven he could hit in the clutch. The Mets were posted as 2½–1 favorites in both Reno and Las Vegas. It was said to be the most lopsided line since the 1950 Philadelphia Whiz Kids faced the fearsome Yankees.

"I saw the odds in the paper today and I couldn't believe it," said Vegas native Marty Barrett.

Deep in talent, the Mets were also the most disliked team in baseball. National League opponents thought they were overrated showboats. Well, showboats at least. New York players were known for their curtain calls and high-fives during batting practice, and Carter especially had been unpopular since his days in Montreal when they dubbed him "Camera Carter." There were four Met biographies out in the summer of '86, and Gooden had a rap album in record stores. It seemed that every New York radio station produced its own Mets theme record, including "Lenny and the Mets," a takeoff on Elton John's "Benny and the Jets," and the Mets own VHS cassette was a hotter item than Playboy's latest video. At the ballpark slick Mets marketing men played the "Let's Go Mets" video enough times to make one's skull implode.

"I know we're not liked around the league, but who cares?" said Hernandez.

Bruce Hurst was named Boston's starting pitcher for Game One of the 83rd World Series. It was an easy decision for McNamara: the Series started three days after Clemens's Game Seven victory over the Angels, and Hurst was Boston's strongest pitcher in the final month of the regular season.

There would be plenty of deserving players who had waited longer, and other heroic figures in the 1986 World Series, but Hurst was the undiscovered master performing at the top of his game precisely when it mattered most. He was ready to blossom while the whole world watched. Within two weeks young lefties across America would try to copy Hurst's follow-through signature—left leg bent at the knee and turned upward with spikes reaching for the sky.

Bruce Vee Hurst was born in St. George, Utah, in 1958, the youngest of five children of Mormons John and Beth Hurst, and he spent his entire youth in the fresh air and open spaces of that state. St. George is a mountain town (population 20,000) near the point where Nevada, Arizona, and Utah collide in spacious silence. The Hurst home was at 650 South Street and was surrounded by a brick wall. Young Bruce spent hours throwing rubber balls at the bricks, fantasizing about pitching in the World Series. His father worked for the state road commission and his mother was part owner of a Ben Franklin–Ace Hardware store. Hurst's parents separated when he was four and his father moved to Odgen, 350 miles from St. George.

As a youngster Bruce found the plate elusive and several times walked more than a dozen in little league games. Kent Garrett, a former player at Brigham Young, coached Hurst in Pony League and taught the young lefty how to pitch. Hurst was a first baseman and pitcher in Pony League and played baseball and basketball at Dixie High School. There weren't any pro scouts hanging around the high desert of St. George, and Hurst was pitching in a vacuum until Garrett organized a team to play in the Utah State Legion tournament in 1975. The St. George lefty struck out 17 against the top-seeded club and spent the afternoon filling out age-weight-height cards for pro scouts. He had an arm and body built for baseball. He was six three and 185 pounds with big legs and a low center of gravity. He threw hard and had the undeniable benefit of being left-handed. Right-handed prospects are difficult to sort out, but legitimate lefties are rare and pro scouts are always looking for southpaws. The bird dogs all found St. George the next year. Hurst went 9–1 for the Dixie Flyers in his senior season and was drafted by the Red Sox in the first round.

He kept playing basketball while he was in the minors and was a guard/forward for the Dixie Junior College basketball team that placed third in the 1979 National JUCO tournament. Hurst could dunk, but he knew the NBA had no use for a slow, six three guard. In 1980 Hurst made the jump from double-A to the major leagues, but it developed that he was not mentally ready for the big show. He was a sensitive young man uncomfortable with the basic approach of tobacco-spitting Sox manager Don Zimmer. Late in the 1980 season in Baltimore Hurst had a bad relief outing and botched a rundown play. Zimmer waddled out to the mound, took the ball, and told Hurst to "go home and grow up." The rookie left the clubhouse in mid-game and ran down Baltimore's 33rd Street, looking for a pay phone to call his brother. He then returned to the park and took the bus back to the Cross Keys Inn after the game.

Hurst spent three months of the 1980 season at Pawtucket and was in triple-A at the start of the '81 season when he quit again. He jumped the team (telling only roommate Wade Boggs) and flew from West Virginia to Pawtucket to pack his bags for Utah. He was newly married and figured that six years in the minors was long enough; he could still get his college degree and start life over again. Sox farm director Ed Kenney gave Hurst a lengthy pep talk and three days later he pitched his way out of Joe Morgan's doghouse, eventually compiling a 12–7 record for the PawSox. When he returned to the big leagues, Ralph Houk had taken over for Zimmer, and Hurst went 2–0 with the Sox in September of

'81. He never went back to the minors and he never quit again.

Hurst had an image problem his first years in Boston. He had soft brown eyes and a high-pitched voice and everybody knew he'd quit twice. He refused to throw sliders because he thought they produced bone chips, and he sometimes whined about Boston's Stonehenge defense. Hurst was a perfectly mediocre 12–12 in 1983 and again in 1984. He had the arm, but he was Boston's Mr. Milquetoast—considered too timid and "too Mormon" to be a big winner.

"Bruce didn't have enough bulldog in him," remembers owner Haywood Sullivan. "Being more aggressive just wasn't his nature."

"I heard that I was timid," Hurst recalls. "It was the first thing I had to overcome. The other thing I heard was that I was immature. How do you defend that? One person might say that you are, and another person might say you're not. I may be quiet compared to the typical baseball player, but nobody knows how I was raised. I'm from a small town, but I always wanted to win as much as anybody. I felt bad when it was said that I was timid because I was Mormon. I don't think it should be put in that light. I don't think I'm timid and shy. The way I am doesn't mean I don't have a real drive to do well and be competitive."

Before the start of the 1986 season Hurst sat on a United Airlines charter and looked at the stat sheet underlining the mediocrity of his big league career. He was 42–46 with a lifetime ERA of 4.59. "If I say I'm a better pitcher than the numbers show, it sounds like a cop-out," he explained. "Yet, it's hard for me to admit that I'm just a mediocre pitcher. I say I feel I'm a better pitcher than my statistics show."

He is. Hurst had a 5–3 record, a 2.79 ERA, and was leading the league in strikeouts when he went down with a groin pull in May '86. He missed seven weeks and struggled when he returned, but went 5–0 with a 1.07 ERA in September. He finished the season with a 13–8 record, a 2.99 ERA, 4 shutouts, and 167 strikeouts in 174.1 innings. He has a heavy fastball, a big breaking ball, and a new forkball, which makes him especially tough on right-handed hitters. He isn't afraid to pitch inside in Fenway Park, and he had the best pickoff move on the team. His strikeout ratio was better than Clemens's, though Hurst insists, "I'm not a strikeout pitcher."

Barrett said, "I don't think people understand how good Bruce Hurst really is. I think he's the toughest pitcher in baseball. I know that when he was coming back from his groin injury, he did some pitching against us. I faced him and I never saw anything like it. He freezes right-handed hitters with that curveball, and if he's freezing righties, what do you think he's like against lefties?"

Once part of a left-handed troika, which included John Tudor and Bobby Ojeda, the Sox had rejected offers for Hurst and dealt the other young southpaws. Tudor and Ojeda became National League stoppers, which put more pressure on Hurst, but he finally rewarded management with an outstanding season in 1986. And Boston's sports talk shows stopped poking fun at the Sox for turning down St. Louis's offer of four pitchers for Hurst at the 1985 winter meetings.

Hurst is close to fellow pitchers Clemens and Nipper, but his best friend in Boston is fellow Mormon and star Danny Ainge, a former major league baseball player who now starts in the backcourt for the Celtics. Hurst and Ainge talk every few days and go to each other's games whenever possible. Their homes are near each other and Michelle Ainge and her three children spend a lot of time with Holly Hurst and her sons, Ryan and Kyle. Bruce Hurst pitched to Danny Ainge four times in the minors. Ainge went 2–4, hitting a double and "a single that spun his cap," according to Ainge. Ainge said the double was a rocket off the wall, but Hurst remembers it as a soft blooper over the infield. Ainge also stole second off his friend.

In addition to baseball and basketball Hurst is passionate about golf and fishing. He does not drink, gamble, or swear, and he has to stay away from sweets because he has a tendency to put on weight. He does not subscribe to a local newspaper but knows all the scores and is unfailingly polite to male members of the media. Hurst started the season with a 2–7 record in 1985 and bravely went on every television station to answer questions about trade rumors and his demotion to the bullpen. He could be extremely candid. "We're disappointed if the Celtics get eliminated early," he admitted in the spring of '86, "because when they drop out, it puts us on the front page and we like to lie in the weeds as long as we can." Women reporters don't find Hurst easy. He is particularly uncomfortable when women scribes wander into the clubhouse and says, "I think it's wrong. They shouldn't be in there."

If he hates anything more than women reporters, it is probably New York City. The Big Apple has always looked rotten to the young man from St. George, Utah, and Bruce Hurst did not plan on finding out how late the bars stayed open when the Red Sox checked into New York's Grand Hyatt Hotel on the afternoon of Friday, October 17, 1986.

McNamara's day got off to a bad start. He appeared on *Good Morning America* with host Charles Gibson and bristled when Gibson noted that Woodrow Wilson was President when the Sox won their last World Series. "Hey, you're not funny," said McNamara. "Seven o'clock in the morning, that's not funny."

The Sox manager knew that the Mets were vulnerable against left-handed pitching. Hurst's presence at the start of Game One would put speedsters Lenny Dykstra and Wally Backman on the bench, and strip the over-rated Strawberry of most of his power. New York's players had no fear of Hurst and felt they'd already seen the best pitching on the planet when they beat the Astros in six thrilling, low-scoring games during the National League Championship Series. At Friday's off day workout Carter said he'd never faced Hurst; Hernandez said, "I have no interest in the American League"; and Knight talked only of the Astros, saying, "Cy Young himself couldn't have been better than what we faced. In the whole six games I never saw a good pitch to hit."

Bobby Ojeda was another popular interview subject. Ojeda was the best of the Boston–New York crossover players. After struggling in Fenway throughout the 1980s, Ojeda went 18–5 with a 2.57 ERA for the Mets. He was the principal figure in the deal that sent Schiraldi, Wes Gardner, LaSchelle Tarver, and John Christensen to Boston after the 1985 season. The Mets didn't have any other former Red Sox, but Boston had former Mets Sambito, Schiraldi and, of course, Seaver. The greatest overlap was in the front office where Sox GM Lou Gorman had been Frank Cashen's right hand man when Cashen assembled the Met powerhouse. Gorman was the man who drafted Dwight Gooden, Dykstra, Strawberry, Roger McDowell, and Rick Aguilera. Gorman made the trades that brought Hernandez, Ron Darling, and Sid Fernandez to New York. Gorman was also the man who said $25,000 was too much money for Houston native Roger Clemens when the Mets drafted Clemens in the twelfth round in 1981.

Ron Darling, the Mets' Game One starter, also had a severed allegiance. Darling grew up rooting for the Sox while playing his high school ball at St. John's in Shrewsbury, Massachusetts. He spent every free weekend in Fenway's right-field bleachers, and in 1975 procured center-field seats from a sick neighbor who couldn't attend the Sixth Game of the World Series. Bernie Carbo's dramatic pinch home run landed not too far from where Darling was seated, and the Mets pitcher said Carlton Fisk's game-winner in the twelfth provided him with his greatest thrill as a fan. Darling was a sophomore at St. John's when St. Peter's of Worcester had big senior first baseman/pitcher Rich Gedman. Darling faced Gedman once at Logan Field in Worcester and intentionally walked his bulky, bespectacled opponent.

Seventeen of the twenty-four Red Sox had never seen Shea Stadium and former Mets Schiraldi and Sambito talked to Boston's hitters about how to handle the ear-shattering sounds of jets landing next door at LaGuardia. The trick, said Schiraldi, was to step out of the batters box and wait until the jets passed overhead.

The usual designated hitter controversy generated some interest. The DH had been used in alternate years starting in 1976, but 1986 was the first time it would be employed according to ballparks. There would be no DH for the games at Shea, but the designated hitters would bat instead of pitchers when the series moved to Boston. "We think this is a better solution than having some of our teams not able to use their DH at all during the World Series," said American League President

Bobby Brown. Tim Lollar, Joe Sambito, and Calvin Schiraldi were the only Sox pitchers who had ever hit in the big leagues. While Boston's bewildered pitchers took batting practice in Shea, Johnson planned to use Danny Heep and Kevin Mitchell as designated hitters in Fenway. The managers would be most affected by the alternating DH rule. McNamara hadn't managed without a designated hitter since leaving the Reds in 1982.

Anyone could see the Sox weren't as healthy as the Mets. Seaver was on the shelf and Buckner had strained his Achilles' tendon in the third inning of the playoff finale. Boston's veteran first baseman was barely able to walk after the Angel series, and it was assumed that he would miss the weekend games in New York. To the amazement of everyone, including his teammates, Buckner arrived at Friday's workout wearing special high-cut baseball shoes, reminiscent of the glory days of Y. A. Tittle. He said he could play. "They're going to have to shoot me to keep me out of this game," said Buckner. "But then again, they might do that."

Boggs, the first batting champ to appear in a World Series since George Brett in 1980, remembered how much it hurt to watch the World Series on television in prior years. "There are the guys you played against all year and they're in the playoffs and World Series, and you just got back from fishing or something."

After a light workout and heavy interviews Hurst dressed in the pitcher's row of the visitors' clubhouse. Shaking his head in amazement, he said to Clemens, "I don't know how you do it."

Mets GM Frank Cashen took the Red Sox hierarchy to dinner Friday night and said later, "We had some great toasts for each other." After the dinner Cashen hosted a huge World Series bash at Pier 59 on the bank of the Hudson River. While Hal Linden, Glenn Close, Roberta Flack, the cast of *Beehive*, and Chita Rivera turned out to entertain, the highlight of the night came when Carly Simon, who rarely performs in public, took the stage and sang history's most sensuous version of "Take Me Out to the Ballgame."

Nobody does it better.

Game One (BOSTON 1, NEW YORK 0)

Shea Stadium is a neon green patch of turf encased in a concrete bowl, flanked by long airstrips, gray terminal buildings, junk yard dogs, and torched Chevys. The Flushing temperature was a chilly 51 degrees and there was a wind of 9 miles per hour gusting under a full moon when Wade Boggs stepped to the plate to face Met righty Ron Darling at 8:31 on the evening of October 18, 1986. Boggs grounded to third, Marty Barrett followed with a single to right, and Bill Buckner hit into a doubleplay to end the inning. The rest of the Series went much the same way for the top three men in the Boston lineup: Boggs didn't hit much, Barrett hit everything in sight, and Buckner seemed to make the final out in every inning, leaving cleanup man Jim Rice to test his leadoff skills over a 7-game period.

Game One was a pitcher's duel, won when Rice walked to leadoff the seventh, took second on Ron Darling's wild pitch, and scored when Rich Gedman's routine grounder skidded under the glove and between the legs of Mets second baseman Tim Teufel.

A 1–0 game is lost on a World Series audience. World Series baseball fans are like conveniently devout Catholics who attend mass only on Easter Sunday. When

the home team gets to the fall classic, true baseball loy-
alists are joined by the white wine and red glasses
crowd, those bandwagoneers who think ERA stands for
the Equal Rights Amendment and who drive Volvos
with "Save the Whales" bumper stickers. These tren-
dies watched Bruce Hurst and Ron Darling fire dueling
zeroes and wondered what happened to all that excitement they heard about during the playoffs. Those who
watch baseball only during the World Series often think
the sport is boring because it lacks the speed, violence,
and timepiece artificiality of games people love to bet
on. In their eyes Game One of the 1986 Fall Classic
was probably a bore.

In fact Game One *was* a tad dull. Most 1–0 games are
baseball masterpieces, filled with overpowering pitching, stellar defense, and mind-bending strategies, but
much of the action in the Hurst-Darling duel was routine. Darling struck out 8 and gave up only 3 hits before
he was lifted for a pinchhitter after 7 innings. Hurst
tossed 124 pitches, gave up 4 hits, and struck out 8 in
8 innings. With 2 on and 0 outs in the sixth, he baffled
Strawberry (the Straw got low-fives from his teammates
during pre-game introductions) with 3 consecutive
curveballs. Strawberry gave the third curve a long look
and walked back to the dugout. Hurst's other small jam
came in the seventh when Boggs dove to spear Mookie
Wilson's sharp grounder that was heading toward the
hole and would have scored Teufel. Boggs got off the
canvas in time to throw out the speedy Wilson. Hurst
batted 3 times and struck out thrice, which explains why
Spike Owen got two intentional walks, twice as many
as he received in his first 1,716 American League at
bats.

Sox manager John McNamara got away with a daring
move when he lifted Hurst for pinchhitter Mike Green-

well in the ninth. The Sox had the bases loaded with 2 outs when Mac elected to pull Hurst for Greenwell. The rookie outfielder flied to center and Calvin Schiraldi came on to pitch the ninth. Schiraldi walked leadoff hitter Strawberry, then benefited from the presence of Dave Stapleton, who'd been inserted for defensive purposes after Buckner grounded to short to end the eighth. Stapleton took Ray Knight's bunt, wheeled, and threw to second to force Strawberry. Pinchhitter Wally Backman flied to left, and Schiraldi fanned pinchhitter Danny Heep to end it. Hurst was asked if he yelled for Stapleton to throw to second when Knight bunted, and the Sox lefty answered, "I was in the dugout."

McNamara was much more candid in victory than he would be later in defeat. "That wasn't an easy decision," he said, when asked about lifting Hurst. "If it doesn't work out and it happens in the ninth inning that we don't win the ballgame, I know my neck and my body might be in the Charles River."

The Lach Factor came into play in the same inning that McNamara made his big gamble. With 2 on and 1 out in the ninth, Dave Henderson singled to left and Boston third base coach Rene Lachemann boldly waved Dwight Evans around third. Evans was out at the plate and said he'd been tripped slightly by Met third baseman Ray Knight, but Lach got the lion's share of the blame.

It didn't matter. One run was enough for Hurst and Schiraldi and the Shea team was forced to leave a wakeup call for their bats. They hit an aggregate .189 in 6 games against the Astros, and managed only 4 singles in 9 innings against Hurst and Schiraldi. The Mets said they didn't see many lefties who threw off-speed pitches. They said Hurst reminded them a little of Astro

Bob Knepper, but admitted Hurst was tougher than the Houston junkman.

Teufel stood tall, just as he had on Gedman's infamous grounder. New York's platoon second baseman didn't hide or make excuses. "The ball took a big hop and I should have had my glove down," he told the crowd of reporters around his locker. "With a man on second there's no excuse. That's my job." Asked about Hurst Teufel said, "I'm sorry, I'm only taking error questions right now."

Darling, the Yale whiz, took no comfort in pitching well in defeat, but did not blame the part-time second baseman. "Hurst's pitching beat us," said the handsome righty. (He was still smarting from a bizarre collison with Henderson when he ran to back up home plate after Teufel's error. There Darling crashed into who else? as he rushed toward the plate to give Rice a signal to slide.) Darling was involved in 13 no-decisions in 1986, and in September pitched in 2 1–0 games that the Mets lost.

Hurst was one Red Sox player well-versed in history. Asked if he could name the last Sox pitcher to toss a 1–0 shutout in the first game of a World Series, Hurst answered, "Babe Ruth."

Ruth's 1–0 victory came against the Cubs in 1918, the last time Boston won the World Series.

Game Two (BOSTON 9, NEW YORK 3)

This was supposed to be baseball's answer to the Lincoln-Douglas debates—Roger Clemens and Dwight Gooden throwing heat in the cool of the night.

Joe Sambito took the subway to the ballpark, just as he had the evening before. On the day after a victory most baseball people do everything exactly as they did the day before. If scrambled eggs for breakfast and a half hour nap produced a win, it'll be more scrambled eggs and another nap the next day. Unfortunately for Sambito and Ed Romero, the Flushing IRT line was struck with a power failure and they had to catch a cab to the tune of $11.

Before Game Two Met third baseman Ray Knight drew a crowd of reporters. He was distressed when he saw he wouldn't be in the lineup against Clemens, and some veteran Met watchers thought Davey Johnson might be starting to panic over New York's scoring drought. Knight had flown his seven-year-old son, Brooks, to the city for the game (he was named after Brooks Robinson), but the boy's father was going to be on the sidelines watching Howard Johnson play third. "I'm just hurt," said Knight.

The 1986 Nobel peace prize winner Elie Wiesel threw out the first ball, and New York crooner Billy Joel sang the anthem. Joel was accompanied by his wife, Christie Brinkley, and Al Nipper took time to get a ball autographed by the megabuck fashion model.

The mound duel never materialized as both starters exited before the sixth inning. Pitching on three days' rest for the third straight time, Clemens was weak and wild and couldn't finish the fifth, even with a 6–2 lead. Clemens's only earlier exit in 1986 was the night he took a line drive off the elbow in the second inning against Baltimore.

Gooden fell apart after the Sox insisted he remove a Band-Aid from his glove hand in the second inning. The turning point came in the third inning when it was still scoreless. After Spike Owen led with a walk, Clemens attempted to sacrifice Owen to second; Keith Hernandez pounced on Clemens's bunt, needlessly rushed himself, and threw a one-hopper that Raphael Santana couldn't handle. The top of Boston's order ripped 3 straight hits off Gooden and it was 3–0. Still walking on air, Henderson blasted a homer to start the fourth and Met manager Davey Johnson contributed when he let Gooden bat with 2 on and 2 out in the bottom of the fourth. Gooden grounded to first to end the inning, then fell behind 6–2 in the fifth when Dwight Evans launched a heat-seeking missile onto the roof of a press tent beyond the fence in left-center. Dr. K was Dr. Longball.

Boston batters scored 6 runs on 8 hits off Gooden and bashed a quartet of Met relievers for another 10 hits and 3 runs in the final 4 innings.

The Sox had plenty of defensive heroes. Boggs did his Brooks Robinson imitation, making three sparkling plays when the Mets scored twice in the third. Evans followed his fifth-inning home run with a splendid diving catch of a Dykstra leadoff bolt in the fifth, and Boston's justifiably maligned bullpen (Crawford and Stanley) blanked the Metropolitans for the final 4.2 innings. Crawford, the man who did not win a game during the 1986 season, had a World Series win to go with his ALCS victory.

Shea started to empty during the middle innings and things grew a little ugly once the Sox blew it open. A golf ball whizzed past Rice's legs as he braced to catch Johnson's routine fly in the seventh. Many of the 55,063 were gone when Hernandez lofted one to center to end it, but Billy Joel and Christie were still keeping the faith in their VIP box.

Buckner, who had two hits and ended three more innings, was becoming something of a folk hero with his Air Buckner shoes, but teammates were slightly skeptical about his situation. When Evans was asked about Buckner's courage, the veteran right-fielder said, "A lot of guys with this team are playing hurt." Meanwhile a healthy Don Baylor wasn't playing at all. Baylor sat for the second straight game as McNamara opted to use Greenwell with the bases loaded and no outs in the seventh. Pinch-hitting for Crawford, the rookie struck out against Met lefty Jesse Orosco as Baylor sat in silent fury.

The Mets were in a deep pothole, but had recent history to encourage them. Only one team had ever won a Series after losing the first two games at home: the Kansas City Royals in 1985. Yet the Red Sox had momentum. They were playing without pressure and hadn't been beaten since Henderson's historic home run in Anaheim, outscoring the opposition 29–9 in 38 innings and while winning 5 straight. A lot of the Sox were wearing "Rene Lachemann Fan Club" caps when they returned from their grapple in the Apple. "I wouldn't wear one outside the park," joked Henderson. "I might get mugged."

Game Three (NEW YORK 7, BOSTON 1)

The scene shifted to Fenway Park and the Mets furnished every conceivable variation on the old cliché "our backs are to the wall."

In this case the wall was the celebrated Boston landmark, which rises 37 feet from the warning track in left field. The Great Wall of China and the Berlin Wall are probably the only walls that have inspired more thoughts and prose than Fenway's gigantic green slab. As much a part of the civic landscape as the Boston Common, the Old North Church, and Fanueil Hall, The Wall makes Fenway special—giving the ancient ballyard the cozy feeling of a miniature golf course.

The width of the wall and its close proximity to home plate have made it a tempting target for generations of American League right-handed sluggers. Newcomers never believe that it is only 315 feet down the left field line, and Sox management does its best to contribute to the conjecture. Tape measures are not allowed on the field and reporters who try to pace the left field line are chased off. The sign says 315, and that's all there is to it.

When the Cincinnati Reds came to Boston to open the '75 World Series, sluggers Johnny Bench, Tony Perez, and George Foster challenged the validity of the sign. Prompted by the doubts of these veteran players, *The Boston Globe* sought out an expert at reading aerial photographs and hired him to determine the exact dimensions of Fenway Park. Using a computer, trigonometry, and special lenses developed for aerial reconnaissance during World War II, this man calculated the dimensions of the field and came up with a startling discovery. All the figures came out precisely as the Sox signs claimed except for the left field line, which measured 304.779 feet. When the *Globe* called Sox publicist Bill Crowley and informed him that the paper had conclusive proof that the left field line measurement was false, Crowley would not corroborate the *Globe*'s findings. One day later the paper ran a page one story on their discovery. The accompanying picture treatment was not unlike the aerial reconnaissance photographs that proved there were Russian missiles being assembled in Cuba during the Kennedy Administration.

When the Mets first appeared in Fenway for a charity game on September 4, Rick Aguilera questioned the distance, but there was no outcry from the Mets hitters. Gary Carter smiled and swung to an easy victory in a home-run hitting contest and New York won the exhibition 7–3.

Met manager Davey Johnson cancelled an off-day workout after his club fell behind 0–2 in the Series, saying he wanted to give his players some rest. Johnson reasoned that his weary troupe had seen the park recently enough; and the no-show also enabled his Mets to steer clear of a national press who were raising doubts about the Mets' alleged greatness.

Some of the NL champs wandered into Fenway despite the cancellation of the workout. Darling had to do his throwing and Game Three starter Bobby Ojeda agreed to hold a press conference. Ojeda's appearance was proof that he had changed since leaving Boston when, during his troubled tenure, the California left-hander referred to newsmen as "media maggots." "I left some blood here. I left some tears here," Ojeda told the press the day before Game Three. He would be the first pitcher in Series history to start against the team he played for one year earlier.

The rest of the Mets took the day off. Wally Backman went bowling and rolled a 184, while Keith Hernandez took a four-hour nap.

The Sox came to Fenway for a workout and McNamara announced that Al Nipper would pitch Game Four. Nipper's appearance assured that Hurst would have four days' rest before pitching Game Five and gave

Clemens five days off before Game Six. The 2–0 lead had a lot to do with McNamara's decision and Nipper was looking forward to his first start since the final weekend of the regular season.

Oil Can Boyd was the star of the day. He talked to the media for half an hour and dazzled newsmen who had never heard Canspeak. Fortunately the press conference was taped and a transcript was distributed later in the day, presumably furnished by the Berlitz School. Unlike the homogenized seven-minute press conference in Anaheim, the Sox let the Can be the Can and the results were refreshing and flammable. "I feel I can master those guys," said Boyd.

On the eleventh anniversary of Carlton Fisk's majestic moonshot off the left field foul pole, the World Series returned to Boston on Tuesday, October 21. It was a clear, unseasonably warm (66 degrees) autumn evening. In the Sox dugout during batting practice Bill Buckner looked at the tarp that protected the well-worn perimeter of the playing field and said, "You know why this is here? They're afraid one of these New York guys might shit on the field."

After Tip O'Neill threw out the first ball, the Can took over and the Mets snapped their slump with 5 hits and 4 runs off him in the top of the first. Lenny Dykstra christened the game with a homer down the right field line and New York's next three batters cracked hits. After yet another Strawberry strikeout, the Sox botched a rundown play in which Gedman and Owen took turns waiting too long to make throws. Silence covered the Fenway lawn like a giant Joe Mooney tarpaulin.

"I saw what Boyd said in the papers," said Dykstra. "We didn't take too kindly to it. The only one that got mastered tonight was him."

Ojeda had all the runs he needed as the former Sox lefty coasted through 7 innings allowing 5 hits and 1 run before handing the ball to Roger McDowell.

So much for local hallucinations of a Sox sweep. Boston was on the brink of losing the home field disadvantage. The Sox lead was down to 2–1 and McNamara was turning the ball over to Al Nipper. The flammable Nipper hadn't pitched in two and a half weeks and owned a 5.38 ERA, the highest earned run average of any World Series starter since Hal Gregg took his 5.87 mark to the mound for the Brooklyn Dodgers in 1947.

Game Four (NEW YORK 6, BOSTON 2)

Darrell Johnson was at Fenway Park. Ol' DJ had been scouting for the Mets since 1983 and the Red Sox were his project throughout September and October. The man who managed Dwight Evans and Jim Rice was responsible for telling Met pitchers what to throw Evans and Rice. DJ's presence anywhere in Boston was sure to evoke memories of the 1975 Series, when he was second-guessed for lifting pitcher Jim Willoughby for pinchhitter Cecil Cooper with two out and none on in the bottom of the eighth of a 3–3 ballgame. Scared rookie Jim Burton came on to pitch the ninth and was tapped for the winning run when Joe Morgan broke his bat on a looping single. "Jim Burton was a sensitive kid and that ruined him," Johnson said of the subsequent blame that Burton was forced to shoulder.

DJ was also second-guessed for flopping Luis Tiant and Bill Lee in Games Six and Seven of the 1975 Series after three days of torrential rains. Now, in 1986, John

McNamara was DJ's progeny, sitting in the highest of high chairs while Boston's baseball fans dissected his every move. The decision to pitch Nipper in Game Four was widely criticized when the Sox lost Game Three, as critics charged that McNamara was conceding a game when he had a chance to take a 3–1 Series lead.

Nipper was no stranger to controversy and adversity. In college, due to a case of mistaken identity, his parents were told that he'd been killed in an automobile accident. In 1985 his season was sabotaged by an anemic ulcer, which originally was feared to be leukemia. Larry Parrish's spikes interrupted Nipper's 1986 season, and he was nothing more than a towel-waving cheerleader in the championship series. A random inspection of newspapers found Nipper's glad hand reaching out in almost every photo of a victorious Sox pitcher coming off the mound. It took Seaver's injury and Boston's 2–0 lead to get Nipper a start in the World Series, but the maneuver allowed Hurst, Clemens, and Boyd to go back to their normal amounts of rest.

More clear October skies graced the night and it was a comfortable 65 degrees when the starting lineups were introduced. After a Natalie Cole anthem and Bowie Kuhn's ceremonial toss, Nipper took the mound for the first time in seventeen days. The gutty right-hander shut down the Mets for three innings before running into trouble. With 1 out and 1 on in the fourth, Gedman went out to talk to Nipper twice and there appeared to be some confusion in the Boston battery. Only Gary Carter knew what was coming; he drove Nipper's next pitch into the net and the Mets were en route to a 3 run inning.

Steve Crawford relieved Nipper and gave up a pair of homers and 3 more runs. With 1 on and 2 out in the seventh, Dykstra hit a high fly to deep right. Evans drifted back, jumped, and momentarily made the catch, but the ball was jarred from his glove over the fence when he crashed into the bullpen wall. Shades of Henderson in Anaheim. In the eighth Carter hit a monstrous shot over the wall in left and Jim Rice never moved from his stance—a gesture first exhibited by Carl Yastrzemski during the dismal days of the early sixties.

The Sox again were unable to do anything with Darling, who pitched shutout baseball for his 7 innings at Fenway. "My own backyard, where I might never have a chance again," he said. He had pitched fourteen World Series innings without giving up an earned run and was giving his first post-game interview when his wife, Toni, was robbed of $900 and two series tickets as she walked down Brookline Avenue with family and friends.

Barrett had 2 hits for the third straight time, but Boggs and Buckner posted bookend 0–5s as the latter ended two more innings. McNamara, asked if he planned to change his lineup, said, "We've won over one hundred games with this lineup and we've been patient with it. I hope we don't have to be patient until next spring, but we're going to be patient again."

The series was 2–2 and home teams were 0–4. "It's just another sign that baseball makes no sense," said Darling.

The Sox were still confident. They had a rested Hurst going against a tired Dwight Gooden in Game Five.

Game Five (BOSTON 4, NEW YORK 2)

It rained lightly Thursday afternoon and gloomy skies threatened the Fenway finale. But after batting practice was cancelled, the rain stopped and the temperature

hovered in the mid-60s. Dwight Evans was feeling re-
flective. He went into McNamara's office to have some
balls autographed, looked down at the "Red Sox" on
his chest, and said, "Skip, I hadn't thought about it, but
this is the last time we'll put this thing on this year."

When American League President Dr. Bobby Brown
came in to speak with McNamara, Evans joked, "Doc,
check my heart and see if it's working."

On the other side of the clubhouse Buckner was
drinking some magic elixir he'd received from the La
Salette Shrine in Attleboro. "It tastes just like water,"
he said after drinking half the potion.

Along pitchers' row Roger Clemens handed out matted, autographed copies of his 20-strikeout photo. Sammy Stewart was in the middle of blasting McNamara
when Clemens came by his locker. Stewart hadn't been
used in the post-season and was ready to talk when reporters started casual conversation near his locker. "He
has got everybody tore up in the bullpen," said Stewart.
"People don't know what their job is. He brought Nipper down and threw me out of long relief. He just kind
of forgot about some of us."

"Has he talked to you about your roles?" Stewart was
asked.

"No, and he told Al Nipper he doesn't have to say
anything to anybody because he has 'manager' written
on his door. All twenty-four of us put the uniform on
and at one time or another contributed. And it wouldn't
be right to go by someone like myself. There's more
than three of us out there."

Confronted with Stewart's remarks, McNamara said,
"I haven't lost sight of anybody."

Nipper's response: "Why did he have to bring my
name into it?"

Motown legend Smokey Robinson lip-synched

through a stirring rendition of the National Anthem before Game Five, probably the funkiest version since the late Marvin Gaye hushed 18,000 at the Los Angeles Forum before the 1983 NBA All Star game. But while Marvin was live, Smokey was Memorex, and suspicious minds were beginning to wonder if the Sox were using the anthem to help their case in the Tommy Harper civil rights suit. Robinson was the third straight minority to sing the anthem before a Fenway Series game. (In fact, the commissioner's office selects anthem singers for World Series games.) The Sox trotted out Ted Williams for the first ball toss and the Splendid Splinter threw a strike into Rich Gedman's mitt.

Smokey Robinson was followed by the miracles.

At 8:43 Bruce Hurst fired the first pitch of Game Five and further established his invincibility against the Mets. Boston's lefty made himself the Mickey Lolich of the 1986 Series, beating the Mets 4–2 with 9 more powerful innings. Hurst stretched his series shutout string to 15.1 innings, scattered 10 hits, struck out 6, and walked only 1 in a 130-pitch masterpiece, which put the Sox on the threshold of a dream.

It was obvious at the start that Hurst was in command against the Mets, as he froze the New Yorkers with the same fastball, forkball, and curve that had blanked them at Shea. The Mets had talked themselves out of hitting Hurst, just as they had Houston's Mike Scott in the playoffs. Hurst was Sandy Koufax East. "It was a case of too much Bruce Hurst," Davey Johnson said afterward.

Gooden, meanwhile, was a confused young man by the time he toed the rubber to pitch Game Five. He'd seen the Sox solve his fastball Game Two, then watched Ojeda and Darling baffle Boston's batters with assorted slop. Dr. K decided he'd beat the Sox with his curveball, which is a little like a *Playboy* centerfold trying to impress her date in the kitchen. Forty-one of Gooden's 82 Game Five pitches were breaking balls. When he fell behind the hitters, he returned to his fastball and the Sox were waiting on it and slapping it to all corners of the Fenway lawn.

Seattle's gilt-edged gifts to Boston combined to put the Sox ahead in the second. Henderson hit a 1-out Strawberry-aided triple (Strawberry fields forever, but not always well) and scored on a sacrifice fly by Owen. This marked the first time any home team held a lead in the 1986 World Series. In the third Buckner reached first on an error by Rafael Santana and took second on a walk. When Evans cracked a single to center, Buckner ambled around third like a man with a Steinway Baby Grand on his back and hobbled for home. Ten feet from the dish, he flopped headfirst, extended his arms, and ate Joe Mooney's dirt as his hands and helmet scraped across the plate. It was 2–0 and Buckner had etched himself into America's consciousness alongside Charles Schultz's Pig Pen. There probably wasn't a detergent executive in America who didn't think about using Buckner's grimy slide for commercial purposes.

Two innings later Rice led with a triple and scored on a single to right by Baylor. When Evans followed with a single to left, Gooden got the hook and finished his 1986 post-season with no victories in 4 starts. Like Don Newcombe and Vida Blue, he was a staff ace denied victory in a World Series while being tagged for 17 hits in 9 Series innings.

Henderson slashed a double to left to make it 4–0 and raise his World Series average to .471. Clearly he had struck some Faustian bargain when he was on the air-phone on the flight to Anaheim. Five World Series games had been played and Henderson was more valuable to Boston than Rice, Boggs, or Baylor.

It got colder and windier as the evening stretched toward midnight, but the late innings were fun for Sox fans. They taunted Strawberry with derisive chants of "Darr-yl, Darr-yl" from the bleachers (Strawberry tipped his cap), then shouted, "Bruce, Bruce, Bruce," as Hurst was fanning Dykstra to end it. Someone walking on Yawkey Way might have thought there was a Springsteen concert playing inside the tall green walls, until the night air was broken by organist John Kiley's rendition of "McNamara's Band."

There were curtain calls for Hurst, Buckner, Barrett, and others when it ended. With two more hits Barrett had smashed the late Thurman Munson's record with his nineteenth and twentieth post-season hits. "Thurman deserves to have someone better than Marty Barrett break his record," said the humble second baseman.

Rice and Hurst agreed to go to the post-game interview to face the national media. Though Rice got things off to a poor start by suggesting that he and Hurst would conduct the session jointly in order to expedite the process and when a reporter objected, Rice erupted, saying, "Take a hike, buddy. We got families to go home to!"

Rice got his temper under control, however, and granted an unusually civil interview. McNamara was also in good spirits. He was enjoying his temporary status as the Series genius. He'd survived the Nipper gamble and his Sox were going to New York to win one game with 24–4 Clemens, working on five days' rest and set to mow down the Mets in Game Six. Clemens was 6–0 with a 2.29 ERA when he worked with five days' rest in 1986. Meanwhile the Mets were bringing Ojeda back on three days' rest for the first time in his career.

The Red Sox home uniforms, baseball's tuxedos, were stored in mothballs when Hurst packed his road grays for the weekend in New York. "I really feel comfortable pitching right now," said Hurst. "It's a lot of fun for me. I just want it to go on." Mentally he'd hung up his spikes for the 1986 season.

Game Six (NEW YORK 6, BOSTON 5)

The first trip of the 1986 Red Sox season was a twenty-minute bus ride from Winter Haven to Lakeland, Florida. Seven and a half months and 846 broken bats later, the Sox gathered at Fenway Park, packed for New York City. They planned to return with the World Series trophy in tow.

"It's at hand, but it's not over," cautioned Evans, the estimable veteran of fifteen autumns and one lost World Series. "We're not going to celebrate until the last pitch and the last out."

Ubiquitous TV minicams and a handful of fans watched the Sox board two buses for Logan Airport. Glenn and Cheryl Hoffman carried an infant daughter Sarah, while Marc and Angela Sullivan had three-month-old Loreal Ashley. Jeff Sellers wore his Ray-Bans, and Bill Buckner limped perceptibly as he clambered up the bus steps. When the caravan pulled out from Yawkey Way and turned down Landsdowne Street, a few employees from a nearby lab held their fists in the air. The buses lost all identity when they reached Boylston Street and went on their way. People everywhere in the city were talking about the Red Sox, yet the team was able to roll through town in total anonymity. The next tour through town, one supposed, would be Lindberghesque.

In the front of the lead bus owner Haywood Sullivan stood, holding the stainless steel pipe that runs from floor to ceiling. His face was drawn. He summoned Jim Rice, who was standing with Rich Gedman in the middle of the bus, and traded him some $40 tickets for $30 tickets.

"Got ten bucks?" asked the owner.

"Can you break a hundred?" laughed Rice.

The buses rolled past a downtown office building that was cloaked in a sign that read "Let's Go Red Sox."

The ride to Logan Airport took longer than the flight to LaGuardia would, and when the carriages finally pulled up to an airport security gate, an employee poked his head in, saw the owner and said, "Mr. Sullivan, we don't have any doubts."

Clemens looked like Jim McMahon walking up the stairway of the Sox chartered Eastern aircraft. His new neo-punk hair was short, wet, and combed straight back. He wore sunglasses and carried a folded *USA Today*— the paper for people too busy to watch television—under his arm. Shortly after takeoff a flight attendant wearing a Sox cap announced, "We have a request from a gentleman who asks that no one smoke during the flight." Clemens's problems with cigarette smoke were well-documented by this time and nobody dared light up during the half hour trip. The Rocket Man was even more concerned with the Shea mound, which he felt was too high, partially negating his leg strength.

Back on the ground Strawberry uttered a statement that would have sounded preposterous in April, May, June, July, or August: "I don't think Clemens is a Bruce Hurst."

Don Baylor, Boston's designated sitter, was confident.

"When we pull this one off, it will be one of the sweetest ones ever. It seems like there's divine intervention from somewhere. Being able to come back when we were down to our last strike, our last swing, well, there must be a reason. I think we have to win it. If you sat down and told this story, I don't think anybody would believe it. Talk about being one game away from winning the World Series. We were one pitch away from going home."

When McNamara was asked if he might replace the struggling Buckner (.174) with Baylor at first base, the iling manager said, "It'll probably be Buckner. He was hobbling at one hundred percent today."

The Series needed some spark. There hadn't been a lead change and three of the games were certified blowouts. There was a decided lack of drama and there were few, if any, memorable plays.

Game Six changed everything. Game Six provided some magic moments and gave the eighty-three-year-old American showcase its greatest comeback story.

The temperature was 53 degrees and there was little wind when Boggs led off the game with an infield hit at 8:27. The Sox jumped to a 2–0 lead in the first 2 innings, but even at this juncture there were warnings that the Boston nine might be in for a fall. Anyone who has watched a lot of baseball has seen blown opportunities in early innings come back to haunt a team. The Red Sox smacked 5 hits in the first 2 innings, but stranded 5 baserunners and scored only twice. Jim Rice was unable to score from first on a wall double by Evans. Buckner left the bases loaded with a hard fly to right to end the second. When the night was over, the Sox would have only 5 runs on their 13 hits while stranding 14 runners.

Clemens pitched no-hit ball and regularly hit 95 MPH on the radar gun in the first four innings. The Mets tied it

with 2 in the fifth and it was still 2–2 when Roger Mc-
Dowell relieved Ojeda to start the seventh. Barrett led with
a walk and went to second when Buckner grounded out. A
throwing error by Knight put Sox runners on first and third.
Barrett came home when Evans grounded out (credit the
run to McNamara who averted a double play by having
Rice run on the pitch), but the Lach Factor and Rice's lack
of speed killed things again when he was thrown out at the
plate trying to score on Gedman's single to left.

Clemens retired the Mets in order in the seventh and
had a 4 hitter with 8 strikeouts and only 2 walks. He
had thrown 135 pitches, 91 strikes.

McNamara had two opportunities to use Baylor in the
eighth. With 1 on and 1 out, he sent rookie Mike Greenwell up to bat against McDowell. Greenwell fanned on
3 dirtballs. With the bases loaded and 2 outs, Buckner
(.143) was then allowed to face lefty Jesse Orosco and
Buckner lined to center, stranding 3 more runners (giving him 9 for the game).

"I guess you just don't pinch hit for Buckner in that
situation," a reporter said to Baylor after the game.

"Why not?" snapped Baylor.

The Sox DH finally flashed his feelings. "I'm a fucking cheerleader. I feel the best players should be in
there and I'm not going to be the fucking judge of that."

Seconds after his eighth inning calls, McNamara tossed
another log on the hot stove when he brought Schiraldi in
to protect the 3–2 lead in the bottom of that inning. Clemens had developed a blister on the middle finger of his
pitching hand. The Mets manufactured a run off Schiraldi
in the eighth, guaranteeing that Clemens, like Gooden,
would not win a game in the 1986 World Series.

The rest of Game Six is more familiar to Bostonians
than "The Midnight Ride of Paul Revere."

Henderson homer . . . 5–3 lead . . . two outs, nobody

on . . . Carter single . . . Mitchell single . . . Knight single
. . . 5–4 . . . Stanley for Schiraldi . . . wild pitch, 5–5 . . .
Wilson foul balls . . . Buckner's error . . .

It was totally improbable. If the same four batters had
been thrown soft batting-practice serves by a kind old
coach, surely at least one would have hit a pop-up or a
catchable fly ball. The odds of four straight batters
reaching base in any situation, at any level, are fairly
high. Mike Cieslinski, inventor of a sophisticated baseball board game, which accounts for individual statistics
and patterns, replayed Game Six starting with 2 out, 0
on, and Carter at bat in the tenth. Cieslinski had to roll
the dice 279 times before the Mets won the game again.

"I just wasn't able to close the game," said a hollow-
eyed Schiraldi. "I was a little nervous when I first went
out, but that's no excuse. I just didn't do the job. I don't
deserve any more chances."

McNamara should have listened to those words. The
twenty-four-year-old was not ready for Game Six of the
World Series and he wouldn't be ready when called into
Game Seven. The bloody bullpen gang that took so
much heat in the spring was coming back to gore the
Sox again. The Mets had solved Schiraldi's fastballs and
he didn't have another pitch, nor did he have the temperament or experience for the role he'd been given.

"The sun will come up tomorrow," said Stanley. "But
I don't know if it will come out. It's supposed to rain."

Game Seven (NEW YORK 8, BOSTON 5)

Twenty-four ballplayers and one beleaguered manager
tossed and turned all night in the city that doesn't sleep.
And all the while the rains poured down on Gotham,

granting the Red Sox an extra day to think about how they let the championship slip from their grasp. Commissioner Peter Ueberroth postponed Game Seven Sunday afternoon and opted to play Monday night, a head-to-head duel with the NFL. Maybe Baylor was right about divine intervention as the downpours enabled McNamara to think about bringing Bruce Hurst back to pitch the seventh and deciding game.

During a wet Sunday evening the Sox manager said he hadn't made his mind up yet, but all signs pointed left, toward Hurst. McNamara was on his way to dinner when he spotted Boyd in the lobby of the Grand Hyatt that night.

"We're going with Hurst because he's a lefty," the manager told the brokenhearted Can.

Boyd's chin dropped and he stepped backward to lean against a lobby pillar. He started to cry and pulled the bill of his cap down over his face. "It hurts so bad, but what can I do?" he said. "Bruce is on a roll and Mac thinks the Mets have a better left-handed lineup. It's just that it was my turn and after all I've been through. I'm sorry, but my sensitivities are going to show through every time."

Boyd had tears in his eyes as he walked around the vast lobby with his friend Nipper. They had a beer in the bar, then the Can headed for the door.

"I'm going to party," he said. "I got no reason not to."

Hurst received word when McNamara called him in his room at approximately 11 P.M. Like Hurst, most of the team stayed in their rooms on Sunday. McNamara, Baylor, and Buckner got pep-talk phone calls from Mr. Reach Out and Touch, Reggie Jackson.

Hurst had pitched only one game on three days' rest in 1986, the fifth game of the ALCS. He gave up 7 hits and 3 runs before running out of gas after 101 pitches in 6 innings. Now he would be trying to become the fourth pitcher in sixty-five years to win three games in a single World Series.

Few Sox players faced the media before Game Seven. It seemed like a good idea considering the questions Bob Stanley was asked as he sat in the dugout eating sunflower seeds before the climactic joust. After explaining his wild pitch a few times, the Steamer was asked how he felt about Game Seven. "We're going to win this game and everyone's going to forget Game Six," said the forlorn reliever.

Predictably, a story circulated that Boyd had jumped the team and was on his way back home to Mississippi. Nipper and McNamara denied the rumor and the Can emerged from the clubhouse one minute before the start of batting practice. Another story circulating back in Boston was that a 1960s episode of the television series *Lost In Space* contained a passage in which an alien from the twenty-first century claimed the 1986 World Series was won by the Boston Red Sox. Yet this could not be substantiated.

Buckner got a rousing ovation during pre-game ceremonies and the thirtieth Game Seven in World Series history started at 8:15 on October 27th. The skies were murky and the air traffic, which had been missing from Games One, Two, and Six, was back at full throttle. LaGuardia officials had re-routed the noisy jets the first four Shea dates, but hadn't allowed for a rain delay. It was a damp 53 degrees when Ron Darling retired Wade Boggs on a liner to short for the first out of the 2,122nd and last game of the year.

Evans and Gedman opened the second with back-to-back home runs (Strawberry had Gedman's in his glove) and a single by Boggs pushed a third Sox baserunner across the plate. In the third, Rice 0 RBI in 7 games while batting cleanup, though Buckner certainly reduced his chances) led with a single off the wall in left but was thrown out going for two. Darling was gone by the fourth and replaced with Sid Fernandez.

McNamara's decision to pitch Hurst looked brilliant for five innings. Dykstra and Backman were on the bench and Hurst took a 1-hitter and 3–0 lead into the sixth. Before the Mets came to the plate, Buckner's Game Six error was played on the Diamond Vision scoreboard—a bush-league tactic more Murdoch than Doubleday. Lee Mazzilli got things started with a 1-out pinch single; Hernandez delivered a bone-breaking 2-run single, and the Mets were on their way to a 3-run inning, which finished Hurst.

Meanwhile the Sox couldn't solve Fernandez, and Schiraldi was returned for more punishment in the bottom of the seventh. Ray Knight led with a homer and after two more hits, Schiraldi was lifted in favor of Joe Sambito, then Stanley. The Mets had a 3-run inning, a 6–3 lead, and all worst fears about the Sox bullpen had materialized. Like Boston in the playoffs, New York was now carrying the momentum of their miraculous deathbed recovery and could not be stopped.

To their credit the Sox rallied for 2 runs in the eighth. Buckner and Rice opened the inning with singles off Roger McDowell and both scored on a booming double to right-center by Evans. Incredibly the Sox made no attempt to move the runner over. Lefty Jesse Orosco replaced McDowell, and Evans died at second as Gedman lined to the infield, Henderson fanned, and pinch hitter Baylor grounded to short.

In a move that confounded everyone, McNamara then

turned the 6–5 game over to Al Nipper in the bottom
of the eighth. Clemens was in the pen and so was Oil
Can, a 16-game winner who hadn't pitched in six days.
Also available was leash-bound Sammy Stewart, who
had never given up a run in 12 post-season innings
while he was with the Orioles. Instead, Nipper got the
call. The man with the 5.38 ERA, the man McNamara
ignored for 17 days before using him in Game Four to
save the rotation. Al Nipper was given the baseball in
the bottom of the eighth inning of the final game of the
World Series with the Red Sox trailing 6–5. Before one
could say "Jim Burton," Strawberry hammered an 0–2
pitch and drove it high and far into the foggy night.
Strawberry circled the bases in slow motion. Nipper was
tapped for two more hits, including an embarrassing RBI
single by Orosco that set the count at 8–5. In Games
Six and Seven the Mets had bled Boston's bullpen for
10 hits and 9 runs in 4.2 innings.

Ed Romero led off the top of the ninth. It was the
final indictment of the shallow waters in the Boston
dugout. The Sox went down 1-2-3 with Barrett swinging
and missing at Orosco's last pitch of the 1986 season.
Spliced into the scenes of the Met celebration, America
saw Wade Boggs weeping in the dugout. The Boston
Red Sox had lost the seventh game of the World Series.
Again.

The Boston clubhouse was quiet. Rene Lachemann
broke the silence by popping some balloons with his
cigar. Interviewers asked questions in hushed tones, the
way people talk to relatives of the deceased when they
pass through lines at wakes.

"This hurts us, too," said Hurst. "As much as the fans
hurt, we hurt. Maybe even more." Nipper wept. Schiraldi sipped from a beer cup and stared straight ahead

with those glazed eyes that couldn't comprehend Game Four in Anaheim or Game Six in New York. "I am responsible for what happened," he said. "I ought to feel like this."

"I don't believe in luck," said the heroic Evans. "I don't believe in history either, but maybe I'm starting to. Sixty-eight years is a long time—1918 was a long time ago. It does make you wonder."

In the interview room McNamara attempted to achieve peace with the media. "I want to thank you all for the job you've done," he said at the end of his appearance. "If I've offended anyone, I'm sorry. It gets testy in here sometimes, but I thank you all."

A pair of chartered buses hummed outside the right field bullpen. To get from the Sox dressing room to the waiting buses, Boston players either had to walk through a long, crowded corridor past the Mets dressing room or cross the field. Hurst took the corridor route, stopping to congratulate Ojeda on the way. He bumped into a drenched Ray Knight in the corridor.

"Congratulations, Ray," said Hurst.

"Hey, you were great," responded Knight. "Really, I can't even express to you how great you were and how great all this is."

Hurst kept moving. "They can't call it a choke," he said to no one in particular.

Mike Torrez was a surprise visitor in the area where the buses waited. Torrez predicted a Sox world championship in 1987. Rowdy Met fans could be heard over the noise of the bus engines. When a team that plays in a stadium adjacent to an airport wins a title, there aren't many places to celebrate or congregate. But the fans were doing their best in the first hours of Tuesday, October 28. Suddenly Sox players were pouring out of the bus, running around the wall, and back onto the dimly lit field. Team physician Arthur Pappas was summoned. Sox traveling secretary Jack Rogers had been hit on the head by a bottle tossed from the near-empty stands. McNamara was one of the first to get to Rogers and his son, Lt. Mike McNamara, ripped off his T-shirt and used it to compress the wound until Dr. Pappas arrived. Rogers was prone on the right field turf, bleeding from the head, when the doctor rushed to his side. Sox players in the meantime milled around their fallen friend, cursing the night.

Clemens exploded. "Baseball like it oughta be," he shouted toward the vacant upper deck. A slight echo bounced back. "They throw golf balls out of the stands and now this. Baseball like it oughta be. This place sucks. They ought to blow the whole place up."

After a few scary moments Rogers got to his feet. His head was heavily bandaged (he had a laceration and a fractured skull) and he rode to LaGuardia in an ambulance that preceded the two team buses.

They left some blood on the diamond and an ambulance led the Red Sox away from Shea Stadium and back to the plane for their final trip home. The ride was short and quiet. Publicist Dick Bresciani informed the weary team that the mayor and governor wished to honor the Sox with a parade and ceremony at City Hall Plaza Wednesday. McNamara turned to a reporter and said, "There are several faces on this plane that you will not see in spring training." Of more interest, perhaps, were the faces that would replace them.

It was after 2:30 A.M. when the chartered jet touched down at Logan and the players and their wives boarded buses for Fenway. About one hundred fans greeted the team at the ballpark. A few players waited under the stands for the luggage truck that finally pulled up at about 3:15 A.M. The back door of the big truck was rolled up and several hundred bags stared out from inside.

Bob Stanley shrugged and said, "Mine will be the last one. That's the kind of year it's been."

Stanley's bag was indeed among the last.

EPILOGUE

I N seven special months they took fifteen road trips,
flew 40,000 miles, and spent one hundred nights in
hotels. Appropriately enough their final journey was
through the heart of Boston. That is where the 1986 Red
Sox will stay.

Seven hundred and fifty thousand loyal New Englanders assembled in City Hall Plaza to honor the team
in splendid daylight on Wednesday, October 29. Roger
Clemens, Jim Rice, Bruce Hurst, Bill Buckner, John
McNamara, and about ten others rode in a parade
through downtown Boston and spoke to the thankful
throng. Half of the players passed up the outing, but
those who attended took comfort in the outpouring of
emotion and affection. There were tears and heartfelt
thanks on the stage as Bob Stanley and Rene Lachemann heard cheers normally reserved for Popes and
World Champion Celtics.

261

When the reception was over, Buckner drove west on the Massachusetts Turnpike until he hit Worcester where Dr. Arthur Pappas was waiting with scalpel in hand. Dwight Evans and Tom Seaver had surgery on their right knees the same day. Rich Gedman and his wife boarded a plane for Japan where he was slated to play in All Star exhibition games. Roger Clemens went home to Houston to collect his Cy Young and MVP awards while awaiting the birth of his first child.

Lou Gorman started breaking up the 1986 Red Sox a week later. Seaver and Tony Armas were told that options on their contracts would not be picked up by the club. Free agents Sammy Stewart and Dave Stapleton learned that the ballclub would not attempt to retain their services. McNamara was named American League Manager of the Year and continued to defend all of his moves without a trace of regret. Bruce Hurst went to a few Celtic games, then returned to St. George, Utah, where he was paraded on a firetruck and handed a key to the city. On November 26, Lachemann took a job as first base coach of the Oakland A's and Boston radio stations played "Walk Away, Rene" long into the night. Debbie Boggs gave birth to Brett Anthony Boggs on November 26 (Wade's number), and seven-pound, thirteen-ounce Koby Clemens ("You knew there'd be a K in there somewhere."—Roger Clemens) arrived at 2:52 P.M. on December 4. The Sox settled out of court with Tommy Harper and signed Joe Sambito to a one-year contract.

In mid-December, McNamara donned a tuxedo and read "The Night Before Christmas" at the Boston Pops annual holiday concert.

The Red Sox failed to make any moves at baseball's winter meetings, but the team again snatched the spotlight when it proved unable to reach a contract agreement with Gedman. The parting was bitter and Gedman wandered into free agency knowing he would not rejoin the team until May 1987, if ever. Gedman was cursed by some fans, while others worried about Boston's prospects without the All Star catcher. Nevertheless, as snow covered the Berkshires, and the Giants and Broncos prepared for Super Bowl XXI, Sox fans bought tickets for the 1987 season.

Baseball, politics, and weather are year-round conversation pieces in the cozy six-state corner of northeast America. In 1986 the Boston Red Sox furnished unforgettable yesterdays and promised exciting tomorrows. They didn't win the Big One, but they stacked cordwood for the hot stove league and brought warmth to the cold New England winter.